Jonathan Edwards and Scotland

For other titles from Dunedin Academic Press please see
www.dunedinacademicpress.co.uk

Jonathan Edwards and Scotland

edited and introduced by

Kelly Van Andel

Adriaan C. Neele

Kenneth P. Minkema

Published by
Dunedin Academic Press Ltd
Hudson House
8 Albany Street
Edinburgh EH1 3QB
Scotland

www.dunedinacademicpress.co.uk

ISBN 978-1-906716-36-3

British Library Cataloguing in Publication data
A catalogue record for this book is available from the British Library

Typeset by Makar Publishing Production
Printed in Great Britain by CPI Antony Rowe Ltd.

Mixed Sources
Product group from well-managed
forests and other controlled sources
www.fsc.org Cert no. TT-COC-2082
© 1996 Forest Stewardship Council

FSC

Contents

List of Contibutors

Rev. Nicholas T. Batzig is pastor of the New Covenant Presbyterian Church (PCA), Richmond Hill, Georgia, and a graduate student at Puritan Reformed Theological Seminary, Grand Rapids, Michigan.

Dr. H. G. Callaway is a shareholder of The Library Company of Philadelphia, Pennsylvania.

Dr. Chris Chun is Associate Professor of Church History at Golden Gate Baptist Theological Seminary, Mill Valley, California.

Richard A. S. Hall is Professor of Philosophy at Fayetteville State University, North Carolina, and the convener of the Jonathan Edwards Society.

Dr. David Ceri Jones is a Lecturer of the Department of History and Welsh History, Aberystwyth University in Wales, .

Dr. Wilson H. Kimnnach is the Presidential Professor in the Humanities, Emeritus, University of Bridgeport, Connecticut, and General Editor of Sermons for the Jonathan Edwards Center, New Haven, Connecticut.

Natalia Marandiuc is a doctoral candidate in the Department of Religious Studies, Yale University, New Haven, Connecticut.

Susan Miller is a doctoral candidate in the Department of English at the University of Glasgow, Scotland, and an associate professor in the Department of Liberal Arts at Nippon Sport Science University, Japan.

Dr. Kenneth P. Minkema is the Executive Editor and Director of The Jonathan Edwards Center and a Research Scholar at Yale University Divinity School, New Haven, Connecticut.

Dr. Adriaan C. Neele is the Associate Editor of the Jonathan Edwards Center and a Research Scholar at Yale University Divinity School, New Haven, Connecticut, and Extraordinary Professor and Research Associate in the Faculty of Theology at the University of the Free State, Bloemfontein, South Africa.

Dr. Kyle Strobel recently completed his doctorate at the University of Aberdeen, Scotland, and is director of Metamorpha Ministries.

Dr. Kelly Van Andel is an adjunct instructor in the Religious Studies Program at the University of New Mexico.

Editors' Introduction

In July 1750, Jonathan Edwards, freshly and summarily dismissed from his pastorate at Northampton, Massachusetts, replied to a letter from his chief correspondent in Scotland, John Erskine. In the letter to which Edwards was replying, his colleague, who knew of Edwards' likely predicament, had suggested that he could procure Edwards a pulpit in Scotland. He would, however, need to submit to the formality of subscribing to the Westminster Confession, the primary platform of the Presbyterian churches promulgated a century before, and to the 'Presbyterian form of church government'. Whether reflecting his frustration with New England's Congregational Way after his bitter and drawn-out dismissal, or striking a diplomatic note to keep his options open—or perhaps both—Edwards responded:

> As to my subscribing to the substance of the Westminster Confession, there would be no difficulty: and as to the Presbyterian government, I have long been perfectly out of conceit with our unsettled, independent, confused way of church government in this land. And the Presbyterian way has ever appeared to me most agreeable to the Word of God, and the reason and nature of things, though I cannot say that I think that the Presbyterian government of the Church of Scotland is so perfect that it can't in some respects be mended.[1]

This sounded promising enough, though Edwards quickly went on to admit that the idea of 'removing with my numerous family over the Atlantic' was 'attended with many difficulties that I shrink at'. And so the tantalizing prospect of Edwards, the great Protestant Atlantic rim theologian and revivalist, coming to Scotland, dissolved almost as soon as it was broached—though this has not stopped historians from indulging in the counter-factual question, 'What if?' In which church, for example, did Erskine, seeking to secure the place of his party, imagine Edwards serving? Perhaps a congregation in Edinburgh, near the university, or some place quieter in the country, where he could focus on writing?

Edwards never made the trip, of course. But in many ways, his influence and legacy in Scotland was almost as significant as if he had actually crossed the ocean with his 'large and chargeable' brood and been given a pulpit or professorship. Arguably more so, since his personal presence may have compromised the esteem in which he was held in many circles by virtue of his publications, correspondence, and reputation. Alas, in the case of the socially awkward and critical Edwards in particular, familiarity could easily breed contempt.

The essays presented in this volume arose out of a conference entitled 'Jonathan Edwards and Scotland', held in May 2009 at the University of Glasgow as part of the Scottish Homecoming observations. This collection is presented as a memorial of that important year for the Scottish people, and as a reminder of the role of religion in their history, for good and for ill. This volume is also meant to contribute to ongoing scholarship into the transatlantic continuities, relationships, and borrowings that marked early modern Euro-America, and to an appreciation of the long and deep connection of Edwards and Scotland.[2]

There was little in Edwards' upbringing that would have marked him as an internationally known religious figure. He was born in 1703 in the colony of Connecticut, of a clerical family that was relatively new to the provincial gentry. Home-taught in the small preparatory school run by his father, Rev. Timothy Edwards, he attended the tiny, fledgling Yale College, at the time hardly distinguished compared to the venerable institutions of Europe. Nonetheless, he possessed uncanny intellectual skills while being nurtured in a dramatically conversionist religious culture. His father and especially his grandfather, Solomon Stoddard, the powerful minister of Northampton for more than sixty years until his death in 1729, were regionally recognized as effective revivalists. As an inheritor of a New England brand of Calvinist evangelicalism, Edwards combined the academic and doctrinal rigor that came out of the Reformation, a nearly mystical pietism, and an eclectic range of reading in Reformed orthodoxy, puritan authors, and the new science of the early Enlightenment.

Though an obscure colonial on a remote edge of the expanding English empire, he set his sights high. His 'downtown' was not Boston but London, and from an early age he ambitiously charted his course to notoriety as a spokesman of 'true religion'. His 'Notes on Style' reflect a self-awareness of his youth and location, both geographically and socially. He would temper his ambition with a 'due modesty', beginning at 'small games' locally before being published in the empire's metropolis.[3]

For all its seeming presumption, Edwards' plans succeeded remarkably well. His first publications—sermons that laid out central themes in his thought[4]—appeared in Boston in the early 1730s. These brought him to the attention of local interlocutors with international connections, such as Rev. Benjamin Colman of Boston. It was Edwards' publications arising out of the revivals of the mid-1730s that he oversaw and witnessed in Northampton and environs, and of the widespread 'Great Awakening' of the early 1740s, that first earned him fame not only in the colonies but in Europe as well, including Scotland. *A Faithful Narrative of a Surprising Work of God*, his description of the Connecticut Valley revivals, provided a template for ministers seeking to achieve and understand similar religious fervor amongst their parishioners. Initially published in 1737 in its fullest form through the offices of the English nonconformist ministers Isaac Watts and John Guyse, Scottish publishers were quick to pick up on the text, publishing it the same year in Edinburgh. This set a precedent, with subsequent titles by Edwards, including *The Distinguishing Marks of a Work of the Spirit of God* and *Some Thoughts Concerning the Revival*, issuing the same year from American, Scottish and English presses. Later, Scots' preference for Edwards meant that his writings would be published *first* in Scotland, and then, at a time when Edwards' reputation waned in America, *only* in Scotland.

In the wake of the Connecticut Valley revivals, and as Edwards began to hear of young English evangelicals such as George Whitefield and the Wesley brothers, he actively sought news of revivals and the interest of religion from abroad. His interlocutors in New England, such as Colman, Rev. Thomas Prince, and provincial secretary Josiah Willard, put him in contact with prominent religious figures in England and Scotland. Edwards' correspondence with Scottish religious figures, such as Erskine, John McLaurin, William M'Culloch, Thomas Gillespie, and William Hog were essential to Edwards in his own work. Edwards and these writers were part of a larger, pan-Protestant, transatlantic 'evangelical network', described by scholars such as Susan O'Brien, Michael Crawford, David Bebbington, and Frank Lambert.[5] O'Brien has written that nothing less than a 'new religious community based on Calvinist evangelicalism came into existence' during the mid-eighteenth century Protestant revivals in Europe and America.[6] Through this far-flung religious republic of letters, participants exchanged news, books, and even donations. For example, accompanying his letters to Edwards, Erskine over the years sent packets containing no less than 54 separate titles—and that is only what we can know from the extant letters, which surely represent only a portion of the total correspondence. Edwards took the information he received and communicated it to his congregation, practicing something like the 'letter days' observed among the Moravians. After he was dismissed from Northampton, Edwards received much-needed cash from Scottish philanthropists such as William Hog. Besides these tangible benefits, Edwards had in his correspondence a forum for the exchange of ideas and, crucially, a means of providing him with a wider, international perspective that was to be key in his evolving vision of the global aspects of the work of redemption.

Revivals for Edwards were a central aspect of God's ongoing work of redemption, and provided him and his Scottish friends with a constant topic of conversation. Scottish evangelists, such as James Robe of the 'Cambuslang wark', emulated Edwards' *Faithful Narrative*—right down to the title—in describing awakenings in their own churches. Their letter-writing grew into a complex of activities: the publication and distribution of sermons and treatises; journals devoted to revival news such as *The Christian History* of Boston, *The Christian Monthly History*, or *The Glasgow Weekly History*; weekly sacrament celebrations that grew from the 'holy fairs' within the Presbyterian communities in Scotland and America; organizations such as associations, prayer groups, and committees; and orchestration of public readings and publicity.[7]

Through his Scottish connection, Edwards became part of the Concert of Prayer movement, which entailed regularly scheduled (usually on a quarterly basis), transatlantic days of prayer for the 'outpouring of the Spirit'. Though it is difficult to locate the origins of such concerts, they were being sporadically observed by 1741 among dissenting communities in England and Scotland. Whether Edwards read about this practice in news-papers or correspondence, or heard about it through the grapevine of New Light revivalist circles, he mentioned it as a good idea in *Some Thoughts Concerning the Revival*, written in 1742 and published in early 1743, by which time the concert had become established in lower Scotland. The following year, a transatlantic, trans-denominational concert was proposed by Scottish evangelicals from McLaurin's circle, and in 1746 they published a 'Memorial' justifying the concert's purpose and explaining its method. Edwards reprinted the Memorial whole as the second section of his *Humble Attempt* of 1747, and in doing so became the most significant American representative of the concert.

Closely associated in revivalists' minds to awakenings was the task of missions. Christopher Mitchell, who previously has done the most work on the connections of Edwards and Scotland, and who is cited in several of the chapters in this volume, has stated that Edwards 'shaped the definition of Scottish missions'.[8] This influence came about largely through Edwards' publication of *The Life of David Brainerd*. Brainerd, a Connecticut native like Edwards, was expelled from Yale College in 1742 for his pro-revival sentiments. He became a missionary sponsored by the Society in Scotland for Propagating Christian Knowledge, working among natives in New Jersey and Pennsylvania. However, the hardships of the missionary life took their toll quickly: Brainerd contracted consumption and died in October 1747 at Edwards' home. Out of admiration for Brainerd and his zealous devotion, Edwards compiled the *Life* from his published and manuscript journals, presenting Brainerd as an exemplar of evangelical piety. The book, first published in 1749 in Boston, and reprinted in Edinburgh in 1765, has been dubbed Edwards' 'most popular work'.[9] This work, along with *A Humble Attempt*, became a key inspiration for later mission movements and for individual missionaries.

Erskine was a, if not the, major source for Edwards of new works on theology, philosophy, and ecclesiology coming from English and Scottish presses, especially once Edwards was ensconced at the remote Stockbridge mission. He was of great assistance in facilitating Edwards' writing projects and disseminating his published works. It was to Erskine, for example, that Edwards in the late 1740s described his effort to write on the 'Arminian controversy', an effort that was temporarily thwarted by the distractions caused by Edwards' contention with his congregation from 1748 to 1750. However, once in Stockbridge, Edwards completed the essay on *Freedom of the Will*, which attacked notions of a self-determined will from a state of 'indifference'. Significantly, one sixth of the subscribers to that book were from Scotland—no doubt thanks to Erskine's efforts. Similarly, Scots accounted for some 15% of the subscribers to Edwards' treatise on *Original Sin*. Erskine sent Edwards the latest tomes by writers such as David Hume, whom Edwards, though he considered Hume a man of genius, judged was 'corrupt'. Also, when Henry Homes, Lord Kames, used Edwards' *Freedom of the Will* in his own *Essays* to support fatalism, Erskine provided Edwards with Kames' book and facilitated the publication, in Scotland, of Edwards' rebuttal.[10]

After the close friendship formed with Edwards over more than a decade of correspondence, Erskine went on to promote Edwards after his death in 1758. He communicated with Jonathan Edwards, Jr., and learned of the transcription work that the son was doing of his father's writings. Out of this came, first, *A History of the Work of Redemption*, one of the 'great works' Edwards, Sr., had described to the trustees of the College of New Jersey in late 1757 as in process, but left incomplete. The first edition of the work appeared in Edinburgh in 1774; a Dutch translation followed two years later, in which Erskine likely had a hand, and it was not until 1782 that the text appeared in New York. Next, a volume of Edwards' *Practical Sermons*, previously unpublished, was issued in Edinburgh in 1788. Then followed, in 1793 and 1796, two more Edinburgh imprints, *Miscellaneous Observations on Important Theological Subjects* and *Remarks on Important Theological Controversies*, composed of entries drawn from Edwards' many notebooks. All of these texts became standard in collected editions of Edwards' works printed in England and the United States in the early nineteenth century.

Beyond Erskine and his contemporaries, we can mention some prominent nineteenth-century Scots who engaged Edwards. In the realm of philosophy, for example, no less than Dugald Stewart, one of the chief formulators of common sense philosophy, admired Edwards' arguments on free will. Thomas Chalmers, leader of the Evangelical Church in Scotland, also drew on Edwards in doctrine and piety, as did theologian John McLeod Campbell. Prominent ministers A. A. and Horatius Bonar of the Free Church of Scotland, and Alexander B. Grosart of the United Presbyterian Church of Scotland, were heavily Edwardsean in their preaching. So much did Grosart admire Edwards, in fact, that he travelled to America and coaxed one of Edwards' descendants, Tryon Edwards, to let him take some of Edwards' manuscripts to Scotland—including the

'Treatise on Grace' and the 'Interleaved Bible'—so that he could transcribe them. Grosart published a volume of selections from these manuscripts in *Selections from the Unpublished Writings of Jonathan Edwards of America* in 1865, with the plan to mount a new collected edition, which, however, did not become a reality.[11] Closer to the present time, revivals in modern Scotland have drawn on the reputation of Edwards. For example, advocates of the Toronto Blessing of the 1990s, which had a Scottish phase and drew the guarded support of the mainline churches, primarily cited Edwards and his revival tracts as their guide.

The essays presented in this volume reflect the importance of Edwards' Scottish and transatlantic influence and exchange, as well as the wealth of material for scholarship, which has been largely undeveloped. Indeed, these essays provide hints for further exploration down various paths. They highlight the breadth and depth of scholarship by those already established in the field, and herald the rise of a new generation of Edwards scholars, for many of the contributions come from graduate and postgraduate students, or scholars early in their careers. While most closely hew to the connection of Edwards and Scotland, these essays also range farther astray at times and touch on themes that, on the face of them, have little to do with Scotland per se, but which treat the broader scope of eighteenth- and nineteenth-century Euro-American religious culture.

The title of the first section, 'International Networks', admittedly, describes all of the essays below in one way or another, but the two contributions under this rubric in particular treat larger issues—namely, preaching and sources—that set our agenda. Through an examination of the exchange of sermon pamphlets, letters, and books that circulated between New England and Scotland, Wilson H. Kimnach considers the preaching brotherhood of kindred spirits that Edwards found in his Scottish counterparts. Citing Sir Walter Scott, he suggests that such preachers, who expressed opinions on the pursuit of authentic Christianity in a difficult time, continued the spirit of the Reformation in their own generation.

Until very recently, scholars have shown a rather woeful lack of awareness and attention to the trajectories and continuities between the Dutch, Scottish, and New England proponents of Reformed orthodoxy.[12] Adriaan Neele seeks to draw attention to this approach through the development and reception of two works that have proved important for Edwards scholarship and Post-reformation Reformed studies: *Theoretico-practica theologia* of Petrus van Mastrict (1630–1706) and Edwards' *A Work of the History of Redemption*. Looking at these two works allows us a glimpse of a much larger field of exchange.

The theme of the next section, 'Evangelicalism and Revivalism', is again one that identifies the work of several authors in this volume, but here our contributors focus on how Edwards served as a catalyst for revivals in Wales and Scotland. David Ceri Jones examines the extent and changing fortunes of Edwards' influence in eighteenth- and early nineteenth-century Wales through a transatlantic perspective, exploring Edwards' influence on Welsh Methodists. He then compares Edwards' reception in Wales to his reception in Scotland through a pan-Celtic lens, demonstrating that the Scottish and Welsh awakenings became periodically intertwined.

Chris Chun then discusses Edwards' influence in eighteenth-century Britain in two major stages. First, he views the Northampton pastor's interaction during his lifetime in the 1740s and 1750s among Scottish Presbyterians. He goes on to consider Edwards' posthumous legacy among English Baptists in the 1780s and 1790s, giving particular attention to Edwards' missiological impulse and the 'sense of the heart', which incited transatlantic awakenings and spurred on the Baptist Missionary Society.

Edwards and his Scottish counterparts' pursuit of revivals and of missions were bound up in their millennialism and their conviction that the spread of the gospel in their time was the fulfillment of biblical prophecy of the end times. Next, therefore, we bring together two essays on 'Millennialism and Missions'. Nicholas T. Batzig discusses the friendship Edwards maintained with John McLaurin of Glasgow through transatlantic correspondence. In doing so, he explores the theological influence that both men had on each other and gives particular attention to Edwards' effort to promote concerts of prayer for the outpouring of the Holy Spirit in his *Humble Attempt*. Edwards, however, was inspired by, and took his cue from, McLaurin and other Scottish evangelicals. In this sense, he was the American facilitator of a Scottish practice.

Edwards' role as a missionary is currently an area that is attracting increasing attention among scholars.[13] Kelly Van Andel examines how the rhetoric of Edwards' Stockbridge sermons to Native Americans created metaphorical geographies of interior and exterior selfhood that shaped religious subjectivity on the mission frontier. Her attention to language highlights the complexity of the mission and Christianizing experience, and calls into question a binary approach to the relationships between coloniser and colonised.

For some time, scholars tended to portray Edwards as an isolated—and largely unappreciated—American figure. This rather romantic image is being replaced, however, as scholars recognize his place as a British philosopher in conversation with, and exercising a significant impact upon, European thought.[14] The three essays grouped under 'Philosophy' bring Edwards into engagement with figures only rarely touched on in discussions of him: David Hume, John Witherspoon, and Immanuel Kant.

Historian of philosophy Richard Hall compares and contrasts Edwards and Hume's understandings of causality, which lead them both to different conclusions. Though raised, like Edwards, in orthodox Calvinism, Hume's understanding brought him to the brink of skepticism and practical disengagement from his philosophical speculations. In contrast, Edwards' conception of causality propelled him to a rational affirmation of God, panentheistically conceived, as the guarantor of the natural order.

Taking the conversation more in the direction of political philosophy, H. G. Callaway focuses on the influence of John Witherspoon (1723–94) and the American conception of religious liberty and church–state separation, as found in the First Amendment. Witherspoon was strongly influenced by debates and conflicts concerning liberty of conscience and the independence of the congregations in his native Scotland. He brought to his work, as president of the (Presbyterian) College of New Jersey, a moderate Calvinism challenging the conception of 'true virtue' as formulated by Edwards. He further advocated the notion of 'Christian magnanimity', which stood in considerable tension with the prior orthodoxy of predetermination and the historical tradition of Calvinistic theocracy.

In a discussion of human will, divine grace and virtue, Natalia Marandiuc compares Edwards' thought with that of Immanuel Kant, whose influence on all of European thought was profound.[15] She acknowledges the differences that existed between their respective views on virtuous action and emphasises that both Edwards and Kant based their thought on at least two similar assumptions. First, they both posited that the idea of a self-determining human will implied an infinite regression of causes, which could not be logically accommodated within a finite universe. Second, they both conceived the human will as being comprised of 'two ingredients', two operative principles, or two loves, which are ranked and condition one another. Overall, Merandiuc argues that in a carefully defined sense, Edwards' thought mirrors Kant's logic on the relationship between the human will and divine grace, and that grace is similarly invoked by both as the root source of the possibility of true virtue.

Recent scholarship on Edwards has also highlighted the central role he gave to beauty in his theology, which in turn identifies aesthetics— the heading of our final section—as an important category.[16] Edwards and John Keats, separated in time by half a century, would seem to be an unusual pairing, but their sensibilities reveal some interesting congruities. Susan Miller compares and contrasts Edwards and Keats' conceptions of beauty and detects the common linguistic ground that they shared, including the sentiment that beauty on earth provided a glimpse of divine beauty.

Finally, ending on a heavenly note, Kyle Strobel considers a topic that rarely receives attention: the nature and purpose of the beatific vision in Edwards' thought.[17] Through discussion with John Owen's christocentric analysis of the beatific, on the one hand, and of Francis Turretin's patricentric orientation on the other, Strobel traces key Reformed formulations of the mysterious and mystical vision and ends with Edwards' trinitarian depiction of the heavenly vision of God. He argues that Edwards both commends and advances the position of Owens, emphasizing that humanity should focus on the God who gives the vision, rather than on the vision that is received.

Acknowledgements

Kelly van Andel, who at the time that the 'Jonathan Edwards and Scotland' conference was held was completing her doctoral work, was instrumental in organizing the gathering and handling the many on-site details that are known only to those who have had the dubious pleasure of being the 'point person' for scholarly gatherings. On behalf of the Jonathan Edwards Center at Yale, which co-sponsored the conference, and of the presenters, the editors of this volume would like to thank the Department of Theology and Religious Studies and the Faculty of Arts at the University of Glasgow for its assistance, hospitality, and support. We would also like to thank

Philip Hillyer for copy-editing this volume, and Dunedin Academic Press for shepherding it through the publication process.

Notes

1 WJE 16, p. 355.
2 See, for example, the essays in Kling, D. W., and Sweeney, D. A. (eds) (2003) *Jonathan Edwards at Home and Abroad: Historical Memories, Cultural Movements, Global Horizons*, Columbia, South Carolina: University of South Carolina Press, which are cited frequently in the essays below.
3 WJE 6, p. 193.
4 *God Glorified in Man's Dependence* (1731) and *A Divine and Supernatural Light* (1734), in WJE 17, pp. 196–216, 405–26.
5 O'Brien, S. (1986) 'A Transatlantic Community of Saints: The Great Awakening and the First Evangelical Network, 1735–1755', *The American Historical Review*, 91, no. 4 (October), pp. 811–32; Crawford, M. J. (1991) *Seasons of Grace: Colonial New England's Revival Tradition in Its British Context*, New York: Oxford University Press; Lambert, F. (1999) *Inventing the 'Great Awakening'*, Princeton: Princeton University Press.
6 O'Brien, S. (1986), p. 816.
7 See *ibid.*; Schmidt, L. E. (1989) *Holy Fairs: Scottish Communions and American Revivals in the Early Modern Period*, Princeton: Princeton University Press; and Kidd, T. S. (2007) *The Great Awakening: The Roots of Evangelical Christianity in Colonial America*, New Haven: Yale University Press.
8 Mitchell, C. (2003) 'Jonathan Edwards's Scottish Connection', in Kling, D. W., and Sweeney, D. A. (2003), p. 223.
9 Conforti, J. A. (1995) *Jonathan Edwards, Religious Tradition, and American Culture*, Chapel Hill, North Carolina: University of North Carolina Press, ch. 3.
10 Home, Henry, Lord Kames (1751) *Essays on the Principles of Morality and Natural Religion*, Edinburgh: Printed by R. Fleming, for A. Kincaid and A. Donaldson; and Edwards, J. (1757) *Remarks on the Essays*, Edinburgh, n.p.
11 Bebbington, D. W. (2003) 'Remembered around the World: The International Scope of Edwards's Legacy', in Kling, D. W., and Sweeney, D. A. (2003), pp. 183–91.
12 Morris, W. S. (1991) *The Young Jonathan Edwards: A Reconstruction*, Chicago: University of Chicago Press, repr. Eugene, Oregon: Wipf & Stock 2005; WJE 6, 'Editor's Introduction'.
13 See, for example, Davies, R. E. (2006) 'Missionary Benefactor and Strange Bedfellow: Isaac Hollis, Jonathan Edwards' English Correspondent', *Baptist Quarterly*, 41, no. 5, pp. 263–80; Wheeler, R. (2008) *To Live Upon Hope: Mohicans and Missionaries in the Eighteenth-Century Northeast*, Ithaca, New York: Cornell University Press; and McFadden, I. D. (2008) '"Amidst the Great Darkness": The Practical Missiology of Jonathan Edwards at Stockbridge, 1751–1758', STM Thesis, Yale Divinity School.
14 As an example of the former view, see Miller, P. (1949) *Jonathan Edwards*, New York: William Sloane; and of the latter, Fiering, N. (1981) *Jonathan Edwards's Moral Thought and Its British Context*, Chapel Hill, North Carolina: University of North Carolina Press.
15 Harris, J. A. (2005) *Of Liberty and Necessity: The Free Will Debate in Eighteenth-Century British Philosophy*, Oxford: Oxford University Press.
16 See Delattre, R. A. (1968) *Beauty and Sensibility in the Thought of Jonathan Edwards: An Essay in Aesthetic and Theological Ethics*, New Haven: Yale University Press; Mitchell, L. J.

(2003) *Jonathan Edwards on the Experience of Beauty*, Studies in Reformed Theology and History, 9, Princeton: Princeton University Press; and Danaher, W. J. (2007) 'Beauty, Benevolence, and Virtue in Jonathan Edwards's *The Nature of True Virtue*', *Journal of Religion*, 87, no. 3 (July), pp. 386–410.

17 For an earlier treatment that consider Edwards on the beatific within the context of the benevolist debate, see Brand, D. C. (1991) *Profile of the Last Puritan: Jonathan Edwards, Self-Love, and the Dawn of the Beatific*, Atlanta, Georgia: Scholars Press.

International Networks

Chapter 1

'Unfearing Minds':
A Transatlantic Brotherhood of Preachers

Wilson H. Kimnach

The Joseph Badger portrait of Jonathan Edwards—the only one painted from the life, and the one from which all other portraits and images of Edwards have been derived—has always troubled me. It is that periwig. Sometimes I sympathise with Timothy Root's impulse to separate it from the man as inauthentic and therefore an empty icon. After all, Edwards spent his entire life on the American frontier, and he continued to follow it west until called back to Princeton to die. Riding horseback over miles of trails through the woods, occasionally jumping walls or fences, and sometimes dismounting to walk in an open field while singing his devotions to the Lord: surely the periwig played no part in all this. I wonder if he even preached in it at Stockbridge. I realise that in the eighteenth century it was a badge of his status as much as the Geneva collar, but generations have been haunted by that image. That shrewd urbanite Benjamin Franklin knew all about headgear: variously bareheaded or bewigged in his several portraits, he wore an outlandish bearskin cap in Paris to represent his 'Americanness'. Well, let us suppose that Badger had decided to give a little iconic relevance to his portrait by having a nice coonskin cap surmount Edwards' high forehead, maybe with the tail curling elegantly over one shoulder. Would William Hogg, the Edinburgh philanthropist, have paid for that as he did for the one we know? Maybe the Scot would have loved it as a representation of his friend and beneficiary in the Wild West.

Today, as we consider Jonathan Edwards and his preaching brotherhood in Scotland, it is helpful to keep in mind the geographic and political dimensions of their relationship as well as the ecclesiastical one, for all of these dimensions interacted powerfully. It is probably no exaggeration to insist, as has George Marsden most recently, that Edwards was more influential among his Scottish colleagues than among those in America.[1] The young man from the West burst upon the Scottish scene in 1737 when *A Faithful Narrative of the Surprising Work of God in the Conversion of Many Hundred Souls in Northampton, and the Neighbouring Towns and Villages of Hampshire in New-England* was published in London. Before the great revivalist George Whitefield began his epochal crusade throughout the English-speaking world, Edwards provided a vivid account of a seemingly revolutionary awakening that had instilled a new spiritual seriousness in his church and greatly strengthened his clerical hand within the town, as if re-establishing the spiritual coherence of old Puritan communities. Edwards' grandfather, the Rev. Solomon Stoddard, had maintained spiritual and political dominance over this same frontier community for sixty years, but by the time Edwards came to assist him in his last years the community was socially fragmenting. After Stoddard's death the young preacher had striven mightily in the pulpit to regain some of Stoddard's old hegemony, and his *Narrative* demonstrated that by the mid-1730s his efforts were being rewarded. Edwards quickly followed up by publishing a memorial volume of *Discourses on Various Important Subjects* (1738), consisting of his first published treatise, 'Justification by Faith Alone' (a greatly expanded sermon or 'discourse'), and four other sermons, all but one preached during the revival. This volume, the only collection of sermons Edwards was ever to publish, also contains a remarkable preface in which Edwards defines a personal homiletical stance in relation to the trends of the day.[2] In the perspective of history, the preface even implies much of the rest of his literary career.

The preface is remarkably self-conscious and self-justifying from the start, for Edwards immediately states that his church insisted upon publication of the volume and financed it despite serious competing economic demands, and in a modest gesture he suggests that their love for these sermons may have had more to do with their own state of mind when originally hearing them than with 'any real worth in them'. He then goes on to observe that there was at first a hostility to the 'old Protestant' doctrine of justification by faith that he preached. Indeed, he insists that he suffered 'a very open abuse' for preaching it and that only the success of the revival had vindicated him. As the preface develops it becomes clear that the real antagonist is Enlightenment era rationalism—identified by Edwards with Arminianism—and its antipathy to 'fine distinctions' in theological argument. In fact, Edwards' assertion is confirmed by the rhetoric of some contemporary Anglicans and liberal clergy who accused Calvinistic conservatives of being 'metaphysical', implying that they obscured Scripture narrative and the evident truths of the gospel in clouds of abstract speculation. Edwards agrees that mere verbal complication should indeed be discarded, but goes on to insist that many fine discriminations are inescapable if one is to appreciate Scripture teachings in all their real depth and complexity:

> though they contain something that is easy, yet they also contain great mysteries, and there is room for progress in the knowledge of them, and doubtless will be to the end of the world; but 'tis unreasonable to expect that this progress should be made, in the knowledge of things that are high and mysterious, without accurate distinction, and close application of thought . . .[3]

In the same spirit, Edwards apologises for his sermon style in the age of John Tillotson, arguing that these sermons were preached

> mostly at a time, when the circumstances of the auditory they were preached to, were enough to make a minister neglect, forget, and despise such ornaments as politeness, and modishness of style and method, when coming as a messenger from God to souls, deeply impressed with a sense of their danger of God's everlasting wrath, to treat with them about their eternal salvation.—However unable I am to preach or write politely, if I would, yet I have this to comfort me under such a defect, that God has showed us he does not need such talents in men to carry on his work, and that he has been pleased to smile upon and bless a very plain, unfashionable way of preaching. And have we not reason to think that it ever has been, and ever will be, God's manner to bless the foolishness of preaching to save them that believe, let the elegance of language, and excellency of style, be carried to never so great a height, by the learning and wit of the present and future ages?[4]

Well! With this peroration Edwards brings his defensive argument to a climax. Now I have never heard Edwards accused of being an ineffective preacher or a less than powerful writer, even by his enemies. Clearly, in this preface he is assuming a literary posture such as polemical writers do when preparing to engage in culture war.

The Scottish clergymen who became correspondents and supporters of Edwards in the years after these publications—John Erskine, Thomas Gillespie, John McLaurin, William McCulloch, and James Robe, to name the most significant—are said to have cherished Edwards' 1741 sermon on *The Distinguishing Marks of a Work of the Spirit of God* as a practical guide for their own revival efforts. However, I suspect that those who saw his *Discourses on Various Important Subjects* volume, and read its preface, may have experienced a more personal frisson. The voice of Edwards in the preface is clearly that of a provincial figure, significantly more removed than they from downtown, that is, London, yet the arguments of the sermons must have struck them as those of a uniquely talented writer, perhaps young and self-conscious but perceptive and even precociously aware of the challenges they all faced from the dominant urban culture. His emphasis upon Scripture over reason, mystery over simplicity, and homiletical power over modish literary style in preaching touches upon significant preoccupations in the history of Scottish preaching. Since the days of John Knox, the Scottish pulpit emphasised the close reading of Scripture; indeed, a dogged pursuit of essential meaning over large tracts of biblical narrative was yet a staple of Scottish preaching. Moreover, Edwards' insistence upon the touchstone of awakening as a practical test of efficacious preaching mirrored his correspondents' emphasis upon revival and the importance of lay involvement. Perhaps most of all, Edwards' challenge to those who relished witty and sophisticated preaching must have captured echoes from Scottish pulpit history. One thinks of the Scottish field preachers during the persecution of the Covenanters who were reputed to have exercised great powers of eloquence and leadership, but whose power may well have derived as much from the drama of the circumstances under which they preached, or—to use Edwards' term—from the 'frame' of the listeners' minds at the time of preaching.

The recovery of authenticity, or true religion, in both Scotland and North America had become the shared burden of Edwards and his Scottish brethren after the decline of English Puritanism, and they attempted to renew the momentum of reformation on both sides of the Atlantic. In conducting such a campaign, there were great challenges they encountered, especially the challenge of the Papacy, the challenge of prelacy, and the challenge of patronage.[5] These were historic challenges in Scotland from the inception of the Reformation, but they proved to be continuing challenges, and Edwards seems to have felt all three of them as directly in America. It has been long since observed that those who wish to go back in time move west. Thus the Puritans, who sought to recover a primitive church, ultimately moved to the 'howling wilderness' of North America. Even Europeans of a more secular mentality who hankered for a simpler and freer life—such as had allegedly existed before the complications of civilization in a distant golden age—also migrated to American shores. And the process continued to evolve there, whether in the case of Solomon Stoddard who moved west of Thomas Hooker's outpost to become another charismatic patriarch in a way that would have been improbable in Boston, or in the case of his contemporary and neighbor, Edward Taylor, who apparently moved to the frontier primarily to embody his experience in outmoded seventeenth-century poetry. Ever after, they who wished to go back and reclaim something lost to the present moved west in America. To make a fresh start, 'Go West, young man!'

Edwards also thought that the great millennial tide was moving ineluctably westward, the tide that would carry the world back to Christ.[6] But we must remember that the frontier Edwards knew was overshadowed by that first challenge to the Scottish church, the Papacy. In America the threat appeared as the French and Indian War (along with Queen Anne's War and King George's), and despite the division in military history into three separate wars, hostilities were sustained or threatened throughout Edwards' life. It was the frontier of massacres and Indian captivities, but for Edwards it was above all the arena of practical confrontation with the Antichrist. In a special notebook Edwards kept meticulous score of battles won and lost, of tonnages of ships sunk and other material data of warfare, as of a code that might reveal the dynamics of God's millennial agenda. A man of peace but a realist beyond pacifism, Edwards argues in one of his Stockbridge sermons that 'the affair of war is one of the most important of all the affairs of the universe: the state of the world of mankind principally depends upon it'.[7] He was thus able to sympathise with his Scottish brethren in 1745 when the French underwrote a Papal resurgence in Scotland in the person of Bonnie Prince Charlie and his Highlanders:

> How far God may punish the nations of Great Britain by him, we cannot tell .... but it now becomes us ... to cry to him, that he would overrule all for the advancement of the kingdom of Christ, and the bringing on the expected peace and prosperity of Zion.[8]

The massacre of Culloden and the attendant depredations of the English in Scotland were later overlooked by Edwards in a celebratory letter to the Rev. William McCulloch:

> God has done great things both in Scotland and America ... wherein his providence is on many accounts exceedingly remarkable: in Scotland, in the suppression of the late rebellion; and in America, in our preservation from the great French armada from Brest [that aimed to recapture Louisburg].[9]

In these events Edwards saw earthly salvations worthy of comparison with those in the age of Moses, and of course the essence was victory over the agents of Antichrist.

Perhaps closer to all concerned was the second challenge, the threat of prelacy: an imposition of the English episcopal church government upon Presbyterian Scotland, and in New England the emergence of Anglicanism. The main threat in the two countries was, however, felt primarily in different eras. Scotland's trial was mainly in the seventeenth century after James VI and I had begun the campaign to unite his kingdom ecclesiastically according to his slogan, 'No bishop; no king'. He and his Stuart successors kept at it intermittently until the Glorious Revolution put an end to them, but in the seventeenth century they perpetrated violence against the resisting Scottish Covenanters comparable to that of the Duke of Alva in Holland. For Edwards and New England, the threat was a much gentler but more intimate phenomenon, particularly when the Rev. Timothy Cutler, rector of the supposedly conservative Yale College, went over to the Church of England, carrying two tutors with him. Cutler had been Edwards' chief academic mentor, and his declaration for Episcopacy, his 'apostasy' as it was known in New Haven, greatly abetted fears and inflamed rumors that the Anglican Church was going to attempt a takeover of the country, sending in missionaries and perhaps even enlisting the civil powers to subvert the last bastion of Puritanism. In both Scotland and America, the issue of 'Anglicanization' was as much a social and political affair as a religious one: seemingly an attempt by the central government and the forces of wealth and power to make the provinces toe the line. For their part, the independent-minded Scots and New Englanders both hearkened back to the Protestant Reformation in their past and saw the present as its treasured legacy. It is touching to read Edwards' breathless response to John Erskine in 1748, wherein he celebrates the

> remarkable and joyful accounts [your letter] contains of things that have a blessed aspect on the interests of Christ's kingdom in the world: such as the good effects of the writings of Mr. West and Mr. Lyttelton on some at Court; . . . the hopeful true piety of the Archbishop of Canterbury; his and the King's disposition, not only to tolerate, but comprehend the dissenters, and their indifference with respect to the liturgy, ceremonies and Episcopal ordination . . . [10]

Edwards seems to have felt that Congregationalists and Presbyterians might rejoice in a little benign neglect from London, if nothing more.

The third challenge—patronage—may seem to have been primarily a Scottish problem; however, a closer look reveals some striking convergences in the experiences of Edwards and his Scottish brethren in relation to this complex and pervasive practice. In Scotland church congregations of course desired what they took to be appropriate pastors, but the Church of Scotland had the authority to install pastors regardless of congregational preferences. One of Edwards' chief correspondents, the Rev. Thomas Gillespie, minister at Carnock, became a martyr/hero of this conflict when he decided to defend a congregation from such an imposition by the Church. In 1752, a neighboring congregation at Inverkeithing had no relish for a minister that the Church wished them to have, but the General Assembly instructed Gillespie to assist in the settlement anyway. He refused and was depositioned by the Church, retiring to Dunfermline where for six years he preached to a congregation without ecclesiastical connection. Finally, other sympathizing ministers joined with him to form a Presbytery and they established the Relief Church.

Edwards was horrified to hear of his friend's expulsion from the Church. He wrote to Gillespie:

> 'Tis to be wondered at that such a church, at this time of day, after the cause of liberty in matters of conscience has been so abundantly defended, should arrogate to herself such a kind of authority over the consciences of both ministers and people, and use it in such a manner,

by such severity to establish that which is not only so contrary to that liberty of Christians wherewith Christ has made them free, but so directly contrary to her own professed principles, acts and resolutions entered on public record.

Moreover, Edwards could not help but surmise that

at the bottom, besides a zeal to uphold the authority of the church . . . many of the clergy of the Church of Scotland have their minds secretly infected with those lax principles of the new divinity, and have imbibed the generous doctrines (as they are accounted) which are so much in vogue at the present day, and so contrary to the strict, mysterious, spiritual, soul-humbling principles of our forefathers. I have observed that these modern, fashionable opinions, however called noble and generous, are commonly attended, not only with a haughty contempt, but an inward, malignant bitterness of heart towards all the zealous professors and defenders of the contrary spiritual principles, that do so nearly concern the vitals of religion, and the power of experimental godliness.

Significantly, Edwards admitted that 'I don't pretend to know how the case is: I only speak from what I have seen and found here in America in cases something similar.'[11]

This letter was written in 1752, just two years after Edwards had experienced 'something similar' in his own dismissal from the church in Northampton. Of course Edwards' case seems quite the opposite from Gillespie's on the surface, in that a popular uprising within his own congregation overturned Edwards' pastorate upon his attempted modification of their communion practice. However, it is clear that Edwards saw himself as reasserting the traditional Puritan practice respecting qualifications for communion after the Northampton church had arbitrarily introduced a radical liberalization under his grandfather Stoddard. Paradoxically, the earlier minister was a modernist who charged ahead of the niceties of the half-way covenant, while his successor was a strict constructionist of the Puritan Way. But more to the point of Gillespie's case, Edwards also saw himself as a victim of the system of civil and ecclesiastical patronage that had evolved in the Connecticut Valley, for Solomon Stoddard and his ministerial colleagues in Hampshire County had constructed a ministerial association of Presbyterian mold that oversaw ecclesiastical affairs within the Valley. Thus, when Edwards differed with his congregation, a council of churches in the region was called. This council contained some sympathisers but also some opponents, and when the vote of the council was taken the opponents prevailed by one vote, in part because one of the supposedly sympathetic lay representatives failed to show for the meeting.

But in Edwards' eyes, a larger issue may have been the cabal of the influential Williams family against him, compounded by the recent death of his most powerful political and social backer, Col. John Stoddard. Throughout his career in Northampton and Stockbridge, Edwards was bedeviled by his cousins of the Williams family and their in-laws. In a 1753 letter to one of his American patrons, Edwards is blunt about the Williams clan:

> There has for many years appeared a prejudice in the family of the
> Williamses against me and my family, especially ever since the great
> awakening in Northampton, about eighteen years ago [1735]....
> When the late great controversy began between me and my people
> concerning terms of communion [1750] ... the family of the
> Williamses deeply engaged themselves in this controversy, on the side
> of my opposers, who were principally upheld, directed and animated
> by them in that controversy ... [12]

The death of Col. John Stoddard—son of Solomon, head of the selection committee that picked Edwards to assist his grandfather, power broker of Northampton and the western New England frontier, religious and political sophisticate—did in fact deprive Edwards of his protector and most astute advisor in things broadly political. Had there been no Williams clan and had Stoddard lived, it is hard to imagine Edwards being fired in 1750, despite certain social divisions inherent in the community and errors in judgment he himself admitted to in another letter to Gillespie.[13] In other words, even in the supposedly autonomous congregations of eighteenth-century colonial New England, the civil and ecclesiastical powers occasionally worked out surprisingly effective methods of oversight and control.

Perhaps the most interesting aspect of this incident, however, is what Edwards did upon his dismissal. John Erskine and his clerical brethren immediately offered to find Edwards a pulpit in Scotland, as did other friends and admirers in Virginia and Connecticut. The Scottish offer must have been especially tempting since Edwards saw Scotland as both close to the centre of the learned world that fascinated him and yet relatively sympathetic to evangelical Calvinism. However, probably because he saw

himself as pursuing a good that had been lost in the past, he plunged westward. Indeed, he moved west of the more settled frontier into real Indian
territory. Stockbridge had been founded by Col. John Stoddard as an Indian
mission in 1736, and it was now Edwards' chosen refuge. Of course, by this
time Stockbridge had become a full-blown company town, sustained by
the Society for Propagating the Gospel in Foreign Parts and land specula-
tors by the name of Williams. Yes, the same ones. Edwards was more than
ever dependent upon the most direct and literal patronage, and he seems
to have spent much of his time in Stockbridge resisting the Williams clan's
efforts to exploit the Indian mission for their own profit, and politicking
(by letter) among the American and English patrons of the mission. Thus
any insults offered to Gillespie by the Church of Scotland actually pale by
comparison with the political combat endured by America's philosophical
theologian on the wild frontier. In the last extant letter Edwards wrote to
Gillespie, he concludes:

> As we, dear Sir, have great reason to sympathise one with another,
> with peculiar tenderness, our circumstances being in so many respects
> similar, so I hope I shall partake of the benefit of your fervent prayers
> for me. Let us thus endeavor to help one another (though at a great
> distance) in traveling through this wide wilderness, that we may have
> the more joyful meeting in the land of rest, when we have finished our
> weary pilgrimage.[14]

But such struggles were born in the courage of faith, and despite their
suffering under the varied threats and constraints of the Papacy, an imperial
state church, and a hierarchical society, Edwards and his Scottish brethren
seem to have been carried well through. Revivals and missions provided
sources of great encouragement, even if the latitudinarian Church of
England was comfortably beyond another Puritan uprising. Separated by
miles of ocean and wild country, Edwards and his Scottish correspondents nevertheless dreamed millennial dreams and plotted together for the
triumph of true religion. For Edwards, the years between 1743 and 1757
were particularly challenging, but during this period the Scots provided
him with a kind of recognition and fraternal warmth that was apparently
difficult to get, or possibly to accept, from those more proximate. He wrote
to William McCulloch early on in 1744, 'I consider myself as writing to a
candid Christian friend and brother, with whom I may be free and bold,

and from whom I may promise myself excuse and forgiveness.'[15] Shortly after, he wrote to the Rev. [John McLaurin]:

> When the day is so dark here in New England, it is exceeding refreshing and reviving to hear … of religion's being to such a degree upheld in the power and practice of it, in those parts of Scotland that have been favored with the late revival, … under the labors and conduct of such pious, solid, judicious and prudent instruments, that Christ there makes use of.[16]

By comparison, Edwards lamented the decline of the American revivals into warring parties of New and Old Lights (or Sides), the result of undisciplined enthusiasm and incompetent leadership. As he explained to John Erskine:

> 'The cry was, 'O, there is no danger, if we are but lively in religion and full of God's Spirit and live by faith, of being misled! … Let us press forward and not stay and hinder the good work, by standing and spending time in these criticisms and carnal reasonings!' … This was the language of many, till they ran on deep into the wilderness and were taught by the briars and thorns of the wilderness.[17]

Of course Edwards may not have been made fully aware of the divisions within the Scottish pulpit community, such as that between the Evangelicals and the Moderates, the former largely adhering to an archaic sermon form not unlike Edwards' own, expounding the gospel stereotypically in a chanting voice, and sedulously avoiding all stylistic enhancements, while the latter cultivated a new sermon form of more open structure, lectured learnedly on moral themes, and cultivated the graces of eighteenth-century literary style. Certainly, the differences in Scotland were parallel in terms of educational and class appeal to many of the differences between Old and New Lights in America. John McLaurin may not have made it clear to Edwards that some considered him as among the Moderates while Erskine was typed an Evangelical, especially inasmuch as McLaurin's sermons would have appealed to Edwards as thoroughly evangelical in substance, while original in thought and graceful in expression. Edwards did express shock upon learning of Ralph and Ebenezer Erskine's secession from the Church of Scotland, but on the whole his letters do not manifest much awareness of the fractiousness of contemporary Scottish religious life, though this may have been a matter of Edwards' policy too.[18]

For if Edwards was losing faith in America's aptitude for achieving efficacious revivals, he was newly inspired by the idea of global religious networks. Indeed, he repeatedly insisted to his Scottish friends that they lived in a miraculous age, and while stepping adroitly aside every time someone tried to bring up the practical issue of the Millennium—insisting that there were doubtless many trials and periods of disappointment to be endured before that day—he welcomed new measures preparing the world for it. By the mid-1740s, Edwards had completed a three-stage critique of religious experience with his treatise on *Religious Affections*; he had initiated a post-revival program to consolidate and perpetuate the fruits of revival in his Northampton congregation with the renewal of their church covenant, and he was looking for a new model of Christian leadership, a model that he would shortly identify with the self-sacrificing heroism of the missionary to the Indians, David Brainerd. When, in 1744, John McLaurin and his Scottish colleagues informed Edwards of the plan to organise their separate congregations in a concert for prayer, uniting the people in offering collective prayer to God for the pouring out of his Holy Spirit upon the church, Edwards seized upon the idea, doubtless as one that would be less disruptive and divisive than the American revivals had been, and, perhaps more important, more likely to be sustained over years rather than months.

During the initial two-year phase of the concert, Edwards' correspondents informed him, both Scots and English had been moved to participate. He read their letters to his Northampton congregation as a stimulus in furthering this post-revival program, although his people were not quick to commit to the concert, at least in significant numbers. Edwards himself, however, seemed immediately excited by the possibilities of this spiritual network:

> I hope the time is hastening, when God's people in all the different
> parts of the world, and the whole earth shall become more sensibly,
> as it were, one family, one holy and happy society, and all brethren,
> not only all united in one head, but in greater affection, and in more
> mutual correspondence, and more visible and sensible service of
> God; and so that in this respect, the church on earth will become
> more like the blessed society in heaven, and vast assembly of saints
> and angels there.[19]

Increasingly troubled by spats with parents over the wayward conduct of their children and by the spiritual intractability of his congregation, Edwards responded intensely to kindred spirits, however far removed, and dreamed of harmonious societies.

Finally, despite his demanding agenda during the mid 1740s, Edwards entered energetically into his major Scottish-American collaboration with *An Humble Attempt to Promote Explicit Agreement and Visible Union of God's People in Extraordinary Prayer for the Revival of Religion and the Advancement of Christ's Kingdom on Earth, Pursuant to Scripture-Promises and Prophecies concerning the Last Time*. In a letter to the Rev. William McCulloch in 1747, Edwards mentions the Concert for Prayer, observing:

> I have taken a great deal of pains to promote this concert here in America, and shall not cease to do so, if God spares my life, as I have opportunity in all ways that I can devise. I have written largely on the subject, insisting on persuasives and answering objections; and what I have written is gone to the press.[20]

The 188-page promotional tract (dated 1747) issued from the press, after some delays, in 1748. Based upon a sermon Edwards preached in February 1747,[21] the tract is amplified by materials drawn from other sermons, letters to his Scottish correspondents, and, especially, Edwards' 208-page manuscript, 'Notes on the Apocalypse'. Probably intentionally, the original sermon is Scottish in style, being heavily exegetical, the opening of the text constituting nearly a third of the sermon manuscript, while Edwards' norm was a page or two. This is also reflected in the tract, but the overall argument is perhaps most remarkable for its publication of material from Edwards' speculations on the Apocalypse that he had hitherto kept to himself, such as those regarding the slaying of the witnesses and the interpretation of the sixth vial.[22]

This collaborative effort—Edwards' tract pointedly reprints the Scottish Memorial in its entirety—was heartily endorsed upon publication by the Scottish ministers; indeed, the Rev. John Willison wrote, 'I wish it were universally spread, for I both love and admire the performance upon subjects so uncommon.'[23] But endorsement in America, whether in the tract's preface signed by five Boston ministers or, later, from the eminent revivalist, the Rev. George Whitefield, was somewhere between guarded and tepid. It seems that the Scots may have been more prepared for the intellectual adventure of applying the Apocalypse than persons associated with the earlier revivals in America. That this radical biblical narrative was more amenable to the Scots may be indicative of a more positive perception of the revival experience in Scotland than in America, at least by the end of the 1740s. It may also bear out the thesis of an early Scottish literary historian, David Irving, that Scots are more interested in *things*, whereas the English are satisfied with mere verbal elegance, and thus the Scots are more hospitable to history, moral philosophy, and philosophical criticism than the English.[24] If these Scots really were so oriented, then they had found their true soul-mate in Jonathan Edwards, for whom ideas were eminently *things*, or authentic entities, whose locale could only be adumbrated by the most artfully poised words. As he observed to John Erskine while analyzing the arguments of Lord Kames's supporters regarding the will, 'These men... aim at they know not what... substituting a number of confused, unmeaning words, instead of things, and instead of thoughts'.[25] In the end, *An Humble Attempt* apparently did sell better on the other side of the Atlantic than in America, for of seven separate English language editions of *An Humble Attempt* published, only three were printed in America.[26]

All in all, in a time of international wars between Roman Catholic and Protestant powers that necessitated the garrisoning of Edwards' frontier home, a time during which the philosophical theologian assumed the outdoor role of missionary to the Indians, a time when he nevertheless produced the most enduring literary monuments from his lifetime of meditation on a theology that would make New England's Calvinist heritage persuasive to the Enlightenment: at such a time Jonathan Edwards found a circle of kindred spirits in distant Scotland good company indeed. They exchanged sermon pamphlets and expressed opinions on the pursuit of authentic Christianity in a difficult environment. John McLaurin, brilliant preacher and leader of the Concert for Prayer movement, may have been most comparable to Edwards for intellect and spiritual depth. James Robe emulated Edwards in producing his own *Short Narrative* of Scottish revivals and excited Edwards with his talents as a publicist and editor of *The Christian Monthly History*. William McCulloch had Edwards' respect as leader of the Cambuslang revival and was a recipient of many letters from Edwards. Thomas Gillespie shared the bond of one who had suffered professional humiliation for cause of conscience, and thus Edwards shared with him the most detailed analysis he gave anyone of the debacle of his Northampton pastorate.[27]

The last to befriend Edwards, John Erskine, was perhaps his best friend, in life and beyond. Erskine catered to Edwards' insatiable hunger for information about the learned world. 'You would much oblige me, if you would inform me what are the best books that have lately been written in defense of Calvinism', Edwards wrote in his earliest extant letter to Erskine, and later in the same letter, 'I should be glad if you would inform me more particularly in your next [letter] . . . what the state of infidelity in Great Britain is'. A man of substantial means, Erskine not only supplied Edwards with information but sent him packages of the latest important books, books from London and Edinburgh reflecting the best both friend and foe could offer. Indeed, the letter containing the above quotations begins with an inventory of Erskine's latest package, including a copy of John Taylor's treatise on *Original Sin*, the efficient cause of Edwards' last major treatise.[28] And after Edwards' death Erskine collaborated with the Rev. Dr. Jonathan Edwards, Jr. to publish *A History of the Work of Redemption* (1774), *Miscellaneous Observations on Important Theological Subjects* (1793), and *Remarks on Important Theological* Controversies (1796), so the benefactions of John Erskine flowed in both directions, to the great profit, in life and after, of his friend in need.

Today it is easy to forget the tenuousness of the bridge between Scotland and Edwards' America in the mid-eighteenth century, fabricated as it was by the exchange of paper documents, manuscript and printed. There were the ocean voyages in vulnerable wooden sailing ships, sometimes during periods of open warfare at sea. Once in the port of Boston, friends—occasionally remarkably forgetful—were required to pick up the mail and to find relatives, other friends, or just travelers who were going west over the Bay Path to the frontier. It was a three days' journey to Northampton on the rough road connecting scattered villages, past farms and the occasional parsonage where a night's rest might be had. After 1750 there was the complication of forty additional miles on even more primitive paths into country where fewer people would have traveled, a place to which passage from Boston might have been most facilitated by a coasting ship, sailing south from Boston into Long Island Sound and up the Connecticut River to one of the small clearings in the forest indicating a landing and a connecting trail. Edwards received letters and packages months after they were sent, and he was never surprised to discover one had gone missing. For his part, he often wrote multiple drafts of a single letter in the hope that one would get through to Scotland. He also wrote most letters with a more or less explicit directive that they be circulated among his correspondents or even published by James Robe in his journal. One way or another, whether in frontier village or deep in Indian territory, Edwards kept his hand extended, and he always found a responsive hand extended equally from the provinces of Scotland.

As Sir Walter Scott wrote, describing John Erskine in *Guy Mannering*, 'Such...must have been the preachers to whose unfearing minds, and acute, though sometimes rudely exercised talents, we owe the Reformation.'[29]

Notes

1 Marsden, G. A. (2003) *Jonathan Edwards: A Life*, New Haven: Yale University Press, p. 309. The most extended recent analysis of this phenomenon is in Mitchell, C. W. (1997) 'Jonathan Edwards's Scottish Connection and the Eighteenth-Century Scottish Evangelical Revival, 1735–1750', Ph.D. diss., St. Mary's College, University of St. Andrews, Scotland.

2 The preface is reprinted in WJE 19, pp. 793–98. The sermons are distributed through-out vol. 19 in chronological order with other sermons.

3 *Ibid.*, p. 796.

4 *Ibid.*, p. 797.

5 This tripartite structure of issues was suggested to me by a lecture in the Lyman Beecher Course of 1886, delivered at Yale University by the Rev. Dr. William M. Taylor and published as Taylor, W. M. (1887) *The Scottish Pulpit from the Reformation to the Present Day*, New York: Harper & Brothers, p. 15. My use of the concept is very different from his.

6 See especially *Some Thoughts Concerning the Revival*, in WJE 4, p. 353.

7 *God's People Tried by a Battle Lost*, in WJE 25, p. 689.

8 Letter of Nov. 1745 to a Scottish Correspondent [McLaurin], in WJE 16, p. 197.

9 Letter of 21 Jan. 1747 to William McCulloch, in *ibid.*, p. 219.

10 Letter of 14 Oct. 1748 to John Erskine, in *ibid.*, pp. 259–60.

11 Letter of 25 Nov. 1752 to Thomas Gillespie, in *ibid.*, pp. 545–7.

12 Letter of 30 Jan. 1753 to Sir William Pepperrell, in *ibid.*, p. 554.

13 Letter of 1 July 1751 to Thomas Gillespie, in *ibid.*, p. 380–4.

14 Letter of 8 Oct. 1753 to Thomas Gillespie, in *ibid.*, p. 610.

15 Letter of 5 Mar. 1744 to William McCulloch, in *ibid.*, p. 142.

16 Letter of Nov. 1745 to a Scottish Correspondent [McLaurin], in *ibid.*, p. 180.

17 Letter of 23 Nov. 1753 to John Erskine, in *ibid.*, p. 538.

18 See Letter of 12 May 1743 to James Robe for Edwards' guarded response to the Erskine secession, in *ibid.*, p. 110.

19 Letter of Nov. 1745 to a Scottish Correspondent [McLaurin], in *ibid.*, p. 183.

20 Letter of 23 Sept. 1747 to William McCulloch, in *ibid.*, p. 237.

21 *The Suitableness of Union in Extraordinary Prayer for the Advancement of God's Church*, in WJE 25, pp. 200–6.

22 The texts of the 'Notes on the Apocalypse' and *The Humble Attempt* are printed in WJE 5. See the editor's introduction for a discussion of themes applied in the tract, especially pp. 29–48.

23 Quotation in WJE 5, p. 87.

24 Irving, D. (1804) *Lives of the Scottish Poets*, Edinburgh: Alex. Lawrie & Co., vol. 1, pp. 182–4.

25 Letter of 25 July 1757 to John Erskine, in WJE 16, p. 708.

26 WJE 5, p. 85.

27 Letter of 1 July 1751 to Thomas Gillespie, in WJE 16, pp. 380–7.

28 Letter of 31 Aug. 1748 to John Erskine, in *ibid.*, pp. 248–50.

29 Scott, W. (1815) *Guy Mannering; or, the Astrologer*, Edinburgh: Archibald Constable & Co., ch. 37.

Chapter 2

Exchanges in Scotland, the Netherlands, and America: The Reception of the *Theoretico-practica theologia* and *A History of the Work of Redemption*

Adriaan C. Neele

My friends, if your Ears be open, there are Three Things that you may hear this Day … I. To offer some Remarks concerning the Covenant in general … II. Offer some reasons of the doctrine: the great Mystery of the Covenant of Redemption, … and III. Draw some Inferences for Application.[1]

Thus wrote the eighteenth-century Scottish preacher Ralph Erskine (1685–1752), in a sermon entitled *Christ the people's covenant*—preached (1722), published in Scotland (1725, 1747), translated and published in Holland (1743), received by Jonathan Edwards in a package from Scotland (1749),[2] and published at Boston (1770). This example touches on the extent of intercontinental correspondence, publications, translations, and covenant theology. More generally, it relates to two fields of scholarship: Edwards and Post-Reformation studies.

Since about 1980, both the studies on Jonathan Edwards and on the Post-Reformation era have seen a considerable increase and development.[3] At the same time, however, while scholarship on Edwards seems to suffer from a growing lack of awareness and attention to the fact that eighteenth-century New England is somehow connected to the continental intellectual thought of the seventeenth century—an understanding that was present in the preceding generation[4]—scholarship on the Post-reformation Reformed period shows a tendency to focus primarily on European developments at the exclusion of early American history and theology, particular that of New England.[5]

In such broad contexts of Edwards and Post-Reformation studies, furthermore, one observes, that, on the one hand, the theologian of Northampton and Stockbridge, while residing at the frontiers of New England, was an active participant of a transatlantic community of evangelical exchanges.[6] As such, attention has been given to Edwards and the Scottish connection, the possible influence of Edwards upon the Scottish clergy, and the other way around.[7] The majority of these studies focus on the New England–Scotland epistolary exchanges, and the revivals, though it is recently proposed to include the Netherlands, and in particular the Dutch Great Awakening, in these appraisals.[8] On the other hand, however, these studies lack the broader historical-theological background, and in particular, of the trajectories and continuities between the Dutch, Scottish, and New England proponents of Reformed orthodoxy.

Therefore, in this chapter I will, first, explore the connections between the Netherlands, Scotland and early America, relevant to academics, translations, publications, correspondence, and theological cross-influences. Secondly, to provide representative examples of these connections, I will trace the development and reception of two works that crossed the Atlantic and were known in Scotland, and important for both fields of scholarship, that on Edwards and Post-Reformation Reformed studies: *Theoretico-practica theologia* (*TPT*) of Petrus van Mastricht (1630–1706) and the *History of the Work of Redemption* (*HWR*) of Jonathan Edwards. My aim, thereby, is to discover if any undercurrent is present before, during, and after the periods of eighteenth-century intercontinental correspondence and revivals. In particular, is there a kinship present among these New England, Scottish, and Dutch theologians, pastors, and religious practitioners—and if so, what kind of kinship?

Therefore, in the first part of this contribution I will focus on the context of the completion of the *TPT*, presented within the academic context of Mastricht's stay at Utrecht from 1676 to 1706: the university, colleagues, correspondence, and students, particularly as they relate to Scotland and New England, as well as the reception of the *TPT*. In the second part, I place the reception of the *HWR* in the Dutch context of 1776, and review its structure and content in light of the *TPT*, and conclude with some final remarks.

The *Theoretico-practica theologia*: Context and Reception

The University of Utrecht in the seventeenth century had grown from a humble beginning in 1636 to a prestigious and internationally acclaimed academy by the time of the death of its chancellor and chair of theology, Gisbertus Voetius (1589–1676). For more than forty years Voetius had lead the Academy with the motto of his inaugural address of 1636, *Scientia cum pietate conjugenda* ('science [or academics] joined with piety'). The faculty of theology was recognised throughout Europe as the apex of Protestant scholasticism and orthodoxy. Voetius' formative influence, through his *disputationis* on Reformed theology, was widely known and long-remembered, as attested in a letter of 1748 by Thomas Gillespie (1708–74) to Jonathan Edwards.[9] Voetius' colleagues Johannes Hoornbeeck (1617–66) and Andreas Essenius (1618–77) have long been regarded as standing in his shadow as one of the foremost advocates of the *praxis pietatis* of Reformed theology. However, their major works were much admired internationally throughout the seventeenth and eighteenth century. New England pastors such as Edwards, and physicians such as Samuel Woodward (1750–1835), read the *Summa controversiarum religionis* of Hoornbeeck, and Essenius' systematic theology, the *Compendium theologiæ dogmaticum*, became the standard textbook at the divinity school of the University of Edinburgh in the seventeenth and eighteenth century, and formative for a generation of Scottish divinity students, Ralph Erskine (1685–1752) and Thomas Boston (1676–1732) among them.[10] Essenius' appointment in 1654 at the Utrecht academy was due to Samuel Rutherford's (1600–61) turning down the chair of the faculty of theology. The senate of the university, the Reformed church, and city counsel of Utrecht, had tried, during seven months of intense correspondence between Aberdeen and Utrecht, to persuade the Scottish theologian of St. Andrews to come to the Utrecht Academy. Even the Scottish church of Rotterdam consulted with Rutherford's brother, James Rutherford, sergeant of the Scottish garrison based in Holland, in support of the request of the Academy.[11] However, Rutherford stated in a letter to the senate his surprise that the Academy invited him, as there was already an 'eminent theologian' in Utrecht, namely, Essenius. Shortly thereafter, both Voetius and Essenius passed away and Mastricht was called from the University of Duisburg, Germany, to succeed Voetius in the chair of theology.

Mastricht was not unfamiliar with the Utrecht Academy. In 1647, while he came from Cologne to be treated in Utrecht for his crippled foot,[12] he stayed there for the study of theology under Voetius and Hoornbeeck, the latter his former pastor and catechism teacher at the Reformed and international refugee church at Cologne. Mastricht received a thorough education: didactic-dogmatic theology, which included the *loci communes* as presented in the Leiden *Synopsis purioris theologiæ*; an introduction to the *Summa Theologia* of Thomas Aquinas; and an acquaintance with the scholastic *disputationes* of Voetius' Saturday morning teachings. The study program was a result of Voetius' 1644 publication, *Exercitia et bibliotheca studiosi theologæ*, a comprehensive 700-page introduction to theological literature and a five-year program of theology. In summary, Mastricht received a scholastic methodological schooling, including the knowledge of the medieval scholastic definitions and distinctions, whereby theology must be known and practiced.[13]

Before his graduation in 1652 Mastricht, as commonly was done at the time, visited other universities for study, among them Leiden University, where he probably studied under the great covenant theologian Johannes Coccenius (1603–69), and at the universities of Heidelberg and Oxford. Following his graduation he returned to Germany to take up a vicariate at Xanten, Cleve, followed by a five-year pastorate in Glückstadt in the north of Germany on the Denmark border. In Glückstadt, an international transfer point between the Netherlands, Scotland, eastern Germany and the Baltic states, he finished his first major theological treatise, *De Prodromus*.[14] This work shows already the contour of Mastricht's fourfold and integral approach to theology: exegesis, doctrine, elenchtic, and *praxis*. Following Glückstadt he served between 1662 and 1677 at the universities of Frankfurt an der Oder and Duisburg, respectively as professor of Hebrew, and Hebrew and philosophy. While at Frankfurt he published a method of preaching,[15] which later became the introductory disputation to his major theological work, the *TPT*, and in Duisburg his major philosophical work *De Gangraena*,[16] a work widely acclaimed, not only by the Reformed church and academy but also by Lutheran and Roman Catholic theologians.[17] Furthermore, at Duisburg he commenced in 1676 with *disputationis* on the doctrine of God, which he continued without interruption upon his arrival at the Utrecht Academy in 1677.[18] In Utrecht followed a flow of publications with a wide range of theological topics, such as the nature of theology, Roman Catholic teachings, the work of redemption, and the assurance of salvation.[19] His work, in the form of disputations, treatises and other publications culminated ultimately in 1699 in his *magnum opus*, the *Theoretico-practica theologia*—a work completed amidst his daily work with his colleagues, correspondence, and students.

In 1679, while Mastricht concentrated his teaching on dogmatics, ethics, and church history, the Dutch theologian Herman Witsius (1636–1708) was appointed as professor of theology. Witsius had earned recent fame with his publication, *De œconomia fœderum Dei cum hominibus* (*On the Economy of the Covenant of God with Man*)—an influential work that attempted to reconcile the reigning orthodoxy and covenant theology. Witsius' theological works were greatly appreciated by various Scottish theologians, among them Donald Fraser of Kennoway, translator of Witsius' work *Excercitationes in Symbolum* (*On the Apostles' Creed*), and Thomas Bell of the Relief Church, who, upon advice of Edwards' major correspondent John Erskine, D.D. (1720–1803), translated Witsius' *Animadversiones irenicae* (*Considerations for peace*).[20] In New England, it was in particular Edwards who also approvingly cited multiple works of Mastricht's colleague, including, *On the Economy of the Covenant*, the *Apostles' Creed*, and *Miscellanea Sacra*, in his writings such as 'Notes on Scriptures', the 'Miscellanies', the 'Blank Bible', and 'Subjects of Inquiry'.[21]

In addition, there was for some time an ongoing scholarly correspondence between Harvard College of New England and the faculty of theology at University of Utrecht. One topic of exchange concerned the relationship of native American dialects and the Hebrew language, which Mastricht's colleague, the Christian Hebraist Johannes van Leusden (1624–99), rejected. Furthermore, Mastricht was involved in correspondence regarding a gift of Harvard College, John Eliot's 1663 edition of the Algonquin Bible. Moreover, Mastricht wrote approbations, required by Dutch Reformed church order, for the Dutch translation of works by Thomas Shepard of New England, *Sound Beleever*, and probably *The Sincere Convert*.[22]

The international character of the Utrecht academy was constituted in part by the significant presence of Scottish students.[23] The harbor city of Rotterdam was a center of commerce and religious communication, through the Scottish Kirk, between Scotland and Holland since the early 1700s, and served as a safe haven for Scottish exiles preceding the Glorious Revolution of 1688, among them Thomas Halyburton (1674–1712), later divinity professor at St. Andrews.[24] Scottish students studied at the Dutch universities at Leiden, primarily for law, and at Utrecht, principally for theology, though transfers between these academies and cooperative studies regularly occurred.

With respect to Leiden, the defense of Mastricht's student, James Hog (c.1658–1734), a graduate of Edinburgh University, is illustrative.[25] He defended on 20 March 1680 a disputation about the assurance of salvation[26] in the presence of other Scottish students Thomas Hog, Jacob Kirton, Donald Cargill, and John Dickson, who all studied at Leiden. In addition, this defense was attended by two Reformed ministers. One of them, Jacobus Borstius (1612–80) of Rotterdam, was known for supporting the Scottish nonconformists in that city and advancing the Scottish cause by translating and publishing several Scottish works into Dutch, among them the *History of the Churches of Scotland* as well as works by Rutherford, whose *Examen Arminianismi* was printed first at Utrecht for the benefit of the Scottish students of divinity there.[27] The other minister was Jacobus Koelman (1632–95), a prolific theologian and translator of multiple works of Scottish theologians into Dutch, such those of the Glasgow professor of philosophy and preacher Hugh Binning (1627–53), David Dickson (1583–1662), professor of divinity of the College of Glasgow and University of Edinburgh William Guthrie (1620–65), and also Rutherford. In addition, Koelman introduced the translations of the works of Thomas Hooker of New England to the Dutch religious public.[28]

Another example showing that students alternated between universities is Colonel John Erskine, the grandfather of John Erskine D.D., Edwards' primary correspondent in Scotland. Colonel Erskine studied law at the Utrecht Academy in 1686–7 but also attended lectures of theology by Mastricht and visited him several times with fellow Scottish students.[29] He notes, for example, in his diary on 7 June 1686, 'I was a while with Professor van Mastricht: he was very kind and I do take him to have true religion.' However, most of Mastricht's Scottish students did not recall him, an exception being James Hog, who appealed to his teacher during the *Marrow* controversy.[30]

In this academic and international setting at Utrecht, replete with Scottish students and New England correspondence, Mastricht completed his life-long project, a work written over a period of thirty years. Commenced at Glückstadt and finished at Utrecht in 1699, his *magnum opus*, the *Theoretico-practica theologia*, became a major and influential work of Protestant scholastic and Reformed orthodoxy of *theoretico-practica* theology.[31] He could not have envisioned the favorable reception of his *TPT* throughout Europe, and that the work particularly would be recognised and approvingly cited by eighteenth-century theologians in Scotland and even New England.

Edwards, 'America's theologian', wrote in 1746 to his student and colleague Joseph Bellamy (1719–90):

> But take Mastricht for divinity in general, doctrine, practice and controversy; or as a universal system of divinity; and it is much better than Turretin or any other book in the world, excepting the Bible, in my opinion.[32]

Though this quotation may be the most cited but least explained appraisal of Mastricht in Edwards scholarship, one has to realise that Edwards reiterated a common understanding among the New England theologians. Take, for instance, the generous praise of Cotton Mather (1663–1728) in his *Manuductio ad Ministerium*:

> But after all there is nothing that I can with so much Plerophorie Recommend unto you, as a *Mastricht*, his *Theologia Theoretico-practica* ... I know not that the Sun has ever shone upon an Humane Composure that is equal to it.

Mather had written an earlier and grandiose opinion on the *TPT* to a Dutch merchant at Albany, New York: 'The world has never yet seen so valuable a system of divinity ... 'Tis orthodox, 'tis concise, 'tis complete. In one word it is everything.'[33]

Mather's commendation of Mastricht's *TPT* was echoed from Boston into the valleys of New England, throughout the eighteenth century and later, by Benjamin Colman (1673–1747), Joseph Seccombe (1706–60), the anonymous editor of the only English translation of a chapter from the *TPT*, entitled *On Regeneration*, and Samuel Hopkins (1721–1803).[34] Mastricht's work of theology was probably used by Bellamy,[35] and extensively read. Edwards' 'Account Book' records that he lent the work repeatedly, and Edward Amasa Park (1808–1900), at the close of the nineteenth century, notes that Jonathan Edwards Jr. (1745–1801) read the *TPT* seven times.[36] Edwards, Sr., however, referring in his 'Catalogue' of Reading to the *TPT* as a 'Body of Divinity',[37] frequently concurs throughout his *corpus* with the *TPT*. These connections, as I have argued elsewhere,[38] are related to an Edwardsean understanding of the covenant of grace.

In respect to Scotland, the 'Marrowmen', such as Ralph Erskine (1685–1752) and John Brown of Haddington (1722–87), were favorable towards Mastricht's thought on the doctrine of the covenant, probably influenced by Mastricht's student James Hog—a Scottish interest that continued even into the nineteenth century.[39] The influence of Mastricht upon Ralph Erkine's intellectual thought is significant. In his theological debate with James Robe on the question, 'Is an imaginary idea of Christ's human body helpful to faith or is it idolatrous?',[40] Erskine wrote an extensive treatise entitled *Faith no Fancy*. In it he relies profoundly on three Dutch philosophers to demonstrate his epistemology, namely, Mastricht's colleague at Utrecht, Gerard de Vries; his Leiden colleague Adriaan Heereboord, whose book on logic was used in Edwards' days at Yale College; and the 'learned' Mastricht, both the *TPT* and *De Gangraena*.[41] More explicit is Erskine's theological thought, as explicated in his sermons, with a strong emphasis on the covenant, such as *Christ the people's covenant*, a sermon published in Scotland, Holland, and New England. In this communion sermon, Erskine, like Mastricht, moves from the biblical text explication to the formulation of doctrine, followed by a practical application. Though such sermon structure is not that unusual in the Reformed theological trajectory, Erskine espouses a view similar to Mastricht's rather unusual—in the context of seventeenth-century Reformed dogmatics—exposition of the work of redemption, the covenant of grace, both throughout history and with an application for the believer.[42] Erskine exhorts that the God of the covenant is not forgetting Scotland throughout history, in particular the people of Dunfermline, 'with a view to the sealing of the covenant'.[43] Moreover, Erskine, like Mastricht, understands the sacrament of holy communion as a covenant renewal.[44] Furthermore, the reception of the *TPT* in Scotland attests that the Dutch theologians, among them Mastricht, exerted considerable influence on Scottish theology. As one scholar of Scottish religious history has noted, 'Covenant theology ... had been imported from Holland, and was destined to occupy a prominent place in the orthodox school in Scotland.'[45]

Thus far, we have seen that the context of the development of Mastricht's *TPT* shows continuing interaction with Scotland and New England, in correspondence, and among colleagues and students. Its reception was more positive in New England than in Scotland. Though Mastricht's work was acknowledged by three generations of eighteenth-century theologians and pastors in New England, it is in scholarship 'often mentioned but rarely explored.'[46]

Mastricht's *magnum opus* consists of two parts: the first part comprises eight books, which could be described as systematic theology, or as Mastricht states, addressing the nature of faith.[47] The second major section concerns the character of obedience, presented as an outline of moral theology and *theologia ascetica*. These two parts, that of faith and obedience, reflect Mastricht's defining theology as the 'art of living to God', and in turn consist of two aspects: how one is made spiritually alive and, being alive, how one lives unto God (*Deo vivere*).[48] In regard to systematic theology, Mastricht appears to follow the division of the six Reformed *loci* of theology, with these significant differences: first, faith is not discussed in the context of soteriology but as a commencement of the discussion of theology proper. Secondly, each *locus* is presented in four parts: exegesis, doctrine, polemic, and *praxis*. The formulation of doctrine and practice is a result of and is guarded, for Mastricht, by the exegesis of Scripture. Thirdly, and contrary to what one may expect of a Post-reformation Reformed *systema*, the work lacks a chapter entitled 'eschatology'; instead, the last chapter is called *De dispensatione foederis gratiæ* ('On the dispensations of the covenant of grace'). This chapter consists of a grand narrative from the creation account to Mastricht's own time, and attests to a broad international and up-to-date interest in historical, philosophical, and theological publications.

Mastricht moves in four major sections from the dispensation under the patriarchs and Moses to Christ and ends with a treatment on the dispensation of eternity. In the first section, he is concerned with the propagation, theology, and heresies of the covenant of grace in the era from Adam to Noach to Abraham to Moses.[49] In the second section, he enlarges the discussion by including sacred and world history as well as the progress and regress of this covenant during the period of Moses to David; David to the Babylonian captivity;[50] and the latter to the coming of Christ. The third section, the dispensation of Christ, is the largest of the chapter, in which Mastricht blends theology, sacred and world history, typology and shadows, confessions and creeds, heresies, persecutions, schisms, the rise and fall of the antichrist, and Roman Catholic and Islamic theology, into one and continuing expanding narrative.[51] However, in each section he notes explicitly the propagation or progress, renovation or renewal of the covenant of grace throughout the ages,[52] whereby his exposition of the dispensation of Christ coincides with an analysis of the Apocalypse chapter 6 and the dispensation of eternity with an exposition of the Apocalypse chapters 7–11. In particular, this section of Mastricht's exposition of the dispensations of the covenant of grace differed with a work of one of his students, Moses Lowman (c.1680–1752), whose work *Paraphrase and Notes on the Revelation* became one of Edwards' major sources for both his 'Notes on the Apocalypse' and *An Humble Attempt.*[53]

Mastricht's view on theology and history, or the development of the covenant of grace, is based on the work of redemption. He notes that the exposition of the dispensation of the covenant rests upon and extends his discussion of the application of the work of redemption, as expounded in the preceding bk. 5, based on Genesis 3:15.[54]

One should note, however, that the presentation of church history throughout several dispensations was not uncommon in Post-reformation Reformed theology, as seen in Frederick Spanheim (1632–1701), Mastricht's colleague at Leiden University, whose *Historica Ecclesiastica* Mastricht praises.[55] Further, to present the history of the church in relation to the covenant of grace was worked out to a great extent by Johannes Coccecius,[56] Mastricht's former teacher at Leiden University. In addition, the exposition of the Apocalypse in relation to church history was also done by Mastricht's contemporary Wilhelmus à Brakel (1635–1711).[57] However, Mastricht stood apart in his time, in that he merged the history of the church and the covenant of grace with sacred and world history concurrently and in concert with the exposition on the Apocalypse:[58] an approach of which he writes, 'I had planned for long ... a great work about the adventures of the Church.'[59]

In summary, Mastricht's work contained a fairly strong and almost unique notion of the covenant of grace throughout history. This theological notion was a part of his overall system of *theoretico-practica* theology, whereby history was understood as theology. This Latin tome was translated into Dutch in 1749, prefaced by Cornelis van der Kemp (1702–72), pastor and professor of theology at Rotterdam:

> Here, the major parts of theology are brought together in a manner not seen before; why this book is called a universal system of divinity; 'tis called a treasure, a storehouse ... for the perfection of the theologian.[60]

The History of the Work of Redemption: Context and Reception

The entire translation of Mastricht's work took place between 1749 and 1753, which context is a part of the reception of the Dutch translation and publication in 1776 of Edwards' work, *The History of the Work of Redemption.*

First, the publication of Mastricht's work was accompanied in the period from 1740 to 1760—corresponding to the New England and Scottish revivals—with translations of various Scottish authors such as Ralph and Ebenezer Erskine, Thomas Halyburton, Josiah Smith, and Edwards' correspondent, James Robe (1688–1753).[61]

Secondly, in addition to the publishers, three other persons were involved in this translation enterprise: Hugh Kennedy (1698–1764), the pastor of the Scottish church at Rotterdam, whose publications were critically received by Edwards; the translator Mr. Jan Ross, assumed to be a member of the Scottish church at Rotterdam; and the pastor and philosopher-theologian at Woubrugge, Alexander Comrie (1706–74), a Scot by birth, having as his catechism teachers Ralph Erskine and Thomas Boston (1676–1732), whose major works he translated into Dutch.[62] One thing these publications have in common: a particular attention to the covenant of grace. In particular, the communion sermons aimed for a personal, and sometimes national, 'covenant renewal'.[63]

Thirdly, these publications and Mastricht's translated works were widely read during the time of the Dutch Great Awakening, and in the same period approvingly cited by Edwards of Northampton,[64] whose account of David Brainerd appeared in 1756 in the Dutch language, also translated by Jan Ross but published at Utrecht.[65] The probable reason for this location of publication was the presence of Gisbertus Bonnet (1723–1803), the second successor of Mastricht at the University of Utrecht and correspondent of John Erskine, D.D., of Scotland.[66] At the very least, Bonnet was instrumental in another publication of Edwards, the *History of the Work of Redemption* in 1776, the structure and content of which does not deviate that much from Mastricht's discussion of the dispensations of the covenant of grace.

The *HWR* originated in 1739 as a series of sermons—or, more accurately, a single sermon delivered on thirty consecutive 'preaching occasions'. After Edwards' death, the sermon manuscripts remained for a while in the custody of Joseph Bellamy, who eventually passed them on to Jonathan Edwards, Jr. He transcribed them and sent them to John Erskine, D.D., in Scotland, where they were tailored into a 'continuing treatise' and published in Edinburgh for W. Gray in 1774.[67] John F. Wilson remarks, 'Erskine may never have known how relatively unfinished and incomplete some sections of the Redemption Discourse actually were'—a remark that may also apply to the Dutch edition. Erskine, after acquiring the Dutch language for his correspondence, had in turn sent a copy to Bonnet at Utrecht,[68] where it was almost immediately translated by Engelbert Nooteboom into Dutch and published by the university printer Abraham van Paddenburg in 1776, prior to the first American edition of 1786. But more notably, the Dutch interest in New England theology continued in the eighteenth century after Edwards' death.

Edwards' sermons 2–12, like Mastricht's first two major sections on the dispensation of the covenant of grace, moves from the fall to Noach to Abraham to Moses to David to the Babylonian captivity to the coming of Christ.[69] Here, not only in structure but also in content Edwards was firmly within his theological tradition by commencing the covenant of grace with Genesis 3:15, the protoevangelium. Mastricht not only begins with this text but he used it also as the scriptural foundation for his entire exposition of the preceding chapter on *De Foedere Gratia*.[70] Mastricht comments, although the 'form or the name is not yet present', this text contains 'all the material and essential parts of the covenant of grace'.[71] Likewise, according to Edwards, Christ began his mediatorial work as soon as mankind fell, and the 'gospel was first revealed on earth, in these words, Genesis 3:15'.[72] Edwards calls this 'the first revelation of the covenant of grace':[73] an echo of Mastricht, when he writes, 'immediately after the fall [was] established a covenant of grace.'[74]

The next major section of Edwards' work, sermons 14–24, focuses on Christ's incarnation to his own time: Mastricht collectively treats this period in his discussion on the dispensation under Christ. Both *TPT* and *HWR* show similarities in content about the time of Christ till the Protestant Reformation. Illustrative is the discussion on the Reformation, where both Mastricht and Edwards note the Roman Catholic opposition, specifically but not limited to the Council of Trent,[75] as well as wars[76] and persecutions.[77] Furthermore, both identify the rise of the Socinians and Arminians as hostile to Reformed teachings.[78] On the other hand, the success of the gospel shows for Mastricht and Edwards a reformation in doctrine and worship.[79]

Finally, Mastricht has a separate discussion on the time to come, *de dispensatione sub aeternitate*, an application of the work of redemptive history that addresses the continuation of earth, heaven and hell.[80] Edwards' sermons 27–30 address also the eternal state of the church. More precisely, the seven steps pertaining to the last things, as formulated in the last four sermons of Edwards' redemption discourse, are similar to the seven steps Mastricht formulated in his chapter on the eternal dispensation.[81] Coinciding with Mastricht's discussion of these seven steps, Mastricht provides an exposition of the seven trumpets of Revelation 8–11. On the seventh trumpet, for example, he comments that this woe is to the peace and happiness of the church and to the destruction of its enemies.[82] Edwards' understanding of this last trumpet in sermon 24 seems closer to Mastricht's understanding than to the exposition on the same by Mastricht's student Lowman.[83]

Thus, Edwards, like Mastricht, divides the history of redemption into major sections, of which each is divided into dispensations, periods and *epochas*, though both understand these differentiations in the history of redemption as belonging to the same covenant of grace, which is the golden thread throughout the *HWR*, as it is in Mastricht's chapter on the dispensations of the covenant of grace. So central is this theological concept to Edwards' work that it is suggested[84] that one could almost substitute the title of 'A History of Covenant of Grace' for *HWR*, as, *de historiae foederis gratiae*, an echo of Mastricht's *TPT* preface.

The Dutch readership, then, was not that unfamiliar with the structure and content of Edwards' work. For them, there was a continuity of theological thought, in particular, that of covenant theology. Antecedents were readily found in Mastricht's work, as well as in the immediate context of Edwards' Dutch edition of the Redemption Discourse.

Therefore, I conclude with three observations. First, the reading of Edwards' *HWR* should not be limited to the historical-theological context of England or New England, but should consider Mastricht's *TPT* as its background. As this major work was influential in the formation of eighteenth-century Scottish covenant theology, so the parallels in structure and content between bk. 8 of the *TPT* and *HWR* may point to a marked influence. For Mastricht, the covenant of grace and eschatology are inseparable—a trajectory found in the redemption sermons of Edwards. Actually, for both Mastricht and Edwards, the progressive development of the covenant of grace in history is teleological. The covenant of grace, according to Mastricht, is being directed toward an end or shaped by a purpose: the *telos* of creation or the divine glory in the eternal dispensation. It may be, therefore, that the positive reception of the *TPT* in New England was a consistent presence in the development of New England theological thought. On the other hand, the reception of the *HWR* in Holland is not that surprising—which leads me to the next observation. Secondly, the exchanges between New England, Scotland and Holland took place between people of different denominational affiliations. Nevertheless, there was a latently present kinship, a theological kinship: that of covenant theology. Thirdly, as this essay suggests, the interaction between scholarship on Edwards and Post-reformation studies can open new ways of approaching the continuities and trajectories of historical and theological thought.

Appendix

*A Chronological Bibliography of Dutch Translations of
Religious Works by Scottish Authors, 1740–67*

Thomas Boston

(1741) *Eene beschouwing van het verbondt der genade, uit de heilige gedenk-
schriften: Waar in de onderhandelende persoonen, die dat verbondt
hebben aangegaan, hoe en T'wanneer het gemaakt zy, deszelfs deelen, zoo*

wel voorwaardelyk als beloovende, en de bestiering van het zelve, ieder afzonderlyk overwoogen worden, trans. Alexander Comrie, preface by Hugh Kennedy, Leiden: Johannes Hasebroek; Amsterdam: Nicolaas Byl.

(1742) *Des menschen natuur in deszelfs vier-voudige staat: Van eerste opregtigheyt, geheele bederving, begonne herstelling, en voltrokke gelukzaligheit of ellende. Vertoond in verscheyde praktikale redenvoeringen,* trans. Abel van Keulen, preface by Cornelius van Velzen, Leiden: Johannes Hasebroek, Amsterdam: Nicolaas Byl.

(1752) *De kleine catechismus der kerken Jesu Christi in Engelandt Schotlandt en Yrlandt,* trans. Jan Ros, preface by Alexander Comrie, Groningen: Laurens Groenewolt.

Ebenezer Erskine

(1754) *Godts naam verheerlykt in Christus, De zuchtingen der geloovigen onder hare beswaringen, De verhooging der geloovigen, en De koning gebonden op de galeryen,* trans. Jan Ross, preface by Theodorus van der Groe, Rotterdam: Hendrik van Pelt, Adrianus Douci.

Ralph Erskine

(1740) *De kragt der zonde, en hoe de wet de kragt is van dezelve, geopent en ontfouwt in verscheide predikatien, gepredikt te Kinglassy den 31. July; als ook te Orwel den 7 en 8 Augustus 1727,* trans. Jan Ross, Rotterdam: Hendrik van Pelt, Adrianus Douci.

(1740) *De overeenstemminge der goddelyke eigenschappen, doorstralende in het werk der verlossinge, en in het zaligen van zondaren door Christus Jezus, zynde eene leerrede, gepredikt te Dunfermline den 29 September 1723,* trans. Jan Ross, Rotterdam: Hendrik van Pelt, Adrianus Douci.

(1740) *Het sterven aan de wet, en het leven naar het euangelium. Of Het sterven aan wettische geregtigheit, en het leven volgens eene euangelische heiligheit,* trans. Jan Ross, Rotterdam: Hendrik van Pelt, Adrianus Douci.

(1742) *De zwangere belofte, en hare vrucht; of De kinderen der belofte voortgebragt en beschreven,* trans. Jan Ross, Rotterdam: Hendrik van Pelt, Adrianus Douci.

(1743) *De groote vrage van den evangeliecatechismus: zynde de inhout van verscheide predikatien over Matth. XXII: 42: En de predikatie van de Samaritaansche vrouwe aan de lieden van de stadt,* trans. Jan Ross,

Rotterdam: Hendrik van Pelt, Adrianus Douci.

(1743) *De verzekeringe des geloofs verklaart en toegepast: zynde de inhoudt van verscheide predikatien over Hebr. X:19–22,* trans. Jan Ross, Rotterdam: Hendrik van Pelt, Adrianus Douci.

(1746) *De gelukkige en groote vergaderinge der volkeren tot Schilo: zynde een verhandelinge over Gen. XLIX: 10 voorgestelt in verscheide predikatien, op avondtmaals-tyden, te Kinglassie, te Airth, en te Carnock,* trans. Jan Ross, Rotterdam: Hendrik van Pelt, Adrianus Douci.

(1747) *Blyde boodtschap in zware tyden, over psalm XLVI,* trans. Jan Ross, preface by Theodorus van der Groe, Rotterdam: Hendrik van Pelt, Adrianus Douci.

(1750) *Christus het verbondt des volks,* Rotterdam: Hendrik van Pelt, Adrianus Douci.

(1752) *De trapwyze overwinninge, of de hemel allengkens gewonnen . . . een belovende en volbrengende Godt, de riviere des levens: voorgestelt, in verscheide predikatien, by gelegenheit van het H. Avondtmaal,* trans. Jan Ross, preface by Theodorus van der Groe, Rotterdam: Hendrik van Pelt, Adrianus Douci.

(1758) *Gevoelige tegenwoordigheit, over Gen. XXXV: 13. Kameren van veiligheit, in tyden van gevaar, over Jez. XXVI: 20, 21,* trans. Jan Ross, Rotterdam: Hendrik van Pelt, Adrianus Douci.

(1758) *De groote bazuine des Evangeliums, over Jez. XXVII:13,* trans. Jan Ross, preface by Theodorus van der Groe, Rotterdam: Hendrik van Pelt, Adrianus Douci.

(1761) *Pleit-reden des geloofs op Godts woordt en verbond: Alles voorgestelt in verscheide predikatien, by de bediening des H. Avondmaals,* trans. Jan Ross, preface by Georgius Hogendorp, Rotterdam: Hendrik van Pelt, Adrianus Douci.

(1762) *De wet van Godts huis,* trans. Jan Ross, Rotterdam: Hendrik van Pelt, Adrianus Douci.

(1763) *Den zondaar verheugd in Gods heiligdom, onder het geloovig gebruik maken van Christus, als de ware geestelyke spyzen der zielen: Zynde den inhoud van 10 uitmuntende leer-redenen, meest op Avondmaals tyden gedaan,* Rotterdam: Hendrik van Pelt, Pieter Holsteyn.

(1767) *De bron van alle zegeningen, of Het grote schathuis geopent: beneffens de gevende liefde van Christus, en de aannemende eigenschap des geloofs.*

Zynde den inhoud van twee verhandelingen, de eerste over 2 Cor. V. 18. De tweede over Gal. II. 20, trans. Jan Ross, Utrecht: J. van Schoonhoven, S. de Waal, G. van den Brink, Jzn.

Thomas Halyburton

(1745) *Gedenk-schriften, in zig behelzende het leven, de bekeeringe, en merk-waardige gevallen van . . . Begrepen in vier deelen. Waar by gevoegt is, een verhaal van zyn laatste woorden*, Rotterdam: Hendrik van Pelt, Adrianus Douci.

(1747) *Het groot aanbelang der zaligheit: begrepen in drie deelen: in zich behelzende I. Eene ontdekkinge van des menschen staat en toestandt van nature, II. Des menschen herstellinge door het geloove in Christus, III. Des christens plicht*, preface by Hugh Kennedy, Rotterdam: Hendrik van Pelt, Adrianus Douci.

James Robe

(1743) *Geloofwaardig en kort verhaal van 't heerlyke werk Godts, geopenbaart in de overtuiginge en bekeeringe van een groot getal zielen in de gemeinte van Cambuslang, en in andere plaatsen van Schotlandt*, preface by Hugh Kennedy, Rotterdam: Hendrik van Pelt, Adrianus Douci.

(1743) *Nader en uitvoeriger verhaal van 't heerlyke en uitmuntende werk Godts; gewrogt in de bekeeringe van veele zielen in verscheidene gemein-tens van Schotlandt, inzonderheit tot Kilsyth*, preface by Hugh Kennedy, Rotterdam: Hendrik van Pelt, Adrianus Douci.

(1743) *[Tweede] Nader en uitvoeriger verhaal van 't heerlyke en uitmun-tende werk Godts, gewrogt in de bekeeringe van veele zielen in verscheidene gemeintens van Schotlandt, inzonderheit tot Kilsyth*, preface by Hugh Kennedy, Rotterdam: Hendrik van Pelt, Adrianus Douci.

(1744) *Derde stukje of Vervolg wegens het Nader en uitvoeriger verhaal van 't heerlyke en uitmuntende werk Godts, gewrogt in de bekeeringe van veele zielen in verscheide gemeintens van Schotlandt, inzonderheit tot Kilsyth*, preface by Hugh Kennedy, Rotterdam: Hendrik van Pelt, Adrianus Douci.

John Smith

(1751) *De uitmuntende levenswyze en predikdienst van den zeer vermaarden euangelie-prediker en reiziger George Whitefield: onpartydig voorgestelt en naar het leven afgemaalt in eene leerreden over Job XXXII. 17. Mitsgaders eenige geestelyke oeffeningen en bevindelyke aantekeningen van jufvrouw Ross, op den weg naar den hemel*, Rotterdam: Hendrik van Pelt, Adrianus Douci.

Notes

1 Erskine, R. (1725) *Christ the people's covenant*, Edinburgh?: n.p., pp. 8, 5; *ibid.* (1770), Boston: William M'Alpine, p. 4.

2 *The Works of Jonathan Edwards Online*, vol. 32, Letter B78 (Letter from Thomas Foxcroft, June 26, 1749).

3 On Edwards studies, see Minkema, K. P. (2004) 'Jonathan Edwards in the Twentieth Century', *Journal of the Evangelical Theological Society*, 47 (December), p. 662. On studies of the Post-Reformation era, see Muller, R. A. (2003) *Post-Reformation Reformed Dogmatics: The Rise and Development of Reformed Orthodoxy, ca. 1520 to ca. 1725*, Grand Rapids: Baker Academic, vol. 4, pp. 479–545.

4 Miller, P. (1938) *The New England Mind: The Seventeenth Century*, Cambridge, Massachusetts: Harvard University Press; Morris, W. S. (1991) *The Young Jonathan Edwards: A Reconstruction*, Chicago: University of Chicago Press; repr. Eugene, Oregon: Wipf & Stock, 2005; Elwood, D. J. (1960) *The Philosophical Theology of Jonathan Edwards*, New York: Columbia University Press; Fiering, N. (1981) *Jonathan Edwards's Moral Thought and Its British Context*, Chapel Hill, North Carolina: University of North Carolina Press.

5 Early American history and theology would fall within the divisions of the Post-Reformation Reformed era proposed by Muller into early orthodoxy (*c.*1565–1640), high orthodoxy (*c.*1640–1725), and late orthodoxy (*c.*1725–75). Muller, R. A. (2003), vol. 1, pp. 31–2.

6 Lesser, M. X. (2008) *Reading Jonathan Edwards: An Annotated Bibliography in Three Parts, 1729–2005*, Grand Rapids: Eerdmans.

7 On the Edwards–Scotland connection, see Orr, J. (1903) 'Jonathan Edwards; His Influence in Scotland', *Congregationalist and Christian World (1901–1906)*, 88 (October), p. 467; Simonson, H. P. (1987) 'Jonathan Edwards and his Scottish Connections', *Journal of American Studies*, vol. 21, no. 3, pp. 353–76. On Edwards' influence on the Scottish clergy, see Durden, S. (1976) 'A Study of the First Evangelical Magazines, 1740–1748', *Journal of Ecclesiastical History*, 27 (July), pp. 255–75; O'Brien, S. (1986) 'A Transatlantic Community of Saints: The Great Awakening and the First Evangelical Network, 1735–1755', *The American Historical Review*, 91 (October), no. 4, pp. 811–32. On other networks from the seventeenth to the nineteenth century, see Vaudry, R. W. (2003) *Anglicans and the Atlantic World: High Churchmen, Evangelicals, and the Quebec Connection*, Montréal: McGill-Queen's University Press. See WJE 2, p. 466, n. 2: 'There are some interesting parallels between the work of the Scottish evangelical ministers of the period and the activities of Jonathan Edwards in New England.'

8 On correspondence, see Mitchell, C. W. (2003) 'Jonathan Edwards's Scottish Connection', in Kling, D. W., and Sweeney, D. A. (eds) (2003) *Jonathan Edwards at Home and Abroad: Historical Memories, Cultural Movements, Global Horizons*, Columbia, South Carolina: University of South Carolina Press, pp. 222–47. On revivals, see Fawcett, A. (1971) *The Cambuslang Revival: The Scottish Evangelical Revival of the Eighteenth Century*, London: Banner of Truth Trust. And on the Dutch *Nadere Reformatie*, see van Lieburg,

F. (2008) 'Interpreting the Dutch Great Awakening (1749–1755)', *Church History*, 77, no. 2 (June), pp. 319–36, which argues that the Dutch revival both is rooted in a Dutch confessional context and connected to events in the Anglo-Saxon world.

9 Printed in WJE 2, p. 497: '(what if I remember right *Voetius* terms *obsessio*, and one in that situation *obsessus*)'.

10 For Edwards on Hoornbeeck, see WJE 2, pp. 301, 471: 'magistri Menachem Rakanatensis, Sect. Bereschit, ex Midrasch Tehillim, citante Hoornebeckio contra Judæos Lib. 4. Cap. 2. p. 354' (the editor's footnote incorrectly identifies him as Anthony Hornbeck rather than Johannis Hoornbeeck). Woodward owned a copy of the second edition (1658) of Hoornbeeck (1653), *Summa controversiarum religionis: cum infidelibus, haereticis, schis-maticis: id est Gentilibus, Iudaeis, Muhammedanis, Papistis, Anabaptistis, Enthusiastis & Libertinis, Socinianis, Remonstrantibus, Lutheranis, Brownistis, Graecis*, Utrecht: Johannis à Waesberge, owned by G. Williams, 1709, Samuel Woodward 'ex dono Dr. Russell', and A. Holmes, 1817 (private collection); Woodward, a graduate of Yale, is probably the Connecticut doctor from Torrington, who served also as Speaker of the Connecticut House of Representatives. On the influence of Essenius' (1669) *Compendium theologiæ dogmaticum*, Utrecht: Meinardi à Dreunen, see van Harten, P. H. (1986) *De Predking van Ebenezer en Ralph Erskine. Evangelieverkondiging in het spanningsveld van verkiezing en belofte*, 's-Gravenhage: Boekencentrum, p. 51; and Boston, T. (1776) *Memoirs of the Life, Time, and Writings of the Reverend and Learned Thomas Boston*, Edinburgh: A. Murray, p. 19: 'A few of us, newly entered to the school of divinity, were taught for a time Riissenius's compend, in the professor's [George Campbell] chamber. Publicly in the hall he taught Essenius's compend.'

11 Kernkamp, G. W. (ed.) (1938) *Acta et Decrata Senatus Vroedschapsresolutiën en andere bescheiden betreffende de Utrechtsche Academie*, Utrecht: Broekhoff N.V., vol. 1, pp. 262–71.

12 The Dutch word for 'foot' is *voet*. The name Voetius is the Latinised form of Voet.

13 G.W. Kernkamp (1936) *De Utrechtsche Universiteit 1637–1936*, Utrecht: A. Oosterhoek's Uitgevers Maatschappij, vol. 1, p. 233; Muller, R. A. (2003) *After Calvin: Studies in the Development of a Theological Tradition*, Oxford: Oxford University Press, pp. 110–16. Voetius, G. (1736) 'Reedenvoeringe van de Nuttigheit der Akademien en Schoolen, mitsgaders der Wetenschappen en Konsten', in le Long, I. (1736) *Hondert-Jaarige Jubel-Gedachtenisse der Academie van Utrecht*, Utrecht: M. Visch.

14 van Mastricht, P. (1666) *Theologiæ didactico-elenchtico-practicæ Prodromus tribus speci-minibus*, Amsterdam: Johannes van Someren.

15 van Mastricht, P. (166?) *Methodus Concionandi*, Frankfurt an der Oder: M. Hübner.

16 van Mastricht, P. (1677) *Novitatum Cartesianarum Gangræna, Nobiliores plerasque Corporis Theologici Partes arrodens et exedens. Seu Theologia Cartesiana detecta*, Amsterdam: Jansson.

17 See Neele, A. C. (2009) *Petrus van Mastricht (1630–1706). Reformed Orthodoxy: Method and Piety*, Leiden, Boston: Brill, pp. 42–3.

18 van Mastricht, P. (1677) *Theologiæ Theoretico-Practicæ disputatio quinta, De Existentia Et Cognitione Dei*, Wilhelmus Mercamp, Duisburg: Franc. Sas.; *idem.* (1677) *De omnisufficientia Dei, pars prior Theologiæ theoretico-practicæ disputatio sexta* Theodorus Groen, Utrecht: Meinardus à Dreunen; *idem* (1677) *Theologiæ theoretico-practicæ disputatio septima De essentia, nominibus et atrributis Dei in genere, Pars 2*, Balduinus Drywegen, Utrecht: Meinardus à Dreunen.

19 van Mastricht, P. (1678) *Disputationum practicarum prima de certitudine salutis ejusque*

natura, Johannes Kamerling, Utrecht: Meinardus à Dreunen; *idem* (1679) *Disputationum practicarum tertia de certitudine salutis, eique opposita præsumptione seu securitate carnali*, pars prima, David de Volder, Utrecht: Meinardus à Dreunen; *idem.* (1680) *Ad illust. episcopi Condomensis expositionem doctrinæ, quam vocat, Catholicæ, diatribe prima de consilio auctoris*, Rutgerus van Bemmel, Utrecht: Meinardus à Dreunen.

20 Witsius, H. (1681) *Excercitationes sacrae in symbolum quod apostolorum dicitur et in orationem dominicam*, Franeker: n.p., and (1677) *De œconomia fœderum Dei cum hominibus, libri quattor*, Leeuwarden, Eelcke Symons Nauta Symons for Jacob Hagenaar. Most of these theologians belonged to the Secession churches such as the Burghers John Brown of Witburn, John Dick, and James Peddie, as well as anti-Burghers such as Thomas M'Crie, and the Scottish Methodist James Hervey and John Colquhoun of the Church of Scotland. On the influence of Witsius' covenant theology in Scotland, see van Genderen, J. (1953) *Herman Witsius, bijdrage tot de kennis der Gereformeerde theologie*, 's-Gravenhage: Guido de Bres, pp. 236–40.

21 For references by Edwards to Witsius' works, see Edwards, J., 'Notes on Scripture' no. 416, in WJE 15, p. 466; 'Miscellanies' no. 1309, in WJE 23, pp. 148, 269–72; entries on Acts 16:27–28, 1 Cor. 14:13, and 1 Tim. 1:9, in WJE 24, pp. 24:981, 1056, 1125; and 'Subjects of Inquiry', in *The Works of Jonathan Edwards Online*, vol. 28.

22 On Native American dialects and Hebrew, see Kernkamp, G. W. (ed.) (1938), vol. 2, p. 51; and on the Eliot Bible, see *ibid.*, vol. 2, p. 90: "'Eodem die,' biedt prof. Leusden de Senaat aan "biblia in Americanam linguam translata" en aan de bibliotheek der Utrechtsche Academie ten geschenck aangeboden, met deze inscriptie: "Bibliothecam celeberrimæ apud Ultrajectionos Academiæ hac sacrorum Bibliorum versione Indica donat Crescentius Matherus, Collegii Harvardini apud Cantabrigienses in Nova Anglia praeses pro tempore." Leusden zal namens de Senaat bedanken en Mather "suis conatibus properum rei Christianae in iis oris successum' toewensen."' The Dutch translations of Shepard were published as Shepard, T. (1686) *De Gezonde Geloovige*, Amsterdam: Johannes Boekholt; *idem.* (1683) *De Ware Bekeering*, Utrecht: Willem Clerck.

23 Kernkamp, G. W. (1936), vol. 1, p. 180. Though we know that the Utrecht senate reprimanded in 1693 70–80 Scottish students—approximately 20 % of the total number of students—for not attending the Anglican Church services, the *Album Studiosorum* of 1689–93 shows about a quarter of that number present. See also (1836) *Album studiosorum Academiae rheno-traiectinae MDCXXXVI–MDCCCLXXXVI*, Utrecht: J. Beijers en J. van Boekhoven; du Rieu, W. N. (1875) *Album studiosorum Academiae Lugduno Batavae MDLXXV–MDCCCLXXV*, The Hague: n.p.

24 Young, D. (ed.) (1825) *Memoirs of the Rev. Thomas Halyburton*, Edinburgh: W. Whyte & Co., p. 79.

25 James Hog graduated from Edinburgh University with an M.A. in 1677, and then studied theology in the Netherlands in the 1680s.

26 van Mastricht, P. (1680) *Disputationum practicarum tertia, de certitudine salutis, eique opposita præsumptione seu securitate carnali*, pars secunda, Jacobus Hoog, Utrecht: Meinardus à Dreunen. James Hog was 'exalted' in the student records of Utrecht from Hog to (Jacobus) Hoog. He was considered as 'one of the holiest ministers in the kingdom [of England and Scotland] having published or recommended the celebrated and edifying tract of the Cromwellian age, called *The Marrow of Modern Divinity*'. Cf. Fisher, E. (12th edn, 1726) *The Marrow of Modern Divinity*, with notes by Thomas Boston, Edinburgh[?]: n.p.; repr. Seoul, New York: Westminster Publishing House, p. 344; Hog, J. (1947), *Wet en Evangelie*, trans. E. Kuyk, Amsterdam: Kuyk, p. 5.

27 For an extensive discussion on the Scottish churches in the Netherlands, see Sprunger, K. L. (1982) *Dutch Puritanism: A History of English and Scottish Churches of the Netherlands in the Sixteenth and Seventeenth Centuries*, Leiden: Brill, pp. 388–90, 431–9. And on Borstius, see van der Haar, J. (ed.) (1985) 'Jacobus Bortius', in *Het Blijvende Woord*, Dordrecht: Gereformeerde Bijbelstichting, p. 35. Rutherford, S. (1668) *Examen Arminianismi conscriptum et discipulis dictatum a doctissimo clarissimoque viro*, Utrecht: n. p. This work received the imprimatur of Voetius and Essenius. See Ryken, P. G. (1999) 'Scottish Reformed Scholasticism', in Trueman, C. R., and Clark, P. G. (eds) (1999) *Protestant Scholasticism: Essays in Reassessment*, Carlisle: Paternoster Press, p. 202.

28 Binning, H. (1678) *Ettelyke gronden van de christelycke religie, klaerlyck geopent, en sonderling tot de practijck gebracht*, trans. Jacobus Koelman, Vlissingen: Abraham van Laren, and Amsterdam: Mercy Brouwning; *idem* (1680) *De ware gemeenschap met God en de geloovigen*, Vlissingen: Abraham van Laren; *idem* (1695) *Des zondaars heyligdom, of: ontdekking van de heerlijke privilegiën, aangeboden aan de boetvaerdige en gelovige, onder 't Evangelium, in veertig predikatiën over Rom. VIII. vers 1–15*, trans. Jacobus Koelman, Utrecht: Wed. van Willem Klerk. On Koelman, see Krull, A. F. (1901) *Jacobus Koelman. Eene Kerkhistorische Studie*, Sneek: J. Campen. On Dickson, see Dikson, D. (1686) *Het Euangelium van Mattheus, kortelijk verklaart*, trans. Jacobus Koelman, Utrecht: W. Clerck. On Guthrie, see Guthrie, W. (1672) *Des Christens Groot Interest*, trans. Jacobus Koelman, Vlissingen: Abraham van Laren. And on Rutherford, see Rutherford, S. (1674) *De brieven van Samuel Rhetorfort*, trans. Jacobus Koelman, Vlissingen: Abraham van Laren; *idem* (1687) *De laatste brieven van Samuel Retorfort*, trans. Jacobus Koelman, Amsterdam: Johannes Boekholt. Koelman's translations of Hooker included Hooker, T. (1678) *De Waare Ziels-Vernedering, en Heilzame Wanhoop*, Amsterdam: J. Wasteliers; *idem*. (1681) *De arme twijfelende Christen, genadert to Christus*, Amsterdam: J. Wasteliers.

29 Macleod, W. (ed.) (1893) *Journal of the Hon. John Erskine of Carnock*, Edinburgh: University Press for the Scottish Historical Society, pp. 192; 184 (April 6, 1686): 'I was seeing professor Van Mastricht, with Mr. Melvel and Pardiven. He gave a large testimony of the church of Scotland, particular to the church discipline, affirming to be the purest that has been since the apostles' days'; p. 219 (January 4, 1687): 'I was seeing Professor Van Mastricht who was most civil and kind to me, and useful company.'

30 This was a Scottish ecclesiastical dispute occasioned by Hog's republication, upon the recommendation of Thomas Boston, in 1718 of *The Marrow of Modern Divinity* by Edward Fisher.

31 van Mastricht, P. (1699) *Theoretico-practica theologia: qua, per singula capita theologica, pars exegetica, dogmatica, elenchtica et practica, perpetua successione conjugantur; accedunt historia ecclesiastica, plena quidem, sed compendiosa, idea theologiæ moralis, hypotyposis theologiæ asceticæ etc proin opus quasi novum. Ed. nova, priori multo emendatior et plus quam tertia parte auctior*, Utrecht: Thomas Appels.

32 For this letter, along with two other relevant letters by Edwards to Bellamy on 11 June 1747 and 9 Jan. 1749, see WJE 16, pp. 216–17, 223, 266.

33 Mather, C. (1726) *Manuductio ad Ministerium. Directions for a candidate of the ministry: Wherein, first, a right foundation is laid for his future improvement; and, then, rules are offered for such a management of his academical & preparatory studies; and thereupon, for such a conduct after his appearance in the world; as may render him a skilful and useful minister of the Gospel*, Boston: Thomas Hancock, p. 85; Silverman, K. (1971) *Selected Letters of Cotton Mather*, Baton Rouge: Louisiana State University Press, p. 306.

34 Colman, B. (1736) *A Dissertation on the Image of God wherein Man was created*, Boston: S. Kneeland and T. Green, pp. 27, 28; Hopkins, S. (1793) *The system of doctrines: contained in divine revelation, explained and defended: showing their consistence and connection with each other: to which is added, A treatise on the millennium*, Boston: Isaiah Thomas and Ebenezer T. Andrews, p. 769; Seccombe, J. (1742) *Some Occasional Thoughts on the Influence of the Spirit with Seasonable Cautions against Mistakes and Abuses*, Boston: S. Kneeland and T. Green, the title page of which has the epigram: '*oportet intelligentem, phantasmata speculari.* Van Mastricht'; van Mastricht, P. (n.d. [1770?]) *A Treatise on Regeneration. Extracted from his System of Divinity, called Theologia theoretico-practica; and faithfully translated into English; With an APPENDIX containing Extracts from many celebrated Divines of the reformed Church, upon the same Subject*, New Haven: Thomas and Samuel Green, p. v.

35 Bellamy, J. (1853) *The Works of Joseph Bellamy, D.D.*, Boston: Doctrinal Tract and Book Society, vol. 1, p. xiv, n. *. Tyron Edwards (1809–1894) notes that Edwards, Sr. lent a copy of Mastricht's work to Bellamy. See Haykin, M. A. G. (ed.) (2007) *A Sweet Flame: Piety in the Letters of Jonathan Edwards*, Grand Rapids: Reformation Heritage Books, p. 85, n. 2.

36 WJE 26, pp. 339, 340; Park, E. A. (1852) 'New England Theology', *Bibliotheca Sacra*, 9 (January), pp. 170–220. See also Sweeney, D. A., and Guelzo, A. C. (eds) (2006) *The New England Theology: From Jonathan Edwards to Edwards Amasa Park*, Grand Rapids: Baker Academic, p. 261.

37 WJE 26, p. 152.

38 Neele, A. C. (2009) *Petrus van Mastricht (1630–1706). Reformed Orthodoxy: Method and Piety*, Leiden, Boston: Brill, pp. 316–20.

39 On the Marrowmen, see Macleod, J. (1974) *Scottish Theology: In Relation to Church History*, Edinburgh: Knox Press, p. 152. On Erskine, see Erskine, E. (1805) *Faith no fancy, or, A treatise of mental images: discovering the vain philosophy and vile divinity of a late pamphlet entitled [sic] Mr. Robe's fourth letter to Mr. Fisher, and showing that an imaginary idea of Christ as man (when supposed to belong to saving faith, whether in its act or object), imports nothing but ignorance, atheism, idolatry, great falsehood, and gross delusion*, Philadelphia: William M'Culloch, p. 31; Kennedy, J. (1979) *The Days of the Fathers in Ross-shire*, Inverness: Christian Focus Publications, p. 134: 'They [the Ross-shire fathers] had no difficulty in regarding the Sacrament of the Supper, as intended by the Lord, specially to seal something other and higher than that which is specially sealed by baptism. They called it, with Mastricht, "sacramentum nutritionis"'; and van Valen, L. J. (1982) *Gelijk de Dauw van Hermon*, Zwijndrecht: Het Anker, second edn, p. 476. On John Brown, see Brown, J. (2002) *The Systematic Theology*, introduced by Joel R. Beeke and Randall J. Pederson, Grand Rapids: Reformation Heritage Books, p. [j]. On Hog, see Hog, J. (c.1710) *Aenmerking over de werking des H. Geests, en het onderscheyd tusschen de wet en 't evangelium, sijnde het korte sommier van sommige huys-oeffeningen over Gal. 3: 2*, trans. Jan Claus, n.p.; Lachman, D. C. (1988) *The Marrow Controversy*, Edinburgh: Rutherford House, pp. 125, 126. On the continuity of the covenant theology in Scotland, see Henderson, G. D. (1955) 'The Idea of the Covenant in Scotland', *The Evangelical Quarterly*, vol. 27, pp. 2–14, the central argument of which is that the term 'covenant' is a keyword for Scottish theological thought, both individually and communally.

40 La Shell, J. (1985) 'Imaginary Ideas of Christ: A Scottish-American Debate', Ph.D. diss., Westminster Theological Seminary, p. 109.

41 *Ibid.*, p. 149. For Edwards and Heereboord, see WJE 6, p. 13. For Erskine's use of Mastricht, see Erskine, R. (1805), pp. 240–1.

42 On Reformed sermon structure, see, for example, WJE 10, pp. 28–36. For Mastricht on the work of redemption, see *TPT*, bk. V.1 (believer), and bk. VIII (history).

43 Erskine, R. (1725, 1770), p. 4: '[God] commends [Christ] for an able Saviour, that will through his work . . . not [be] forgetting Scotland'. See *TPT*, bk. VII.5, pp. 829–45; and Erskine, R. (1725, 1770), p. 4: '[There] is a company of people meeting in *Dunfermline*, about a communion-table'. See also pp. 15, 26.

44 Erskine, R. (1725, 1770), p. 56: 'consider, that you have a good claim and right to this covenant . . . you are welcome to it'.

45 Story, R. H. (ed.) (1890?) *The Church of Scotland, Past and Present*, London: William Mackenzie, p. 216.

46 WJE 14, p. 45: 'The influence of these two authors [Mastricht and Turretin] on JE is often mentioned but rarely explored. Their works included Turretin's *Institutio Theologiae Elencticae* (3 vols., Geneva, 1680–83) and van Mastricht's *Theoretico-Practica Theologia* (Utrecht, 16[99])'.

47 *TPT*, Prologus, 1102: 'Fidei naturam, octo libris hactenus expedivimus'.

48 *Ibid.*, bk. I.1.i, p. 1: 'Theologia . . . est doctrina deo vivendi per Christum'. The definition of theology as *bene vivendi* is, according to Sprunger, the kernel of theology influenced by Peter Ramus (1515–72). Sprunger, K. L. (1966) 'Ames, Ramus, and the Method of Puritan Theology', *Harvard Theological Review*, 59 (April), pp. 148–51. On the trajectory of this definition, see Muller (2003), vol. 1, pp. 154–8.

49 *TPT*, bk. VIII.1.xi, p. 866, 'Primum ergo, epochae patriarchalis curriculum . . .'; *ibid.*, xx, p. 875: 'Secundò hîc consideranda venit series Patriarcharum, [note] sub quâ Ecclesia fuit per hoc curriculum. In hac primus est Noachus'; *ibid.*, xxii, p. 879: 'Tertium curriculum periodi patriarchalis, [note] profluit ab Abrahamo ad Mosis nativitate'.

50 For example, *ibid.*, bk. VIII.2.xxvi, p. 908: 'Secundum ergo epochae Mosaicae curriculum, à Davide pergit usque ad captivitatem babilonicam'.

51 On theology, for example, see *ibid.*, bk. VIII.2.xxv, p. 906: 'Contemplati sumus statum Theologiae & Religionis'; on history, *ibid.*, bk. VIII.3.xliii, p. 1051: 'Quartum impetum in Theologiam reformatam, faciunt Iesuitae, ut iam de universo papismo seu Antichristianismo'; and on Roman Catholi theology, *ibid.*, bk. VIII.2.xxvii, p. 918: 'De quibus videri potest Greg. Nazianzenus Orat. Cont. Iulianum, & Virgilius Aeneid. XI. item Plinius lib. VII. cap. 2'.

52 On the progress and renewal of the covenant, see, for example, *ibid.*, bk. VIII.3.xxi, p. 962: 'Quantum ad Statum Ecclesiae, sub hac aetate; occurrunt penes eam (1) Propagatio Ecclesiae, talis ac tanta'; and *ibid.*, bk. VIII.2.xvii, p. 896, 'Primum ergo foedus, apud Sinai renovatum'.

53 WJE 5, pp. 55–9. Lowman studied theology under Mastricht in 1698.

54 *TPT*, bk. V.1.i, p. 389: 'Foedus gratiae pandemus in prima promissione, protoplastis peccatoribus . . . quae prostat Gen. III. 15'.

55 *Ibid.*, praefatio; Spanhemii, F. (1689) *Summa historiæ ecclesiasticæ. A christo nato ad seculum XVI inchoatum. Præmittitur doctrina temporum, cum oratione de christianismo degenere*, Leiden: Johannes Verbessel.

56 Cocceius, J. (1665) *Summa Theologiae, Summa Doctrinae de Foedere et Testamento Dei*, Geneva: Sumptibus Samuelis Chouët; on the structure of Cocceius' covenant theology, see van Asselt, W. (2001) *The Federal Theology of Johannes Cocceius (1603-1669)*, Leiden: Brill.

57 à Brakel, W. (1700) *Logike latreia, dat is, Redelyke godtsdienst, in welken de goddelyke waerheden des Genadeverbondts worden verklaert, tegen partyen beschermt, en tot de prac- tyke aengedrongen. Als mede de bedeelingen des verbondts in het O.T., ende in het N.T. ende de ontmoetingen der kerke in het N.T., vertoont in eene verklaringe der Openbaringe van Johannes,* Rotterdam: Reynier van Doesburgh.

58 *TPT*, praefatio: 'Adspersa est libro *octavo,* de *dispensatione foederis gratiae* per omnia Ecclesiae secula, *historia Ecclesiastica,* plena quidem'.

59 *Ibid.*: 'Occeperam dudum quasi pro commentario, in breviorem prioris editionis epito- men, opus satis copiosum de *Fatis Ecclesiae.*'

60 van Mastricht, P. (1749–53) *Beschouwende en praktikale godgeleerdheit: waarin, door alle de godgeleerde hoofdstukken henen, het bybelverklarende, leerstellige, wederleggende, en praktikale deel door eenen onafgebroken schakel, onderscheidenlyk samengevoegt, voorg- estelt word; hierby komt een volledig kort-begrip der kerklyke geschiedenisse, een vertoog der zedelyke, en een schets der plichtvermenende godgeleerdheit, enz.; in het Latyn beschreven; naar den laatsten druk in het Nederduitsch vertaalt, benevens de lykrede van den vermaarden hoogleeraar Henricus Pontanus, over het afsterven van den hoogwaardigen autheur; met eene voorrede van den heer Cornelius van der Kemp,* 4 vols., Rotterdam: Hendrik van Pelt; Utrecht: Jan Jacob van Poolsum, vol. 1, preface, p. 3.

61 The bibliography of translations of just these few authors is extensive, but instructive, and has not hitherto been fully enumerated. See the Appendix to this chapter.

62 Kennedy, H. (1752) *A short account of the rise and continuing progress of a remarkable work of grace in the United Netherlands. In several letters from the Reverend Mr Hugh Kennedy . . .. to some of his correspondents in Scotland and at London. In the epistle to the reader, there are some seasonable observations,* London: printed for John Lewis; *ibid.* (1743) *A discourse concerning the nature, author, means and manner of conversion. Prefixed to the Dutch translation of A faithful narrative of the extraordinary work of the spirit of God at Kilsyth, Written by J. Robe,* Edinburgh: R. Fleming and A. Alison.

On Ross, see Nemansky, P. (1992) Jan Ross. Een achttiende-eeuwse vertaler van Engelse piëtische lectuur', *Documentatieblad Nadere Reformatie,* vol. 16, no. 1 (Spring), pp. 43–53; Geschiedenis van de Schotse Kerk te Rotterdam, doopboek http://www. scotsintchurch.com/sicarchives/INDEX, accessed March 16, 2009; J. van Valen, personal communication, March 14, 2009. For Thomas Boston, see the Appendix to this chapter. On Comrie, see Honig, A.G. (1892, 1991) *Alexander Comrie,* Utrecht: H. Honig; rep. Leiden: Groen en Zn.

63 See the Appendix to this chapter.

64 For references to Boston, see WJE 16, pp. 235, 20:461; WJE 24, p. 460; 'Controversies' Notebook, in *The Works of Jonathan Edwards Online,* vol. 27, p. 44. To Ebenezer Erskine, see Smith, J. E. (ed.) (1959), p. 72; WJE 12, p. 330. To Ralph Erskine, see WJE 4, p. 538; WJE 12, p. 330; WJE 16, p. 662. To Thomas Halyburton, WJE 18, p. 90. And to James Robe, WJE 4, p. 535; WJE 16, p. 105.

65 Edwards, J. (1756) *Historiesch verhaal van het godvruchtig leven en den zaligen doodt, van den eerwaarden heer David Brainerd, onlangs bedienaar des evangeliums en leeraar eener gemeinte van christen indianen, te Nieuw-Jersey, alles getrokken uit zyn eigen dag-register, en andere byzondere schriften, welke tot zyn eigen gebruik waren opgestelt,* trans. Jan Ross, preface by G. v. Schuylenborgh, Utrecht: Jan Jacob van Poolsum.

66 This is another major network, not only between Scotland and the Netherlands, but between Utrecht and the Middle Colonies. G. v. Schuylenborgh was pastor near Utrecht, and was involved in translations of some works of Edwards and, during his

study of theology at Utrecht University, provided lodging for Johannes Frelinghuysen, son of Theodorus Frelinghuysen, who was introduced by Schuylenborgh to his wife to-be, Dina van den Bergh, who joined him to Newark. On Dina van den Bergh, see House, R., and Coakly, J. (eds) (1999) *Patterns and Portraits: Women in the History of the Reformed Church in America*, Grand Rapids: Eerdmans, pp. 33–51.

67 WJE 9, pp. 21–6.

68 Wellwood, H. M. (1818) *Account of the Life and Writings of John Erskine D.D.*, Edinburgh: George Ramsay & Co., p. 315: 'He had, for many years, carried on a correspondence with learned men on the Continent, with Professor Bonnet of Utrecht.'

69 WJE 9, pp. 532–3.

70 *TPT*, bk. V.1.i, pp. 389–409.

71 *Ibid.*, p. 389: 'Foedus gratiae pandemus in prima promissione, protoplastis peccatoribus . . . quae prostat Gen. III. 15'.

72 WJE 9, p. 132.

73 *Ibid.*, p. 133.

74 *TPT*, bk. V.1.i, p. 389: 'immediatè post violationem foederis operum'.

75 *Ibid.*, bk. VIII.3. xl, pp. 1048–9: 'Reformanda papalis, eadem fuit, quae aetatis nisi quod capita eius antichristiana . . . per Concilium Tridentinum'; WJE 9, pp. 424–5.

76 *TPT*, bk. VIII.3.xxxix, p. 1046: 'illinc quidem armis & atrocissimis persecutionibus'; WJE 9, p. 426.

77 *TPT*, bk. VIII.3.xliv, p. 1078: 'Agmen ciaudant persecutiones, indeque nata martyria, quae non minus quam schismata obstiterunt propagationi Ecclesiae'; WJE 9, p. 427.

78 *TPT*, bk. VIII.3.xliii, p. 1051: '*Tertium* impetum in Theologiam Reformatam fecerunt *Sociniani*'; *ibid.*, p. 1052, '*Sextum* insultum in Theologiam Reformatam, faciunt *Arminiani*'; WJE 9, p. 431.

79 *TPT*, bk. VIII.3.xl, p. 1045: 'institutaque Reformatione ad verbum Dei, doctrina ab erroribus, cultus ab idololatria & superstitione, regimen ecclesiasticum, à tyrannide Papali, vindicata fuerun'; WJE 9, pp. 432–3.

80 Harry Stout examines the relationship between history and revival in Edwards' theology, and traces Edwards' tripartite discussion of history—the history of redemption on earth and the related history of heaven and hell—in Stein, S. J. (ed.) (2007) *The Cambridge Companion to Jonathan Edwards*, Cambridge: Cambridge University Press, pp. 125–43.

81 *Edwards:*

Edwards:	*Mastricht:*
1) Christ's glorious appearance	Christ's glorious return
2) The last trumpet & destruction of Antichrist	Destruction of the Antichrist
3) The church will be caught up	Resurrection of the dead
4) The righteousness of the church & judgment	The last judgment
5) Judgment of the righteous and wicked	The acquittal of the church & condemnation of others
6) The ascent of Christ and His church	Handing over the Kingdom & the end of ages
7) World on fire and eternal life	Eternal life

82 *TPT*, bk. VIII.4.iv–vii, pp. 1094–5.

83 On the last trumpet, see *ibid.*, bk. VIII.4.ii, p. 1092: 'Exsecutionem, sub buccinatione septem Angelorum, Penes quam narratur. . . .'; WJE 9, p. 496, 502: 'that the last trumpet shall sound, and the dead raised, and the living changed'; see also WJE 14, p. 523, and Edwards' comments on Lowman, WJE 9, p. 252.

85 Bogue, C. W. (1975) *Jonathan Edwards and the Covenant of Grace*, Cherry Hill, New Jersey: Mack Publishing, p. 117.

Evangelicalism and Revivalism

Chapter 3

'Sure the time here now is like New England': What happened when the Welsh Calvinistic Methodists read Jonathan Edwards?

David Ceri Jones

That the thought and writings of Jonathan Edwards made a significant impact on the evangelical revival in England, particularly in its Wesleyan form and among some evangelical Dissenters has been well documented,[1] but it was in revival communities in the Celtic periphery of the British Isles, where evangelicals and Methodists shared a commitment to Calvinist theology, that Edwards was often read most consistently, most carefully and with most profit. Recent work on the evangelical awakenings throughout the mid eighteenth-century British Atlantic world tends to stress their similarities and interconnectedness, but this comparison has tended to operate on a strictly trans-Atlantic, or east–west, axis. In a recent essay Nigel Yates has suggested that the juxtaposition of a pan-Celtic approach might be a useful tool to reveal and explain some of the other interconnections and influences that made-up the early evangelical movement.[2] What I want to do in this essay is to try to combine both paradigms; by exploring Edwards' influence on the eighteenth-century Welsh Methodists, the trans-Atlantic dimension, it will be quickly apparent that the fortunes of the Scottish and Welsh awakenings, the pan-Celtic dimension, became periodically intertwined.

At the outset, though, it is necessary to introduce a caveat by pointing out that the Welsh Methodists did not possess the sort of direct and immediate relationship with Edwards that a number of prominent Scottish ministers clearly enjoyed. Edwards' influence in Wales was neither as hands-on, nor as sustained. There are probably a number of reasons for this. The Welsh did not have as sophisticated a network of actual trans-Atlantic correspondents[3] as the Scots; Welsh migration levels to the colonies were much lower, and there was comparatively little ongoing interchange between the smaller number of Welsh settlers in the New World and the old.[4] In addition, Wales did not possess the kind of university educated semi-professional ministerial body enjoyed by the Scots,[5] nor the accompanying tradition of high level theological discourse, either in the public or private spheres. What both revivals did share was a commitment to a broadly Calvinist soteriology, and access to the revival's most ubiquitous international personality, George Whitefield. These two common factors had bound the Welsh and Scottish evangelicals into a Calvinist-based trans-Atlantic community of saints by the early 1740s. It was through the networks that this community generated that Edwards' influence became most keenly felt in Wales.

In November 1738, following his first face-to-face meeting with his co-revivalist Daniel Rowland, Howel Harris confided in his diary that 'sure the time here now is like New England.'[6] The Welsh revival had begun just two years earlier when Harris, a schoolmaster from Breconshire near the English border, and Rowland[7] a Church of England curate based at Llangeitho in Cardiganshire, west Wales, experienced evangelical conversions and began preaching startlingly awakening sermons independently of one another. When they met for the first time at Defynnog during November 1738, a strategically important meeting at which their two independent mini-awakenings were fused together to create a unified Welsh revival, they set aside time specifically to discuss Edwards' *A Faithful Narrative of the Surprising Work of God*, the British edition of which had been published under the sponsorship of the English dissenting ministers Isaac Watts and John Guyse towards the end of 1737. Harris claimed to have first read Edwards in February 1738 and testified that he found his heart 'boiling with love to Christ' as he read it, and interceded with God to: 'O go on with thy work there and here.'[8] We do not know exactly when Rowland read Edwards, but must clearly have done so by the time he met Harris on this first occasion.

What did Harris mean when he compared the Welsh revival to the Northampton awakening? What did he and Rowland read in Edwards' *A Faithful Narrative*, that seemed to resonate so strongly with their own experience in Wales? The first point that needs to be made is that the appearance of Edwards' book was timely. Harris and Rowland had been working steadily in their pioneering ministries for over eighteenth months, and their activities were just beginning to arouse suspicion and even opposition. Meeting one another and pooling their resources was clearly important, but reading Edwards' *A Faithful Narrative* seemed to confirm to them the authenticity of God's work in their midst, and suggest to them, probably for the first time, that they might actually be part of something far bigger and more extensive than they had initially realised. But they would have read something far more practically useful than just this in its pages. A number of recent writers, including C. C. Goen, in his introduction to the critical edition of *A Faithful Narrative*, have argued that it was probably one of the most important books in the definition and defence of revivalism;[9] Edwards' Northampton revival, which the book described in paradigmatic terms, quickly becoming the benchmark account of genuine religious revival.[10]

Using thoroughly empirical categories, born of his deep immersion in Enlightenment thought and literature, Edwards argued that the authenticity of any religious revival could be deduced from a number of observations. Primary was his conviction that a genuine revival would affect all kinds of people, from both sexes, of all ages and from all ranks of society; this was reinforced by the presence of numerous dramatic conversion experiences and clear evidence of transformed lives; the strength of the spiritual impressions experienced was important, but as with the test of numbers, this was not always as reliable a sign of an authentic work of grace as the other indicators. There was much here for Harris and Rowland to digest and reflect upon; they had both witnessed the accentuation of the religious concerns of many of the members of their respective communities in Breconshire and Cardiganshire. They had both seen frequent and dramatic conversions in response to their preaching, and both could point to many examples of the individual transformations that these conversions had brought about. In early 1739, for example, Harris could write excitedly to George Whitefield:

> I have some more good news to send you from Wales. There is a great revival in Cardiganshire, through one Mr D. Rowland, a Church clergyman, and he has been much owned and blessed in Carmarthenshire also. We have also a sweet prospect in Breconshire, and part of

Monmouthshire; and in the county where I am now [Glamorgan], the
revival prospers . . . In Montgomeryshire . . . there seems to be some
shining beams of the Gospel of grace.[11]

Edwards' taxonomy of a genuine religious revival was fleshed out
with two carefully constructed case studies of the conversions of Abigail
Hutchinson and Phoebe Bartlett, both of which became models by which
others could explain and assess what they had themselves experienced.
Harris had already begun organising his converts into small cell groups, or
societies; the first of these was established in early 1736, and within four
years a network of some fifty of them were fully operational in south-east
Wales. These societies had strict rules of entry, and even stricter rules for
those who had managed to pass that first hurdle and wished to remain
members. The societies became the forum in which individual conversion
experiences were assessed; the reading of Edwards at such a critical juncture
in the Welsh revival undoubtedly helped Harris and Rowland to do this by
enabling them to fine tune their theology of conversion. Having said this, it
was perhaps the vocabulary of revivalism, picked up from Edwards, which
proved the most enduring legacy of their reading of *A Faithful Narrative*. As
Edwards talked about 'a considerable revival of religion', 'an unusual religious
concern' or 'no small effusion of the Spirit of God', so the Welsh Methodists
began to talk of 'demonstrations of the divine love and favour', of 'amazing
power' and that 'God was [among] us indeed'.[12]

Much of the scholarly work on Edwards' influence in Britain has concentrated on the way in which John Wesley edited his writings according
to his own theological predilections. But for much of the 1740s there were
multiple parallel readings of Edwards going on in the early evangelical
communities. The split between Calvinistic and Wesleyan Methodists
by 1741 meant that the Calvinists under the direction of Whitefield and
Howel Harris read different versions of Edwards than their Wesleyan near
neighbours. In 1742 the English Calvinistic Methodist printer Samuel
Mason secured the rights to reprint the Boston edition of Edwards' *The
Distinguishing Marks of a Work of the Spirit of God* (1741). It was placed on
sale in Whitefield's Tabernacle and in the Calvinistic Methodist magazine,
The Weekly History and carried the enthusiastic endorsement of George
Whitefield who recommended it 'to the serious perusal of all Christians,
and to ministers of every denomination in particular'.[13] The book, read in

this edition rather than in John Wesley's more popular and much shorter 1744 abridgement,[14] was circulated fairly widely in Wales, being of particular help during the controversies surrounding Howel Harris' adoption of Moravian-style 'blood and wounds' theology and his passionate advocacy of the prophetic gifts of his new 'companion', Mrs Sidney Griffith, in the later 1740s.[15]

By 1749 these two issues were causing major problems in Wales. In that year Thomas Bowen, an exhorter from Montgomeryshire, wrote to Howel Harris outlining a dispute which he was having with a fellow exhorter Thomas Jones, who happened to be part of Harris' inner circle. Bowen accused Jones of using 'unguarded expressions' and confusing language about the efficacy of the blood of Christ. It is not too much to infer that this criticism was also being simultaneously levelled squarely at Harris himself, who had become notorious for the use of such language by this time. However, Bowen's accusations went a step further as he criticised Jones, and once again by implication Harris, for his enthusiasm, especially Jones' tendency to use wild and exaggerated hand gestures and bodily contortions during his preaching, and his and Harris' seemingly unanswerable claim that their views about the blood of Christ were views which had been revealed to them directly by the Holy Spirit. It was at this point that Bowen dragooned Edwards into the support of his case. Drawing on his reading of *The Distinguishing Marks of the Work of the Spirit of God*, Bowen used Edwards' warnings against a reliance on what he called 'private impressions' of the Holy Spirit to rebuke some of the excesses of the Welsh Methodists, and Harris in particular, for using claims to direct inspiration to, as Bowen put it, 'ascend the chair of infallibility in . . . points that are ambiguous'.[16] In the same way that Edwards had been forced to defend the Great Awakening against the excesses of some of its preachers,[17] he was now being deployed by certain well-read Welsh Methodists in the task of defending and defining genuine religious experience from the counterfeit.

However, it was Edwards' commitment to the establishment of an international prayer network that brought him and his writings to the attention of a greater range of the Welsh Methodists during the later 1740s. The idea of a 'Concert for Prayer' had first taken shape in July 1743 among a group of Scottish evangelical ministers who had set aside part of every Saturday evening, every Sunday morning and the first Tuesday of the last month of each quarter of the year for earnest intercessory prayer for a fresh outpouring of the Holy Spirit.[18] The full potential of these special periods of prayer was realised by John Erskine, who was to become minister of the strategically important Old Greyfriars Church in Edinburgh,[19] who persuaded many of the most prominent evangelical leaders of the day to join what quickly became an international intercessory network aimed at stimulating fresh revivals. Erskine worked closely with Jonathan Edwards,[20] whose *A Humble Attempt to Promote Explicit Agreement and Visible Union of God's People in Extraordinary Prayer* (1747) became the manifesto of this new community.

Both the Scots and many of the colonial American evangelicals were already on board, so Erskine circulated a private document to some leading British evangelicals,[21] outlining the rationale for the prayer network, in a pitch for wider support. John Wesley enthusiastically signed up on behalf of himself and his preachers almost immediately,[22] and the same proposals were sent to Howel Harris in Wales during 1745. Harris had first been introduced to Erskine by George Whitefield, and the two had maintained a close correspondence since 1741. Harris had sent material to him for inclusion in the Scottish evangelical magazine, *The Glasgow-Weekly History*, and Erskine had done the same for the London-based version of the magazine. By 1745 Harris had assumed the leadership of English Calvinistic Methodism on account of Whitefield's extended absences in America, and so brought Erskine's proposals before the monthly gatherings of the English and Welsh Calvinistic Methodists at Trevecka in March 1745. Following the Scottish example very closely, he recommended that a regular day of prayer should be set aside once every three months and that every Sunday morning should be set aside 'on account of ye late work in England, Scotland, Wales & America, both to praise God for it & intercede & pray for it[s] furtherance & to be humbled for ye sin that attended it'.[23] For a while it looked as though Erskine's network would lead to an impressive coming together of many of the main strands within the revival, recapturing the unity that had existed before the acrimonious splits between the Moravians, Wesleyans and Calvinists in England in the early 1740s, at least that was what Harris seemed to be hoping for when he signed up for the venture.[24] But in the end the network was only entered into spasmodically by the Calvinistic Methodists in both England and Wales, and came to represent one of the last really realistic opportunities for healing many of the rifts that had opened up within English Methodism in the early 1740s.

Having said all this, it was William Williams, Pantycelyn, who sustained the most prolonged and thorough engagement with Edwards' work. Following the disruption of Welsh Methodism in 1750 and the enforced retirement of Howel Harris, Williams came to the forefront of the leadership of the Welsh Methodist movement, together with Daniel Rowland steering it through the difficult waters caused by the split. Williams quickly emerged as the main theological writer in the Welsh revival and from the later 1750s began publishing theological works that defined and gave structure to it. The influence of his close reading of Edwards is not far from the surface in many of his writings.

In 1762 there was a fresh outbreak of revival in Wales, this time centring on Llangeitho; this revival was more dramatic and ecstatic than many of those which had taken place in the previous decades and as a result aroused more severe opposition, particularly on account of many of the bizarre ecstatic bodily manifestations, including sobbing, jumping and dancing, that regularly occurred.[25] To answer those who wished to discredit the revival on account of these excesses, Williams produced two apologetic works: his *Llythyr Martha Philopur* was published in 1762, and was followed shortly afterwards with *Atteb Philo-Evangelius* (1763). Both works demonstrate the full extent of Williams' debt to Edwards. Martha Philopur was a typical, if fictitious, female Methodist convert, while Philo-Evangelius was a model local Methodist society leader. In Williams' hands Martha described her experience; phrases like 'I received the Word in fullest ecstasy'; 'While you preach . . . I do my utmost to restrain myself . . . and I often cannot stop my tongue from crying out, "God is Good"'; 'I leap and shout for joy, in so great salvation, that I never knew before',[26] occurred again and again in her narrative. In the sequel Williams used the character of Philo-Evangelius, to counsel Martha and explain the place and role of such phenomena to the Methodists themselves in the first instance, but also to all those who were keen to discredit them. Williams, through Philo, wrote:

> It is not only by means of outward manifestations . . . that I conclude that God is in the Church and is visiting his people. Apart from the heavenly inclination on their spirits inciting their tongues to a living

praising of God, this fire burns in the life and behaviour of so many of them . . . They are zealous, not for the secondary matters of faith, but for the essential issues of salvation. Faith and love are the chief graces they cry for.[27]

The Edwardsean line of reasoning here is clear; Edwards had argued that extraordinary physical manifestations were inevitable in times of religious revival, whether in the form of 'tears, trembling, groans, loud outcries, agonies of body, or the failing of bodily strength',[28] but the acid test of the authenticity of a person's religious experiences was not to be judged by the strength of emotion, but whether they believed correct notions about the divinity of Christ, whether there was a conscious and decisive turning away from sin, a greater love of the Bible and a greater regard for the worship of Christians. Williams readily admitted that Edwards' *The Distinguishing Marks of the Work of the Spirit of God* (1741) was 'the best book I have seen to that purpose: it gave me more light in some things',[29] and assured his readers in the closing lines of *Atteb Philo Evangelius* that if anyone was still unconvinced by Williams' two books he would reissue a new edition of Edwards' work to finally settle matters.[30]

In the second place, Williams' long involvement in the Welsh revival led him to think carefully about the place and role of religious revivals in the broader historical process. Like Edwards once more, Williams wrote history that attempted to place the revival in which he participated into a larger overarching historical meta-narrative. Although there is no evidence to suggest that Williams read Edwards' *A History of the Work of Redemption* (1773), the parallels between their teleological historiographies is striking. In *Atteb Philo-Evangelius*, Williams argued that before Harris and Rowland arrived on the scene in 1735, 'Ignorance covered the face of Wales, hardly any gospel privilege could stand against the corruptions of the day' until their revival begun a couple of years later and 'light broke forth as the dawn in many parts of the world . . . and O wonderful morning! The Sun shone on Wales'.[31]

From this starting point, Williams extrapolated that the dawn of the current revival in Wales was but one of a whole series of dawns that the Church had experienced since the days of the Apostles. In what appears to have been a combination of both a linear and cyclical view of history, Williams argued that the sun had initially shone on the early church for about '300 years'—there was undoubtedly a nod here in the direction of traditional Protestant appeals to a pre-Catholic Celtic church as well[32]— but had then faded for over a thousand years before a series of proto-evangelicals like John Wycliffe, Jerome of Prague, the Bohemian Jan Hus, the Waldenses and the Albigenses, had attempted to recapture the primitive simplicity of the apostolic church. The Reformation was merely the most dramatic of these new dawns, but even it was followed by a further succession of sunrises and sunsets, albeit in quicker succession, as the fortunes of Protestantism in England and Wales waxed and waned throughout the sixteenth and seventeenth centuries. The most recent night, that between the Glorious Revolution and the mid-1730s, was merely a short hiatus in the grand narrative of the spread of Christianity to the ends of the earth before the dawning of the millennial reign of Christ.[33]

The writing of what Michael J. McClymond calls 'universal chronicles' of this kind was far from unusual in the early eighteenth century.[34] Edwards had argued, in his *History of the Work of Redemption*, which was after all a greatly expanded series of sermons, first preached in 1739 in the lull between the Northampton revival and the beginning of the Great Awakening, that major turning points in history were always accompanied by powerful and widespread religious revivals. These revivals, he said, were God's customary way of working within history and they would become both more frequent and more wide-ranging until the world was gradually Christianised and the millennial age ushered in.[35] The optimistic mindset that lay behind this eschatologically-driven view of history, as David Bebbington reminds us, lay behind much of the activism of later eighteenth- and nineteenth-century evangelicals.[36]

Which leads neatly into the third area of overlap between Williams and Edwards: Williams also incorporated a very prominent eschatological perspective into his histories. Inspired by the appearance of the Northern Lights over his home in Carmarthenshire in October 1769,[37] Williams penned *Aurora Borealis* (1773), a quasi-scientific description of the natural phenomenon, but one from which Williams also drew some spiritual observations and lessons.[38] He interpreted the lights as a portent of the end times, as a prophetic signal that the spread of the gospel would continue and increase in its reach, much as the Northern Lights themselves covered the skies. He wrote:

> As the Northern Lights spread across the sky, so also the gospel in
> time will cover the earth as well … All the earthquakes that happened
> in 1755 and 1756 … all the Wars in Asia, Europe and America are
> merely a fulfilment of the Lord's Word … and when I see them and
> similar things I am ready to believe that summer is at hand.[39]

This was very similar to the sort of typology which Edwards frequently adopted, and which was most fully developed in his *A History of the Work of Redemption*. But in many respects the most interesting of Williams' quasi-eschatological publications was his *Pantheologia*, a seven-part publication published in instalments between 1762 and 1779, the subtitle of which gives the most complete sense of its contents: 'A History of all the Religions of the World; namely the Pagan Religion, Islam, Judaism, and Christian, which comprises the three branches, the Church of Rome, the Greek [Orthodox] Church, the Protestant Church …'. To both Williams and Edwards, the fate of the 'heathen' was an essential component of their end-times speculations, and one that preoccupied much of their attention. While its important not to make too much of this comparison, since much more work has been done on Edwards' more sophisticated interest in comparative religions than Williams', it is possible to make a number of broad observations.

Williams, in Enlightenment fashion, had clearly been collecting information for a major survey of all of the world's religions for many years before the publication of *Pantheologia*.[40] Edwards similarly filled many notebooks with material on the various world religions throughout his life, but unlike Williams he never made extensive use of them in any of his writings, despite harbouring a wish to write a major book showing that any evidence of true religion among the heathen was the result of God's revelation rather than natural law as the Deists of his day argued. Recently, Gerald McDermott has paid close attention to the material in Edwards' notebooks and made a strong case for Edwards' adoption of enlightened and generous attitudes towards non-Christian religions. Based on his view that 'pagans' had received some knowledge of God, however rudimentary, from the Jews and from the *prisca theologia*, Edwards tentatively speculated that there might be vestiges of true religion in the non-Christian religious traditions.[41] Despite plenty of evidence that Edwards and Williams read some of the same authors, particularly travel works describing various world religions, Daniel Defoe, Humphrey Prideaux and Isaac Watts, Williams' thought was probably not moving in the same radical direction. Williams was not really given to speculative theology in the same way as Edwards, and was probably not possessed with the same kind of original insight as Edwards either, but he was committed to introducing his fellow Welsh men and women to some of the latest knowledge of the day. In some of the early pages of *Pantheologia*, for example, he wrote:

> It is lamentable that the white, monoglot Welshman in Britain differs so little from the white monkey in India ... the illiterate Hottentot far outstrips him in all universal knowledge ... But whoever considers that there is no locality in Europe (if the monoglot Welsh know what 'Europe' means) which possesses so few books of national and ecclesiastical history in their own language as obtains in Wales ... When a monoglot Welshman hears the words 'philosophy', 'mathematics', 'geography' and such like, he scarcely thinks other than that they are words of enchantment.[42]

Williams did not speculate further, but it is surely possible that had Edwards produced his projected work critiquing some of the assumptions of Enlightenment religion, then Williams might well have taken up his interest in world religions once again. It was their shared eschatologically driven view of history that lay behind Edwards' and Williams' interest in other world religions. They both thought that the millennium was fast approaching, their revivals were part of its inauguration, and that the conversion of the heathen was imminent, whatever form that was actually to take. This kind of thinking was to play a key role in the birth of the modern missionary movement, and it was no accident that it was from the pages of Jonathan Edwards that William Carey, the founder of the first missionary society, the Baptist Missionary Society, was to find inspiration.[43]

This essay has explored the Welsh engagement with Jonathan Edwards' writings and ideas throughout the eighteenth century, and argued that it was both thorough and sustained. Yet for much of the eighteenth century it was Edwards' practical works on the nature of religious revival that were most avidly read and used. It was not until the beginning of the nineteenth century that some of Edwards' writings were actually translated into Welsh[44] and a more detailed engagement with his major theological ideas and works took place, particularly among those elements within Welsh

Methodism, and nonconformity more generally, who were adopting elements of the Edwardsean 'New Divinity' in their desire to combat both High or Hyper-Calvinism on the one hand and Arminianism on the other, both of which were on the rise in Wales by that point.[45]

Notes

1 See Hindmarsh, D. B. (2003) 'The Reception of Jonathan Edwards by Early Evangelicals in England', in Kling, D. W., and Sweeney, D. A. (eds) *Jonathan Edwards at Home and Abroad: Historical Memories, Cultural Movements, Global Horizons*, Columbia, South Carolina: University of South Carolina Press, pp. 201–21.

2 Yates, N. (2007) 'Wind, Rain and the Holy Spirit: Welsh Evangelicalism in a Pan-Celtic Context, 1750–1850', in *Bishop Burgess and his World: Culture, Religion and Society in Britain, Europe and North America in the Eighteenth and Nineteenth Centuries*, Cardiff: University of Wales Press, pp. 103–20.

3 Jones, D. C. (2004) *'A Glorious Work in the World': Welsh Methodism and the International Evangelical Revival, 1735–1750*, Cardiff: University of Wales Press, pp. 285–91.

4 Williams, G. (1979) 'A Prospect of Paradise? Wales and the United States, 1776–1914', in *Religion, Language and Nationality in Wales*, Cardiff: University of Wales Press, pp. 217–18.

5 Holmes, A. R. (2006) 'The Protestant Clergies in the European World', in Brown, S. J. and Tackett, T. (eds) *The Cambridge History of Christianity: Enlightenment, Reawakening and Revolution, 1660–1815*, Cambridge: Cambridge University Press, p. 113.

6 Aberystwyth, National Library of Wales (NLW), Calvinist Methodist Archive (CMA), Howel Harris' Diary 35, 27 November 1738.

7 For Howel Harris and Daniel Rowland, see Tudur, G. (2000) *Howell Harris: From Conversion to Separation, 1735–1750*, Cardiff: University of Wales Press; Evans, E. (1985) *Daniel Rowland and the Great Evangelical Awakening in Wales*, Edinburgh: Banner of Truth Trust.

8 Aberystwyth, NLW CMA, Howel Harris' Diary 35, 22 & 23 February 1738.

9 WJE 4, pp. 28–30.

10 Crawford, M. J. (1991) *Seasons of Grace: Colonial New England's Revival Tradition in Its British Context*, New York: Oxford University Press, p. 132.

11 Aberystwyth NLW, CMA, The Trevecka Letters, no. 136, Howel Harris to George Whitefield, 8 January 1739.

12 Quoted in Evans (1985), pp. 70-3.

13 Lewis, J. (ed.) (1742), *The Weekly History*, no. 53 (10 April), 4.

14 Wesley, J. (1744) *The Distinguishing Marks of a Work of the Spirit of God. Extracted from Mr Edwards. Minister of Northampton, in New England*, London: W. Strahan.

15 Tudur (2000), chapters 7 and 8.

16 Aberystwyth NLW, CMA, The Trevecka Letters, no 1847, Thomas Bowen to Howel Harris, 30 January 1749.

17 Kidd, T. S. (2007) *The Great Awakening: The Roots of Evangelical Christianity in Colonial America*, New Haven: Yale University Press, chapter 9.

18 Fawcett, A. (1971), *The Cambuslang Revival: The Scottish Evangelical Revival of the Eighteenth Century*, London: Banner of Truth Trust, chapter 12.

19 Landsman, N. C. (2004) 'Erskine, John (1721–1803)', *Oxford Dictionary of National Biography*, Oxford: Oxford University Press [http://www.oxforddnb.com/view/

article/8870, accessed 20 Sept 2010]; Bebbington, D. W. (2003) 'Remembered around the World: The International Scope of Edwards's Legacy', in Kling, D. W., and Sweeney, D. A. (eds), *Jonathan Edwards at Home and Abroad: Historical Memories, Cultural Movements, Global Horizons*, Columbia, South Carolina: University of South Carolina Press, pp. 179–80.

20 Jonathan Edwards to a correspondent in Scotland, November 1745, in WJE 16.

21 See Aberystwyth, NLW CMA, Trevecka 3188, 'Reasons for observing certain times in the manner within written to bless the Lord for his late revival of real Christianity'.

22 John Wesley to John Erskine, Lord Grange, 16 March 1745, in Baker, F. (ed.) (1982) *The Works of John Wesley, vol. 26, Letters II: 1740–1755*, Oxford: Oxford University Press, p. 128.

23 'At an Association held at Trevecka, 29 March 1745', Aberystwyth, NLW CMA, Trevecka 2945: Records of Associations, p. 145. For a detailed discussion of Harris' dogged attempts to implement the Concert in Wales, see Evans, E. (2010) 'A Concert for Prayer: Consolidating the Great Awakening', *Cylchgrawn Hanes: Cymdeithas Hanes y Methodistiaid Calfinaidd*, 34, pp. 9–10, 16–17, 19–22.

24 See Jones, D. C. (2003) '"The Lord did give me a particular honour to make [me] a peacemaker": Howel Harris, John Wesley and Methodist Infighting, 1739–1750', *Bulletin of the John Rylands University Library of Manchester*, vol. 85, nos. 2 and 3, pp. 73–98.

25 See White, E. M. (2008) '"I will once more shake the heavens": the 1762 Revival in Wales', in Cooper, K., and Gregory, J. (eds), *Revival and Resurgence in Christian History*, Studies in Church History, 44, Woodbridge: Ecclesiastical History Society / The Boydell Press, pp. 60–1.

26 Translation in Evans (1985), *Daniel Rowland*, pp. 319–20.

27 *Ibid.*, p. 321.

28 Edwards, J. (1742) *The Distinguishing Marks of the Work of the Spirit of God*, London: Samuel Mason, p. 17.

29 Aberystwyth, NLW CMA, The Trevecka Letters, no. 1381; William Williams to Howel Harris, 7 December 1745.

30 Hughes, G. H. (ed.) (1967), *Gweithiau William Williams Pantycelyn*, cyfrol II, Cardiff: University of Wales Press, p. 31.

31 Translation in Evans (1985), *Daniel Rowland*, p. 75.

32 Williams, Glanmor (1967) *Welsh Reformation Essays*, Cardiff: University of Wales Press, chapter 9; Williams, Glanmor (1970) *Reformation Views of Church History*, London: Lutterworth Press, pp. 63-74.

33 Morgan, D. L. (1988) *The Great Awakening in Wales*, London: Epworth Press, pp. 6–7.

34 McClymond, M. J. (1998) *Encounters with God: An Approach to the Theology of Jonathan Edwards*, New York: Oxford University Press, p. 66.

35 See Zakai, A. (2007) 'The Age of Enlightenment', in Stein, S. J. (ed.) *The Cambridge Companion to Jonathan Edwards*, New York: Cambridge University Press, pp. 88–91.

36 Bebbington, D. W. (1989) *Evangelicalism in Modern Britain: A History from the 1730s to the 1980s*, London: Unwin Hyman, p. 61.

37 Hughes, G. T. (1983) *Williams Pantycelyn*, Cardiff: University of Wales Press, pp. 70–1.

38 See Hughes, D. A. (1986) 'William Williams Pantycelyn's Eschatology as seen especially in his *Aurora Borealis* of 1774', *The Scottish Bulletin of Evangelical Theology*, 4, pp. 49–63.

39 Translation in Evans, E. (2011) *Bread of Heaven: The Life and Work of William Williams,*

Pantycelyn, Bridgend: Bryntirion Press, p. 241.

40 Williams, C. G. (1968) 'The Unfeigned Faith and an Eighteenth Century *Pantheologia*', *Numen,* vol. 15, no. 3, pp. 212–13.

41 McDermott, G. R. (1999) 'A Possibility of Reconciliation: Jonathan Edwards and the Salvation of Non-Christians', in Lee, S. H. and Guelzo, A. C. (eds) *Edwards in our Time: Jonathan Edwards and the Shaping of American Religion,* Grand Rapids: Eerdmans, pp. 173–202.

42 Translation in Evans (2011), *Bread of Heaven,* p. 166.

43 This link is explored in some detail in a number of the essays in Stanley, B. (ed.) (2001) *Christian Missions and the Enlightenment,* Grand Rapids: Eerdmans.

44 Edwards', *The Religious Affections* (1746) was translated into Welsh by John Roberts in 1809. *Cyfarwyddiadau ac annogaethau I gredinwyr . . . A glasglwyd, yn benaf, allan o waith . . . Jonathan Edwards,* Bala: R. Saunderson. However, Welsh translations of some of Edwards' other works did not appear until much later in the century. Bebbington (2003), pp. 184–5.

45 See Thomas, O. (2002) *The Atonement Controversy in Welsh Theological Literature and Debate, 1707–1841,* translated by John Aaron, Edinburgh: Banner of Truth Trust.

Chapter 4

The Legacy of Jonathan Edwards:
Eighteenth-Century Catalysts for Revivals
among Presbyterians and Baptists in Scotland

Chris Chun

H. Richard Niebuhr referred to him as 'America's Augustine', and Robert
Jenson dubbed him 'America's Theologian'. Why then should we have a
discussion on the subject of Jonathan Edwards' legacy in general, and in
Great Britain and Scotland in particular? In my view, such consideration
is an essential part of Edwards study, because he called Britain 'my home
country'.[1] Born on American soil, however, having lived and died prior
to the Revolutionary War, many historians forget that Edwards was a
British subject. In fact, Edwards published his first book in England: *A
Faithful Narrative of the Surprising Work of God* (1737), printed in London,
immediately gave him an international reputation as great theologian of
revival.[2] Suffice it to say that the legacy left by Edwards is well remembered
in New England, although only recently have scholars begun to acknow-
ledge Edwards' significance beyond an American context.[3] This essay will
attempt to demonstrate that Edwards was not only 'America's Theologian',
but has a glorious legacy in Scotland.

In eighteenth-century Britain, Edwards' influence can be viewed in
two major stages: (1) during Edwards' lifetime in the 1740s and 1750s
among Scottish Presbyterians; and (2) his posthumous influence on
English Baptists in the 1780s and 1790s. Also in Scotland, subsequently,
one English Baptist minister argued against the Sandemanianism found
among Scotch Baptists, thus further carrying on Edwards' legacy of the
'sense of the heart'. This essay, therefore, will explore the profound influence Edwards had as a catalyst for the missionary awakening and the
revivals.

The Edwardsian Legacy among Scottish Presbyterians and English Baptists

Due largely to the ecclesiastical division caused by the aftermath of the Great Awakening, there were few reasons to be optimistic about the religious climate in New England. In the face of these divisions, Edwards' encouragement came from his trans-Atlantic correspondence, which included an invitation to participate in the ecumenical movement known as the 'Concert of Prayer' in Scotland. Through these organised, regular prayer meetings, the Scottish Presbyterians[4] implemented the 'means'[5] of advancing the revival. Prompted by the invitation, Edwards accepted the challenge of promoting such prayer meetings in colonial America. In February of 1747 he began a series of sermons based on Zechariah 7:20–22. The result of this effort was later expanded into a book, *An Humble Attempt to promote Explicit Agreement and Visible Union of God's People in Extraordinary Prayer for the Revival of Religion and the Advancement of Christ's Kingdom on Earth, Pursuant to Scripture-Promises and Prophecies of concerning the last Time* (1748).[6]

Almost immediately after its publication in Boston, Scottish Presbyterians had access to *Humble Attempt*. In a letter dated August 31, 1748, to John Erskine (1721–1803),[7] Edwards confides some of his frustration with Thomas Prince (1687–1758)[8] who 'forgot' to send a copy of the work. Evidently the 'last year' (presumably 1747) refers to the date when Edwards had sent 'books on the subject of the Concert for Prayer' to Erskine via Prince, but Erskine did not receive it. Edwards then took 'some further care to have the books conveyed' to Erskine, and 'this time', Edwards said, he would surely 'receive it'.[9]

The full title of the *Humble Attempt* well summarises the subject matter of the treatise. Edwards thought that uniting in prayer was a solution to the problems of dissection that he faced following the Great Awakening. The catholicity of the prayer meeting for the common purpose could serve as the means of advancing and even expediting Christ's kingdom, which Edwards believed to be imminent. In the American colonies, Stephen Stein has claimed that the Concerts of Prayer had rather 'limited success'. His assertion builds upon Joseph Bellamy's statement in 1749: 'To this day, I believe not half the Country have ever So much as heard of Mr. Edwards piece upon the *Scotland Concert*.'[10] Michael Haykin agrees with Stein that the initial stages of what began with the 'poor response'[11] but he argues that 'A significant number of congregations in America and Scotland observed the Concert of Prayer throughout the 1750s',[12] especially during the French and Indian War (1754–63). While Edwards' relationship with Scottish Presbyterians is well known, most notably through the work of Christopher Mitchell in 1997,[13] his legacy among English Baptists is lesser known: to this we now turn our attention.

Jonathan Edwards' posthumous influence is closely tied to the beginnings of the Protestant missionary wakening. William Carey (1761–1834) was one of the most significant early leaders of the modern missionary movement[14] and is often called the 'father of modern missions', but he was not alone. One of his friends and colleagues was Andrew Fuller (1754–1815).[15] If Carey's *An Enquiry into the Obligations of Christians to Use Means for the Conversion of the Heathens* (1792) was the ethical catalyst for the missionary awakening, Fuller's *Gospel Worthy of All Acceptation* (1785) was its theological stimulus. In other words, Fuller was the theologian and Carey the activist and visionary of the mission movement. In the midst of a rapid decline among Baptist denominations in England—due largely to Hyper-Calvinism amongst Particular Baptists and Unitarians as well as deistic tendencies among General Baptists[16]—Fuller's *Gospel Worthy of All Acceptation* 'fell like a bombshell on the playground of theologians, [and] Fuller was pilloried by Arminians and Hyper-Calvinists alike'.[17] Fuller's theological ammunition for this dispute relied largely on the distinction made by Edwards in *Freedom of the Will* between 'natural and moral inability'.[18]

Both Hyper-Calvinists and Arminians maintained that unregenerate sinners ought not to be required to perform that which they are incapable of doing. Hyper-Calvinists said they needed to first look for those who have the inner warrant (a Scripture text in their minds) to come to Christ for their salvation and then preach to them exclusively, while Arminians maintained that sinners should not be required to respond to the gospel unless they had the ability to do so. Fuller used Edwardsian reasoning to resolve this difficulty and argued the distinction between natural and moral ability.[19] As a Particular Baptist, Fuller believed that without the grace of 'unconditional election'[20] unregenerate 'heathens' could not respond positively to the gospel. Yet this helplessness was not due to a defect of any natural human faculty. Rather, their inability was of a 'moral' or 'criminal' type.[21] In other words, there are no natural, physical, external factors that would restrain unbelievers from choosing or rejecting the gospel. In this sense, they are 'free' to accept and therefore morally responsible for their choices. If they reject the gospel, they choose to do so in accordance with their own desires. The choices simply reveal who they are as individuals—whether or not they are reprobate or elect.[22] This is why natural ability became for Fuller the basis upon which heathens had the 'duty' to respond in faith and repentance, regardless of their eternal status in the doctrine of election.

Fuller did not usually give as detailed a philosophical account of natural and moral inability as Edwards did. Instead, Fuller's distinctions are more inclined to the implications for salvation. It is as if the results of a complex mathematical formula solved by Edwards were taken to their maximum potential by Fuller and applied to the formulation of a precise theology, which became the basis for what was to become known as the Modern Missionary Movement. It is therefore no wonder that among many evaluations of the impact of Edwards in England, David Bebbington concludes that 'probably most important in the reception of Edwards by the English Baptists was the impact on Andrew Fuller.'[23]

Any historian familiar with Edwards studies (or mission history, for that matter), is aware that *The Life of David Brainerd* is a standard text for domestic and foreign missionaries.[24] However, *Humble Attempt* helped spark the missionary revivals when Baptist pastor John Ryland Jr. received a parcel of books from John Erskine in 1784, including the *Humble Attempt*. Ryland, fully aware of the esteem in which Fuller and John Sutcliff held Edwards, wasted no time in sending them the books, thereby changing missiological history.

The reading of *Humble Attempt* by Fuller, Sutcliff and other Northamptonshire members revived the 'Concert of Prayer' that began in the 1740s in Scotland and New England but had since subsided, and forty years later produced the 'Prayer Call of 1784' in England. The Prayer Call established the practice of using the first Monday of each month for prayer for the advancement of Christ's Kingdom. These calls,[25] plus the 1789 republication of *Humble Attempt*,[26] have been directly linked by historians to both Carey's historic ministry and the formation of the Baptist

Missionary Society (BMS) in 1792, and the London Missionary Society (LMS) in 1795. These events, taken together, were the genesis of the Protestant missionary movement.

The Edwardsian Legacy of the 'Sense of the Heart' in Scotland

Andrew Fuller further ushered the Edwardsian legacy from England to Scotland when he visited his trusted sister denomination in Scotland to raise funds for the newly-formed BMS.[27] As a secretary of the missionary society, Fuller found himself in a rather precarious situation when one of their largest financial supporters, Archibald McLean (1733–1812),[28] with Sandemanian viewpoint, accused Fuller of abandoning the Reformation dogma of *sola fide*. As an English Baptist, Fuller was quite familiar with Sandemanianism,[29] yet he did not have either the time or cause to engage them until he faced the strand of Sandemanianism in Scotch Baptists churches. Fuller's exposure to Sandemanianism came about in the course of his five visits to Scotland during the late 1790s and early 1800s to raise the money needed for the BMS. Fuller was a part of the larger network among Baptist congregations in Britain, one that featured a remarkable unity in its support of overseas missions. This is more the reason why Fuller initially did not wish to engage in a polemical dispute, especially since McLean was a financial supporter.[30]

Notwithstanding, Fuller felt the need to retort to McLean's accusation in *Commission of Christ* charging Fuller with abandoning *sola fide*. Fuller therefore responded to McLean's charges in the *Appendix* to the second edition of *The Gospel Worthy of All Acceptation* (1801), but the debate did not end there, which led to a further publication, *Strictures on Sandemanianism in Twelve Letters to a Friend* (1810). When the dust finally settled, in the assessment of Martyn Lloyd-Jones, Fuller 'really dealt' with McLean to the point where Fuller had 'more or less demolished' the position taken by McLean.[31] What was the theological ammunition that Fuller used to not only acquit himself of such an indictment, but demolish McLean's position? Fuller used Edwards' conception the 'sense of the heart' found in *Religious Affections* to argue against McLean's version of Sandemanianism.

There are familiar historical parallels between the setting of *Religious Affections* in New England and Fuller's dispute with Sandemanianism in

Scotland. In New England, the awakening that rippled throughout the region was complicated by lay preachers, critics of the learned clergy, and by the over-zealous, even bizarre, behavior on the part of alleged converts.[32] These extraordinary manifestations subsequently became the point of contention between the camps of the Old Light and those of the New Light. One of the principal criticisms of the revival, as represented by the Old Light, came from Charles Chauncy (1705–87), who denounced overt enthusiasm and called for a return to what he described as sane, rational religion. In response to Chauncy, Edwards defended the revival against the Old Light as a divine work. Because of the growing controversy over the nature and signs of the gracious operation of God's Spirit, Edwards preached a long series of sermons based on 1 Peter 1:8. Some of the core ideas from these sermons gave expressions to the nature of true religion, which later became the foundation for *Religious Affections*. The historical similarities in Edwards' and Fuller's settings are that just as Chauncy's reaction was against the worst kind of emotionalism in New England, the rejection of affections of the heart by the Sandemanian faith in Scotland may have had its origin in similar background, for 'Sandeman does appear to have been responding to the unduly introspective temper of some circles of eighteenth-century Evangelicalism.'[33]

In any case, McLean, in his Sandemanian persuasion, thought that he was defending the Reformation doctrine of justification by faith alone. The problem, however, was the fact that he adhered to Robert Sandeman's version of it, which emphasized that 'justification comes by *bare* faith.'[34] This entails that, to possess the saving faith in any way other than mere mental assent to what Christ had accomplished, would be tantamount to human endeavor to merit salvation. The faith was wholly passive on the part of the human mind's persuasion. Conversely, this also meant that faith was never active and had no reference to the heart's conviction. Sandemanianism had a clear-cut answer on this issue: the inclusion of will and affection into faith would compromise *sola fide*.[35] Thus, in McLean's mind, Fuller violated this doctrine.

Despite such accusations, Fuller's response is rather charitable: 'I have the pleasure to agree with Mr. McLean in considering the belief of gospel as saving faith', but the point of disagreement is identified by Fuller as the issue of 'What the belief of the gospel includes.'[36] While both McLean and

Fuller agree that divine influence is the ultimate cause of perception and belief, the point of disagreement is the manner in which these casualties occur. According to McLean's maxim, the 'Holy Spirit causes the mind, while carnal, to discern and believe spiritual things'.[37] For McLean, the gospel can be discerned and believed by the mind without any aversion or approbation of the heart. In contrast, Fuller argues that causality is in the Holy Spirit, such that the Spirit 'imparts a holy susceptibility and *relish* for the truth'.[38] At this point, careful readers of Edwards may be able to identify the Edwardsian influence, since he also wrote in *Religious Affections* that 'spiritual knowledge primarily consists in a taste or *relish* of the amiableness and beauty'.[39] In opposing McLean's position, Fuller appears to be picking up both the ideas and the phrases to be found in Edwards' statement.

Edwards did not originally intend his ideas to be used against Sandemanianism. However, Fuller elaborates on these concepts to make his case against McLean's understanding that spiritual knowledge is not merely doctrinal mastery but a type of knowledge that such mastery relishes. Fuller thought that McLean's system of the theory of knowledge in Sandemanianism was erroneous; therefore, Fuller looks to Edwards to find his solutions. By quoting *Religious Affections*, Fuller claims, 'Spiritual understanding consists, primarily in *a sense* of the heart of *spiritual beauty*.' Contrary to McLean's conception of knowledge, this understanding is based on 'sense of the heart'. According to Fuller, the knowledge attained from such understanding is neither mere 'speculation', nor is it 'a clear distinction made between the two faculties of understanding and will, as acting distinctly and separately in this matter'.[40] Here, this English Baptist utilises the pneumatological epistemology found in *Religious Affections* to challenge the epistemology of this vexed Scotch Baptist.

The legacy of Jonathan Edwards in the conception of 'natural and moral inability' is well embedded not only in Fuller and amongst the Northamptonshire Association in England, but also as the predominant theme of the New Divinity School in New England. However, the same could not be said of Edwards' legacy of concerning the 'sense of the heart'. While some later New England theologians spoke of affectional transformation occurring in regeneration, they do not have the compelling and beautiful discussions about the 'sense of the heart' that one finds in Edwards' writings.[41] Yet across the Atlantic, this aspect of Edwards' theological aesthetic was employed as a key component in Fuller's line of reasoning against McLean. Fuller's polemical dialogue with McLean relied heavily upon Edwards to argue that the mind and heart are inseparable constituents in arriving at a spiritual knowledge of faith. Hence Edwards' ideas were employed to further advance the interest of the ministry of BMS in Scotland and beyond.

Conclusion

Many historians rightly point out that David Brainerd's piety functioned as a model for missionaries of the nineteenth century. However, because of the evangelistic restraint of Hyper-Calvinism, the modern missionary movement might never have gotten off the ground if it hadn't been for the metaphysics of 'natural and moral inability' and the 'use of means' found in *Freedom of the Will*. We can speak similarly of *Humble Attempt*: had it not been for Edwards' optimistic outlook and exhortation to communal prayer, the fuel for the rigors of the foreign missions might well have been depleted. Due to Edwards' catalytic influence on the genesis mission-ary awakening, his missiological legacy is far greater than that of simply editing *The Life of David Brainerd*. Furthermore, while the 'sense of the heart' is considered by many to be one of the unique aspects in Edwards' thoughts, this facet of his theological aesthetic is not well transmitted in the writings of his successors in New England. Yet across the Atlantic, in the hands of Fuller, the pneumatological epistemology found in *Religious Affections* became the central argument against those who believed faith to be a completely passive feature of human faculties. In the ministry of BMS, 'Edwards on the Affections' became yet another important legacy in Scotland.

Notes

1 'Cover Leaf Memoranda', in WJE 6, p. 194.
2 Edwards had published two pamphlets and a letter before this point, but his first book was *A Faithful Narrative*; see, Lesser, M. X. (2003) 'An Honour Too Great: Jonathan Edwards in Print Abroad', in Kling, D. W., and Sweeney, D. A. (eds) (2003) *Jonathan Edwards at Home and Abroad: Historical Cultural Movements, Global Horizons*, Columbia, South Carolina: University of South Carolina Press, pp. 287–8.
3 Kling, D. W., and Sweeney, D. A. (eds) (2003); Noll, M. A. (2005) 'Jonathan Edwards' *Freedom of the Will* Abroad' in Stout, H. S. *et al.* (eds) (2005) *Jonathan Edwards at 300: Essays on the Tercentenary of His Birth*, Lanham: University of Press of America, pp. 89–108; McDermott, G. R. (ed.) (2009) *Understanding Jonathan Edwards: An*

Introduction to America's Theologian, New York: Oxford University Press.

4 Edwards' connection to such Scottish evangelicals, such as John McLaurin, William McCullosh, James Robe, Thomas Gillespie and John Erskine is of critical importance in the reception of Edwards in Britain. Of all of them, however, Erskine is the most notable link for our purpose. For broader discussions regarding Edwards' relationship with the Scottish evangelicals, see Mitchell, C. W. (2003) 'Jonathan Edwards' Scottish Connection', in Kling, D. W., and Sweeney, D. A. (eds) (2003), pp. 222–39. See also, O'Brien, S. (1986) 'A Transatlantic Community of Saints: The Great Awakening and the First Evangelical Network, 1735–1755', *The American Historical Review*, 91, no. 4 (October), pp. 811–32.

5 Prayer as a 'means' in Edwards' thinking is found as early as 1743: '[It] is God's will, through his wonderful grace, that the prayers of his saints should be the one great and *principal means* of carrying the designs of Christ's kingdom in the world'. WJE 4, p. 516; my emphasis.

6 The *Humble Attempt* was completed and ready for publication in September 1747, but due to the lengthy printing process in Boston, it was not published until January of 1748.

7 Erskine was a Church of Scotland minister, a prolific author, and an avid reader of theology. Yet for our purpose, his role as the 'hub' for transatlantic correspondence is crucial. According to Yeager, Erskine's preoccupation with books donated many literatures to numerous leading Academic institutions in America including, Harvard, Princeton, Dartmouth, and Yale. Erskine did not begin his epistolary correspondence with Edwards until 1747 but he continued to nurture this relationship until Edwards' death in 1758. His bond with Edwards was cordial, and this is visible in a series of letters by which Edwards confides in Erskine about the painful inner experiences as he faced the Lord's Supper controversy. When Edwards was dismissed from the Northampton parish, he experienced considerable financial struggles. During this time, Erskine extended the invitation for ministerial employment in Scotland. Erskine's loyalty to Edwards was extended in strenuous times as well as after his death. The remaining years of his life, Erskine dedicated much time, money, and efforts to promote Edwards' writings. Such a significant role that Erskine played in the circulation of Edwards' corpus in Britain cannot be overstated. His epistolary friendship with John Ryland, Jr. is particularly noteworthy to consider, since this was the vital link in which Fuller received many of writings of Edwards. For a biography of Erskine, see Wellwood, Sir H. M. (1818) *Account of the Life and Writings of John Erskine, D.D., Late One of the Ministers of Edinburgh*, Edinburgh: Archibald Constable and Company. See also Yeager, J. (2011) *Enlightened Evangelicalism: The Life and Thought of John Erskine*, New York: Oxford University Press.

8 Thomas Prince, Edwards' ministerial colleague in Boston, took care of Edwards' correspondence with the Scots, but his forgetfulness often tested Edwards' patience. It may be hypothesized that Prince's disagreements about Edwards' interpretation of prophecy in Revelation 11 might have contributed to his carelessness in delivering the post.

9 WJE 16, p. 246.

10 WJE 5, p. 48.

11 Haykin, M. (1994) *One Heart and One Soul: John Sutcliff of Olney, his Friends and his Times*, Durham: Evangelical Press, p. 159.

12 *Ibid.*, p. 162.

13 Mitchell, C. W. (1997) 'Jonathan Edwards's Scottish Connection and the

Eighteenth-Century Scottish Evangelical Revival, 1735–1750', Ph.D. diss., University of St. Andrews.

14 Of course, Jesuits were conducting missions long before the Protestant missionary movement. Moreover, before Carey's time the Moravians were also very active with missions. Yet mainstream Protestant involvement, with the new emphasis on Bible translation in missionary enterprise, was pioneered by Carey.

15 For recent study of Fuller's life and thought, see Morden, P. (2003) *Offering Christ to the World: Andrew Fuller (1754–1815) and the Revival of Eighteenth Century Particular Baptist Life*, Studies in Baptist History and Thought, 8, Carlisle: Paternoster Press; Haykin, M. (ed.) (2004) *'At the Pure Fountain of Thy Word': Andrew Fuller as an Apologist*, Studies in Baptist History and Thought, 6, Carlisle: Paternoster Press; see also Brewster, P. (2010) *Andrew Fuller: Model Pastor-Theologian, Studies in Baptist Life and Thought*, B & H Academics. Moreover, emulating the Yale edition of *The Works of Jonathan Edwards*, there is a current undertaking to produce a modern critical edition of the entire corpus of Andrew Fuller's work. The project is expected to comprise at least 15 volumes.

16 'Particular' or Calvinistic Baptists held to a limited atonement, a belief that Christ's death and salvation were specifically designed for the elect. Hyper-Calvinists, however, believed that the call to repent and believe should not be universal, since reprobates do not have the ability to do so. 'General' or Arminian Baptists believed in a general atonement, the belief that Christ died for the whole world—elect and non-elect alike. Thus, the efficacy of Christ's death is available to anyone who voluntarily exercises faith in Christ. In the context of the Enlightenment, the Unitarians (in opposition to the Trinitarians) argued for a single personality of God as reason for their rule, and denied the deity of Christ. Deists believed that God did not interfere with the laws of the universe, including human affairs, and usually rejected supernatural events and divine revelation. In Britain, Unitarianism and Deism were prevalent in the thinking of eighteenth-century General Baptists.

17 George, T. (1991) *Faithful Witness: The Life and Mission of William Carey*, Birmingham: New Hope, p. 56.

18 While Edwards' original intention for the natural and moral distinction was to argue against the 'prevailing notion' of Arminianism, Fuller used the distinction to fight on two fronts, against both Hyper-Calvinists and Arminians. For more on this dispute, see Chun, C. (2006) 'A Mainspring of Missionary Thought: Andrew Fuller on Natural and Moral Inability', *American Baptist Quarterly*, 25, no. 4, pp. 335–55.

19 Fuller defined natural ability as 'the enjoyment of rational faculties, bodily powers, and external advantages'. See Fuller, A. (1785) *The Gospel of Christ Worthy of All Acceptation*, Northampton: T. Dicey, p. 185. In Fuller's view moral ability is closely related to the inclination or 'sense of the heart'. Since sinners do not have this, they cannot use their natural ability to right purpose.

20 See Schaff, P., and Smith, H. B. (eds) (1877) *The Creeds of the Evangelical Protestant Churches, vol. II:* 'Article XIII – XVIII', *The Canons of Synod of Dort*, London: Hodder and Stoughton, pp. 582–5. For Fuller's commitment to the five points of Calvinism (TULIP), see Nettles, T. (1986) 'On the Road Again', in *By His Grace and For His Glory: A Historical, Theological and Practical Study of the Doctrines of Grace in Baptist Life*, Grand Rapids: Baker Books, pp. 108–30.

21 Having already 'considered as well as [Fuller] could' on *Freedom of the Will*, he writes, 'I have frequently been enquiring into the *nature* of that inability so plentifully ascribed

in the scriptures to [the] fall of men. I found this to be chiefly of the *moral* kind; a *voluntary*, and therefore *criminal* and *punishable* inability'. See Fuller, A. (1785) *The Gospel of Christ Worthy of All Acceptation*, Northampton: T. Dicey, p. v.

22 Fuller insists that free agency is in 'the power of being what they are!' In Edwardsean fashion, Fuller states that free agency is 'in the power of following the inclination'. Fuller, A. (1988) *The Complete Works of the Rev Andrew Fuller: With a Memoir of his Life by the Rev. Andrew Gunton Fuller*, vol. 2, Harrisonburg: Sprinkle Publications, pp. 521, 656. For both Edwards and Fuller, freedom is the ability of the individual to be the person that he is, as was the case for Judas Iscariot. See *ibid.*, p. 520, and WJE 1, p. 296. However, this 'free action' is utterly determined by the condition of a person, which in turn can traced to personality, character, upbringing, genetic inheritance, external and internal circumstances of life experience and so forth.

23 Bebbington, D. (2003) 'Remembered Around the World: The International Scope of Edwards' Legacy', in Kling, D. W., and Sweeney, D. A. (eds) (2003), p. 184.

24 See Conforti, J. A, (1985) 'David Brainerd and the Nineteenth-Century Missionary Movement', *Journal of the Early Republic*, 5, pp. 309–29; Conforti, J. A. (1985) 'Jonathan Edwards' Most Popular Work: *The Life of David Brainerd* and Nineteen-Century Evangelical Culture', *Church History*, 54, pp. 188–201. See also Pettit, N. (1986) 'Prelude to Mission: Brainerd's Expulsion from Yale', *New England Quarterly*, 59, pp. 28–50; Walls, A. (2003) 'Missions and Historical Memory: Jonathan Edwards and David Brainerd', in Kling, D. W., and Sweeney, D. A. (eds) (2003), pp. 248–65.

25 The Call was critical to the beginnings of Carey's ministry. According to Thornton Elwyn, 'Northamptonshire Association prayer call was one of the most decisive events in the life of in that period, and probably for all Christendom'. Elwyn, T. (1997) 'Particular Baptist of the Northamptonshire Baptist Association as Reflected in the Circular Letters' *Baptist Quarterly*, 37, no.1, p. 380.

26 In 1789, for the purpose of wider circulation, this prayer movement republished the 'pocket-size' edition of *Humble Attempt*. In describing the significance of the new edition, Iain Murray states, 'It is arguable that no such tract on the hidden source of all true evangelistic success, namely prayer for the Spirit of God, has ever been so widely used as this one'. Murray, I. (1987) *Jonathan Edwards: A New Biography*, Carlisle: Banner of Truth Trust, p. 299. Even if Elwyn and Murray have overstated the significance of these events, it is arguable that the Prayer Call, together with the republication of *Humble Attempt*, paved the way for the formation of the Baptist Missionary Society and the London Missionary Society.

27 The relationship between Scotch Baptists and English Particular Baptists in the early nineteenth century was not of variant branch of their own denomination but of a sister domination.

28 Mclean was born at East Kilbride and he was educated first at Cathcart, then at Cowcaddens in 1746. He taught himself Hebrew, Greek, and Latin. In 1759 Mclean married Isabella, the youngest daughter of William Moore, with whom he obtained a small property, enabling him to set up as a bookseller and printer in Glasgow in 1760. McLean was a Scotch Baptist minister who was raised in the Church of Scotland, but later discovered the writings of John Glas and became convinced of their doctrine in 1762. Mclean became an elder in the Edinburgh Scotch Baptist church after leaving the Church of Scotland in 1768. Mclean was an ardent advocate of Sandemanianism and was an influential writer on many controversial subjects. His most prominent works are *Letters to Mr Glas in Answer to his Dissertation on Infant Baptism* (1767), which is

the first Scottish defense of the baptism of believers by immersion, and *The Commission Given by Jesus Christ to his Apostles Illustrated* (1786), which sets out Scotch Baptist beliefs in full. In addition, he contributed an essay on 'Baptists in Scotland' to Rippon's Annual Register (1795), and a commentary on the Epistle to the Hebrews (1820). See Cooper, T., and Murray, D. B. (2004) 'McLean, Archibald (1733–1812)', *Oxford Dictionary of National Biography*, Oxford University Press [www.oxforddnb.com/view/article/17648, accessed 10 Nov. 2006].

29 According to Lloyd-Jones, in the late 1780s and 1790s Sandemanianism became 'a menace both in England and Wales'. Lloyd-Jones, D. M. (1996) 'Sandemanianism', in *The Puritans: Their Origins and Successors: Address Delivered at the Puritan and Westminster Conference, 1959–1978*, Edinburgh: Banner of Truth Trust, p. 173.

30 On the extent to which Mclean financially supported the work of the Baptist Missionary Society, see Talbot, B. (2003) *The Search for a Common Identity: The Origins of the Baptist Union of Scotland 1800–1870*, Studies in Baptist History and Thought, 9, Carlisle: Paternoster Press, pp. 51–2.

31 Lloyd-Jones, D. M. (1996), p. 173.

32 Westra, H. (1999) 'Divinity's Design: Edwards and the History of the Work of Revival', in Lee, S. H., and Guelzo, A. C. (eds) (1999) *Edwards in Our Time: Jonathan Edwards and the Shaping of American Religion*, Grand Rapids: Eerdmans, p. 151.

33 Haykin, M. (ed.) (2004), p. 227.

34 Sandeman, R. (1759) *Letters on Theron and Aspasio, vol. II: Letter V*, Edinburgh: Sands, Donaldson, Murray, and Cochran, p. 330; my emphasis. Furthermore, Mclean argues that the proclamation is nothing more than persuasion of the human mind: 'they not only declared the gospel-testimony, but called everyone to believe it unto their salvation; and urged this call by every motive and argument which the gospel furnished them with, and which are the strongest that possibly can be proposed to the human mind'. Mclean, A. (1786) *The Commission Given by Jesus Christ to his Apostles Illustrated*, Edinburgh: Printed for W. Gray, Paternoster Row, pp. 85–6.

35 Sandeman, R. (1759), p. 330.

36 Fuller, A. (1988), vol. 2, 'Appendix', p. 393.

37 *Ibid.*, p. 410.

38 As a result, the human agent can 'discern its glory, and embrace it'. In this context, Fuller relies on Edwards' pneumatological epistemology. See *ibid.*, p. 410.

39 WJE 2, p. 281.

40 Edwards quoted by Fuller, A. (1988), p. 411n; Fuller's emphasis. See WJE 2, p. 272. These segments also appear but in much greater length in Fuller, A. (1988), pp. 602–6.

41 I am gratefully indebted to Sweeney for this point, since he does not recall a specific instance where the actual phrase 'sense of the heart' was used. Among Edwardsean traditions in New England the closest notion of 'sense of the heart' may be found in 'tasters' such as Nathanael Emmons and Asa Burton, but their accounts are not nearly as in-depth nor do they explicitly quote Edwards' notion of the sense of the heart as does Fuller. See Emmons, N. (1842) 'Man's Activity and Dependence Illustrated and Reconciled' and Burton, Asa 'Essay XXX' (1824) in Sweeney, D. A., and Guelzo, A. C. (eds) (2006) *The New England Theology: From Jonathan Edwards to Edwards Amasa Park*, Grand Rapids: Baker Academic, pp. 171–86.

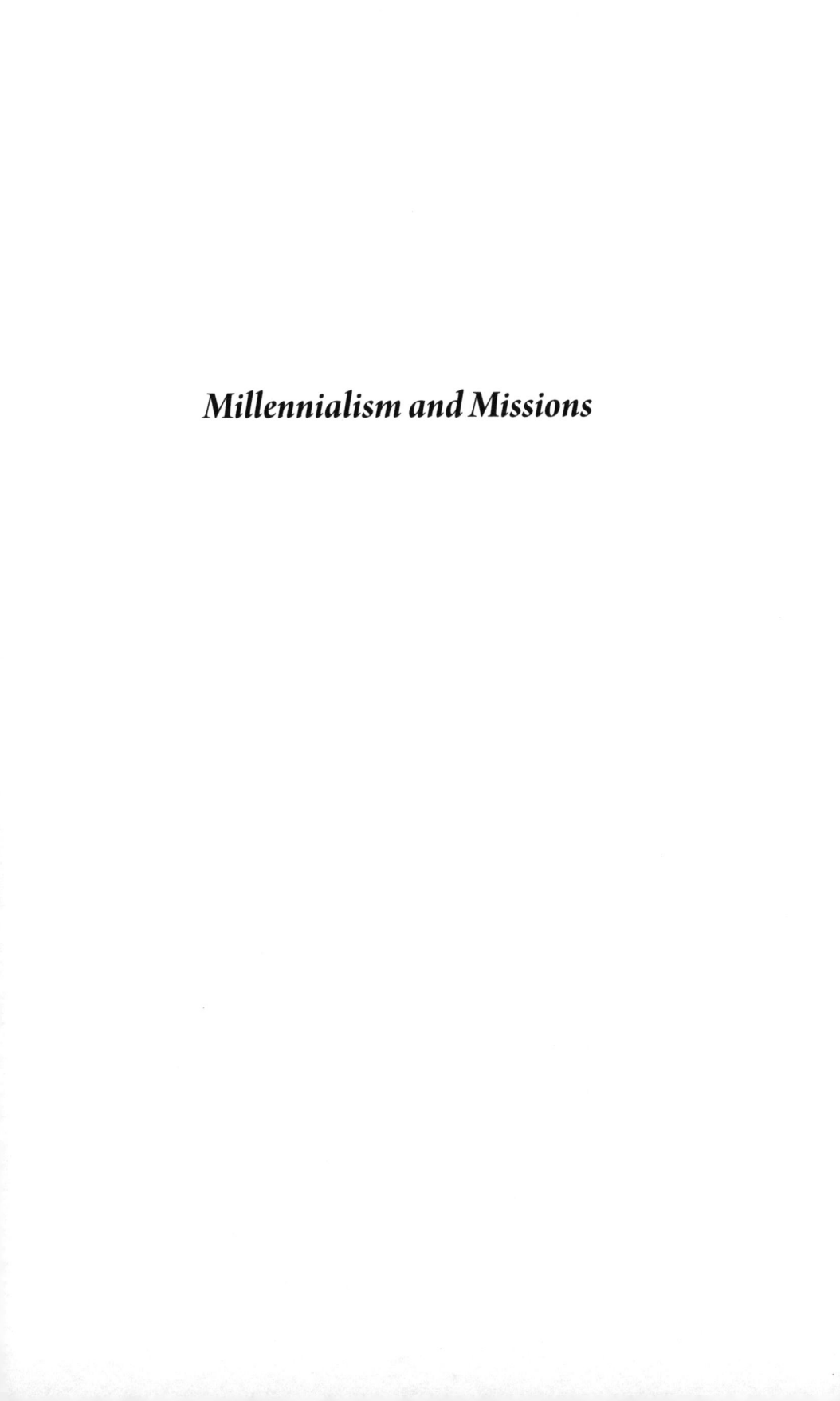

Millennialism and Missions

Chapter 5

Edwards, McLaurin, and the Transatlantic Concert

Nicholas T. Batzig

Throughout human history, the friendship of two uniquely gifted individuals has often resulted in an extraordinary benefit for the world. Such was the friendship of Pierre-August Renoir and Claude Monet. These men of enormous creative ability often traveled together to a particular location in order to garner inspiration for their subsequent works of art. Renoir's works reflect the influence that Monet had upon him. This influence is all the more evident when the one contrasts the works that Renoir brought forth in the company of Monet with the works he produced in the company of Paul Cézanne. The influence that Monet had upon Renoir is evident in one noteworthy example. Renoir's admiration of his friend was captured in his portrayal of Monet painting at his garden behind his French chalet. The painting is unique in that it is reflective of what Monet valued most—capturing the beauty of a landscape. While this painting—in an extraordinary manner—captures Renoir's admiration for Monet, its distinctiveness is discovered in what lies beneath the canvas. Beneath it lays another portrait—one painted by Monet. Having first begun to work on the canvas, Monet then gave it to his friend to paint on. In turn, Renoir produced one of the most memorable paintings of the Impressionist school—a portrait of Claude Monet doing what he did best, and what he loved most.

The benefit derived from the friendship of Renoir and Monet is surely one of the greatest examples in the modern world, but it is illustrative of another friendship of a century earlier—the friendship of Jonathan Edwards and John McLaurin of Glasgow. There is a temptation to envisage Edwards' friendship with McLaurin as a merely formal association—to reduce it down into a means to an end. Though this would be reductionistic, it is somewhat understandable since many of the letters written between the two did not survive. Add to this the fact that neither Edwards nor McLaurin ever crossed the Atlantic—the two never actually met in person. While these reasons help explain why their friendship has been undervalued, the literary evidence overwhelmingly supports the conclusion that this was no casual acquaintance.

Edwards interacted with numerous Scottish ministers; of whom McLaurin is understood to have been the 'catalyst'.[1] On the surface, Edwards' relationship with the Scottish ministers in general, and with McLaurin specifically, may appear to have been less significant than it actually was, but as Christopher Mitchell has so aptly noted:

> Edwards' isolation was real, and the spiritual and intellectual camaraderie offered by his Scottish correspondents was viewed by him, not as a luxury, but rather as the means of meeting a fundamental need in his life and ministry.[2]

While this is certainly true of Edwards' correspondence with James Robe of Kilsyth, John Erskine of Edinburgh, and William McCulloch of Cambuslang, it is particularly so with regard to McLaurin. Edwards personally expressed as much in a letter written to McLaurin in November of 1745:

> I am greatly obliged to you for your large, friendly, profitable and entertaining letter of February last. I esteem my correspondence with you, and my other correspondents in Scotland, a great honour and privilege; and hope that it may be improved for God's glory, and my profit.[3]

A close examination of letters and extant works reveal that their friendship was anything but a mere formal association. To envision it in this way is to ignore an enormous amount of evidence suggesting that the two had a mutual appreciation for the fellowship and intellectual contributions of the other.

By 1742 McLaurin had acknowledged how he had specifically benefited from two works of Edwards that has been published in Scotland. *Surprising Narrative* was first published in Edinburgh in 1737, and *Distinguishing Marks* was published in both Edinburgh and Glasgow in 1742. So great was the influence of the Northampton minister on his Scottish counterpart that the first printing of the *Freedom of the Will* was purposefully held off until 1754. McLaurin desired to secure subscriptions for it throughout

Scotland. Of the 88 copies ordered by McLaurin and Robe, 45 subscriptions were secured. In a gesture of friendship and mutual respect for his Scottish associates, Edwards' willingly held the printing off until sufficient subscriptions were obtained. Edwards' influence on his Scottish correspondents was of such magnitude that, as Mitchell notes, 'Edwards became one of the chief advocates of Scottish evangelical Calvinism in the eighteenth century without ever crossing the Atlantic.'[4] It is surely fitting that a figure of such profundity should be the object of interest to McLaurin; but it is correspondingly appropriate that an individual of such theological magnitude as McLaurin should be of particular interest to Edwards.

Though largely forgotten in the church—even from within the Calvinist tradition to which he belonged—McLaurin was nevertheless a man of extraordinary theological ability. John Brown of Edinburgh, in the preface to the 1830 edition of the *Works of John McLaurin*, described him as 'the most profound and eloquent Scottish theologian' of the eighteenth century.[5] Brown's commendation was noted some thirty years later by McLaurin's son-in-law, John Gillies, in the preface to the 1860 W.H. Goold edition of the *Works of the Rev. John McLaurin*. This edition differed only from the first edition, printed in Glasgow in 1755, by the addition of the brilliant exposition, 'On the Prophecies Relating to the Messiah'. This final essay supplies, on account of its eschatological nature, the theological connection between McLaurin and Edwards in regard to the concert of prayer.[6] Nevertheless, the question remains as to why McLaurin's works have not been reprinted in nearly 150 years.

Born in 1693 in Argylshire, McLaurin was promptly relocated from one home to another. His father—a Presbyterian minister—passed away when John was only 3 years old. His mother died not many years later when he was only 14. Having lost both parents—as well as a younger brother—John and his brother Collin (who subsequently went onto become a Scottish mathematician of extraordinary notoriety) went to live with their uncle, Daniel McLaurin, a minister of the gospel in Kilfinan. There is no evidence to suggest otherwise than that John received exemplary nurture and theological instruction in his new home. Young John's piety and intelligence were immediately recognised during his time of study at the University of Glasgow. After a short stint in pastoral ministry, McLaurin was placed in the running for the chair of Divinity at the

University of Glasgow. This is confirmation that John Brown's praise of McLaurin was far from misplaced. To fill the chair of divinity there one either had to be a man of exceptional theological ability, or—as turned out to be the case with regard to Thomas Leechma,—a man of substantial connections.[7]

McLaurin's Theological Contributions

The relationship between Edwards and McLaurin cannot be fully understood apart from an investigation of the theological contributions of both men. While an abundance of scholarly works concerning Edwards' enormous corpus of writing have been produced, it is not so with the writings of McLaurin. This neglect surely owes to the limited printings his works have undergone. Add to this the small number of sermons and essays included in the published editions, and it becomes abundantly apparent how a man of such capacity could be almost entirely forgotten. McLaurin's theological depth and insight, unmatched by most of his Scottish contemporaries, is manifest from even a cursory reading of his sermons and essays. His style was perspicuous but profound. W. H. Goold expressed his sentiments concerning McLaurin's remarkable ability when he wrote:

> The essay on 'Prejudice Against the Gospel', and the Sermons on 'The Sins of Men not Chargeable to God', and 'On Glorying in the Cross of Christ', are compositions, the two first for profundity and acuteness, the last for impressive eloquence, to which, in the whole range of theological literature, we will not easily find anything superior; and there is not one of the treatises in the volume, which does not contain in them many indications of a mind of extraordinary endowments, subjected to the best of all influences, and employing its best energies in the best of causes. McLaurin's thoughts have, in a remarkable degree, the characteristic marks of original genius; they are singularly pregnant thoughts. They germinate in the mind. There is a living spirit in them. It is impossible to read him with attention, without being, as it were, compelled to exercise your own faculties. He is a writer who requires attention in his readers; but he richly repays it.[8]

McLaurin's adoption of Enlightenment principles was wed to an unwavering commitment to Calvinist doctrine. This was equally true of Edwards. Mitchell has further observed that McLaurin, like Edwards . . . functioned theologically on a level above most of his contemporaries, and displayed the same ability as his New England counterpart to use Enlightenment conceptions for the purpose of explicating and defending orthodox and evangelical Calvinism.[9]

Although he showed a vast approach to learning, both of ancient and contemporary authors, he was at every point a propagator of orthodox and evangelical Calvinism. He never seemed to allow his defense of orthodoxy to supplant his eagerness to promote the central truths of the gospel. An evangelical and Calvinistic christocentrism permeated McLaurin's works. The impact of this evenhanded theological commitment was felt as he actively engaged the effort to 'keep the truth before the minds of the people in the West of Scotland, during the early portions of the moderate ascendancy'.[10] Of Edwards' Scottish correspondents, John Erskine has typically been credited as having been 'the most eminent scholar among [Edwards'] Scottish correspondents', the singular Scottish figure with whom 'he discussed his most important theological ideas'.[11] This claim is susceptible to re-evaluation in light of Edwards' recommendation of a number of McLaurin's sermons and essays.

On numerous occasions, both in his letters and writings, Edwards refers to McLaurin. Some of the more significant allusions include a recommendation of the latter's *Prejudices Against the Gospel.* The subjects to which Edwards appeals in this work include such controversial doctrines as human depravity, eternal punishment, and the imputation of Christ's active obedience. McLaurin's essay is a masterful defense of these doctrines, and is noteworthy, as is evident from Edwards' citations. This particular essay reveals to a large extent the similarity between McLaurin's argumentation and the logical method employed by Edwards. In *Prejudices*, McLaurin utilised the *prisca theologica*, a hermeneutical principle frequently employed by Edwards. For Edwards and McLaurin a sure way to uphold a coherent *weltenshauung* was to root pagan worship in the perversion of Adamic and Noahic revelation. Another interesting connection is seen in a passing remark in which Edwards commends McLaurin's sermon, 'Of God's Chief Mercy', an exposition of Romans 8:32 that influenced Edwards' thoughts on assurance.[12] One final instance will suffice to demonstrate the theological similitude. McLaurin, in his most celebrated sermon, 'Glorying in the Cross of Christ', employs a comparative process by which he contrasted the state of the humiliation of Christ, in the incarnation, with his concurrent divine glory. The particular section in which this comparison appears is reminiscent of portions of Edwards' renowned sermon, *The Excellency of Christ*. In that sermon Edwards exegeted the metaphors of the lion and lamb by explaining that they were representations of the perfections of Christ harmoniously applied to his two natures. Concerning McLaurin's 'Glorying in the Cross', the Rev. James Waddell Alexander expressed the following sentiment: 'There is probably no single sermon in the English language which has acquired a higher place in the esteem of sound theologians and evangelical Christians.'[13]

In short, it should be noted that both men adopted a theocentric, as well as christocentric, approach to preaching, to the doctrines of grace, and to the fundamentals of experiential Calvinism. It is no overstatement to say that the correspondence occurred as a result of their mutual interest in the advancement of these foundational principles as they were seen in light of current opposition as well as revival. And so in a rather wonderful way, these men who found themselves moved by God, joined themselves to one another for necessary intellectual stimulation and spiritual support.

The Connection

McLaurin was the first of Edwards' Scottish correspondents. The relationship spawned out of a deep desire for the glory of Christ and mutual spiritual development. It is difficult to ascertain the precise date of the initial correspondence. It appears to have been sometime in middle of 1743. It is possible that George Whitefield, who frequently traveled between the UK and North America, became something of an intermediary. In a letter from Edwards to James Robe, written in 1743, mention is made of prior communication between he and McLaurin. It has been suggested that the first correspondence occurred sometime in October of that same year. McLaurin was most likely the chief propagator of the Edwards–Scotland connection on account of his admiration for Edwards and from his willingness to contact him. McLaurin was an elder minister of many of Edwards' Scottish correspondents. It appears that many of them worked through McLaurin to deliver books or messages to Edwards. In addition to this, Edwards' vested interests in the Scottish revivals certainly helped foster his relationship with McLaurin.

The events that transpired during the time of the correspondence were significant. In a letter written to William Hogg, a merchant in Edinburgh 'to whom [Thomas] Boston was largely indebted for assistance in getting his *Fourfold State* printed and published', McLaurin expressed sincere desire that funds be collected to pay for a portrait of Edwards—copies of which were to be sold to provide for the needs of Edwards' family. This fact is noteworthy because it was at that same time that things began to heat up on the domestic front for the Northampton minister. The year 1744 was that of the 'Bad Book' episode. This was, in some measure, instrumental in Edwards' 1750 rejection from the pulpit. McLaurin's care and esteem for Edwards is demonstrated most clearly in his desire to have a portrait of him:

> As care has been taken to preserve to us the faces of so many other eminent authors and other persons, it seems a pity if no such respect is put on an author whose past and possibly some future composures may come to be more regarded when the world's taste mends.[14]

McLaurin was ready to support Edwards in the face of opposition and the opinion of the world. In short, 1744 proved to be a year of international admiration for Edwards because of McLaurin's efforts, as well as a year of domestic frustration at home.[15] In addition to this act of kindness, Edwards made mention of an undisclosed gift his Scottish correspondents, directed by McLaurin, wished to give to the seminary at the New Jersey College. He noted this in a letter to John Erskine in 1750:

> I am very glad to hear what Mr. McLaurin informs of the encourage-ments likely to be given from Scotland to New Jersey College, a very hopeful society; and I believe what is done for that seminary is doing good in an eminent manner.[16]

The Concert of Prayer

Although the theological camaraderie and material endowments are not insignificant factors in the history of the friendship of Edwards and McLaurin, there was a matter of greater weight and deeper consideration. In his preface to the *Apocalyptic Writings*, Stephen J. Stein explains:

> A group of Scottish ministers met in October 1744 and agreed to unite in prayer regularly at designated times and in quarterly meetings with the hope that God would revive his church throughout the world.[17]

The precise details of the concert and its continuation have not been difficult to discover. The Scottish ministers engaged in the cause wrote a memorial in which they recorded specific details. Concern for a sustained commitment to the concert lay behind the widespread circulation of the memorial to all the societies involved, as well as to American ministers— of which Edwards was the leading proponent. In October 1747, just three years after the concert began, Edwards wrote *An Humble Attempt*. It was a direct answer to the prescriptions laid down in the memorial.

John Gillies, McLaurin's son-in-law, also recorded in some detail the events leading to the concert together with the memorial. This was published in his 1754 edition of the *Historical Collections of Remarkable Periods of the Success of the Gospel*. In this work, Gillies recorded how the 'concert was first set on foot, spread, and carried on without printing anything about it for some time, in the way of private, friendly correspondence, by letters in 1744'. McLaurin, the originator of the concert,

> encouraged the societies of prayer, which multiplied in Glasgow ... With his approbation there was a general meeting appointed once a month, consisting of a member from each society, with a minister from their pres[byteri]es, to inquire into the state of the societies, and to send more experienced persons to assist the younger sort.[18]

McLaurin's role in the societies cannot be disregarded since he was the organiser of the societies of prayer throughout Scotland. Upwards of thirty societies with at least thirty members each existed just prior to and throughout the initial years of the concert. Nearly one thousand individuals were praying for universal revival in the church.

If October of 1743 is the correct date of the initial contact, the correspondence is tied more directly to the Cambuslang revivals. Both men had an experiential acquaintance with revival—Edwards in Massachusetts, and McLaurin in Cambuslang. Apart from their mutual commitment to pray for continuing revival, both men shared a deep concern for the souls of professed converts. Owning their roles as spiritual apothecaries, the two carefully analyzed the marks of true Christianity. It was Edwards' 1739 Edinburgh edition of *Distinguishing Marks* that propelled McLaurin's pastoral involvement in the Cambuslang revivals. No evidence has been presented to support the suggestion that McLaurin was instrumental in preaching during the days of the Cambuslang revivals. To be sure, there were at least 25 ministers involved, and one can reasonably speculate that McLaurin was one of them. It was William McCulloch's record of the revivals that disclose the central place McLaurin held in regard to Cambuslang. It is estimated that nearly 110 converts were made at one time in the revivals there. The overwhelming need for pastoral assistance served as the catalyst for McLaurin's participation.

There was, of course, another reason for Edwards' interest in the concert. On Edwards' part, the Northampton revivals served as affirmations of his millennial expectations. While it would be a bit anachronistic to classify him as a 'postmillennialist' (since that phraseology is of modern invention), Edwards had distinct millennial expectations that awaited the fulfillment of a large portion of the messianic prophecies of the Old Testament in the Christianization of the world. Consequently, this compelled him to turn his attention to the prophetic passages in the Old Testament which he understood to be speaking of the messianic latter-day glory. This is most evident, among many other places, in Edwards' 1741 sermon *Importunate Prayer for Millennial Glory*. Turning to Isaiah 62:6–7, Edwards wrote, 'We have prophecies left by God in the Scriptures, in the hands of his church, of what God will do in the latter days, which doubtless are to be of some use to the church.'[19]

It is not clear whether McLaurin shared the same millennial expectations as Edwards. It is evident that both understood that the prophecies of the Old Testament found eschatological fulfillment in the incarnation of the Son of God; but there is little evidence to suggest that McLaurin believed the messianic prophecies related specifically to a millennial 'later-day glory'. There is one passing reference to the end-time conversion of Jews and gentiles in *Prophecies Relating to the Messiah*, but the absence of allusions to the term 'millennium' or 'later-day glory', is evidence of McLaurin's focus on the 'already' aspect of a Christ-centered eschatology. McLaurin's writings indicate that if there were any modern category into which he would fit, it would be that of an 'Inaugurated Millennialist'. McLaurin emphasised that Christ's first advent brought with it the full spiritual blessings promised in the Old Testament prophets. This conclusion is reached definitively by a reflection on McLaurin's thoughts expressed in his *Prophecies Relating to the Messiah*. The majority of the author's attention is turned to the engrafting of the gentile nations at the first coming of Christ. This alone seems to provide the interest in the concert of prayer for McLaurin. While God may not have promised revival at every period throughout the history of the church, he had promised to save multitudes of gentiles. The expectation that McLaurin had from the knowledge of the expansion of the covenant was sufficient to unite his heart to Edwards in the cause of the concert. For Edwards, the concert was driven by an expectation of a mass conversion of the world, and the end-time hope of the conversion of ethnic Israel. For McLaurin it was simply driven by the exponential nature of the Abrahamic Covenant in the inclusion of the gentiles.

Edwards' *Humble Attempt* becomes the gateway into a deeper knowledge of the concert. This is specifically so on account of the inclusion of the memorial in the second section of the work. Among the seven suggestions listed in the memorial, the third was a call for 'short and nervous scriptural persuasives and directions to the duty in view'.[20] Edwards' scriptural persuasive, whether 'short and nervous' or not, can certainly be recognised as an attempt to root the continuation of the concert in divine inspiration. *An Humble Attempt* seems to have given the concert momentum in Scotland, though it lacked serious continued influence in America. There was a genuine effort to renew a widespread commitment to the concert of prayer on both sides of the Atlantic. This would continue over the subsequent decade. John Gillies explained, in his *Historical Collections*, that on July 3, 1754, members of the societies for prayer signed the following agreement:

> We whose names are subscribed agree, that the concert for prayer should be continued for seven years after this date ... Members of societies in other places and ministers, to whom the proposal has been mentioned, have also agreed to it. ... It is therefore entreated that all into whose hands this may come, would join in so blessed a mean[s] of promoting the kingdom of Christ. The Lord incline them to comply!

Ten years after the concert, certain Scottish ministers sought its continuation. It is not clear as to how long this extended effort persisted. Gillies' reference, almost a decade later and in the context of a renewed effort in Scotland, demonstrated the significant contribution McLaurin and Edwards played in this global effort to pray down the Divine blessing. A friendship that began as a simple admiration of likeminded theological minds and Christ-exalting hearts, yielded a benefit for the church that has been unsurpassed in subsequent generations.

Notes

1   I am indebted to Christopher Mitchell for the work he has done on Edwards' Scottish correspondents. I wish to thank him for granting use of a chapter from his doctoral dissertation on McLaurin and Edwards. The language of McLaurin being the 'catalyst' comes from Mitchell's essay, 'Jonathan Edwards' Scottish Connection', in Kling, D. W., and Sweeney, D. A. (eds) (2003) *Jonathan Edwards at Home and Abroad: Historical Memories, Cultural Movements, Global Horizons*, Columbia, South Carolina: University of South Carolina Press, pp. 222–47.
2   *Ibid.*, in Kling, D. W., and Sweeney, D. A. (eds) (2003), p. 226.
3   WJE 16, p. 180.
4   Mitchell, C. (2003), in Kling, D. W., and Sweeney, D. A. (eds) (2003), p. 223.
5   McLaurin, J. (1830) *Works of the Rev. John McLaurin*, Glasgow: Printed for William Collins, p. xxix.
6   See Edwards' "Prophecies of the Messiah' and 'Fulfillment of the Prophecies of the Messiah', respectively 'Miscellanies' nos. 891, 922, and 1067, and no. 1068, in *The Works of Jonathan Edwards Online*, vol. 30.
7   Mitchell explains that McLaurin was only defeated on account of Francis Hutchenson, the famous Scottish philosopher. The influence he had at the University of Glasgow served to ensure the election of Leechman.
8   Goold, W. H. (ed.) (1860) *Works of the Rev. John MacLaurin*, Glasgow: J. Maclaren, p. xxix.
9   Mitchell, C. (2003), in Kling, D. W., and Sweeney, D. A. (eds) (2003), p. 227.
10 Taylor, W. (1887) *The Scottish Pulpit from the Reformation to the Present Day*, New York: Harper & Brothers, p. 170.
11 Stephenson, S. A. (1983) 'The Theological and Ministerial Influences of Jonathan Edwards', Ph.D. diss., University of Pennsylvania, p. 187.
12 'Table' to the 'Miscellanies', entry 'Satisfaction', in WJE 13, New Haven: Yale University Press, p. 145.
13 McLaurin, J. (1854) *Glorying in the Cross of Christ*, New York: Anson D.F. Rudolph, p. 3.
14 McLaurin, J. (1830), p. xlviii.
15 Stephenson, S. A. (1983), p. 181.
16 WJE 16, p. 350.
17 WJE 5, p. 37.
18 Gillies, J. (1845) *Historical Collections Relating to Remarkable Periods of the Success of the Gospel*, Kelso: John Rutherfurd, p. 462.
19 WJE 22, p. 372.
20 WJE 5, p. 326.

Chapter 6

The Geography of Sinfulness:
Mapping Subjectivity on the Mission Frontier

Kelly Van Andel

While this essay does not specifically address Jonathan Edwards' Scottish connection, it highlights and frames evangelical Calvinism as articulated by Edwards and promoted by Scottish ministers. Hence, though separated by the Atlantic, we can conclude that the 'geography', or map of the shapes and boundaries of sinfulness, prove similar, if not the same, for Edwards and his Scottish contemporaries and correspondents. Also, because Edwards' missionary efforts are generally applauded in evangelical Calvinist circles such as those in Scotland, I posit that the polemic of 'the geography of sinfulness', as discussed here in terms of 'interior' and 'exterior' rhetorical positioning, has not been fully considered or mapped on either side of the Atlantic. All said, my aim in this essay is to move readers—especially those associated with or sympathetic to Edwards' transatlantic influence on evangelical Calvinist missions—to deeper critical awareness of how the use of language created and creates geographies of interiority and exteriority quite apart from any physical landscape. Such awareness, though, necessitates attention beyond historical generalizations to consider dialectical nuances. It is to such attention that readers are invited to here.

Context
A year after his painful dismissal from Northampton, Jonathan Edwards and his family moved to the frontier town of Stockbridge, Massachusetts, in June 1751. Originally established between 1736 and 1739, Stockbridge was meant to be a model community, a prototype for future missions, where English and Indians would live side by side in peace. For Edwards, while such a community anticipated 'the dawn of the millennium when

every tribe and nation would see the light of God's righteousness and dwell together in harmony (cf. Isaiah 60)',[1] it simultaneously propounded that Indians, if not adults, should 'renounce the coarseness and filth and degradation, of the savage life, for cleanliness, refinement, and good morals',[2] which were understood to accompany the acquisition of Christianity. In reality, then, the mission conceivably existed more as an experiment in English civility than millennial harmony. Indeed, the English believed that the Indians might be more effectively evangelised if they learned to live with the colonials, according to the principles of English civilization, which they would then adopt in place of their own. [4]

In many respects, a precursory glance at Edwards' understanding of the Indians and the mission can easily assign the construction of subjectivity at Stockbridge into the either/or binary of coloniser and colonised, oppressor and oppressed, and accommodation and resistance, respectively. In *To Live Upon Hope: Mahicans and Missionaries in the Eighteenth-Century Northeast*, Rachel Wheeler challenges what we might call this 'route binary' of English and Indian colonial subjects through her claim that 'the overly simplistic narratives of accommodation and resistance that have long dominated the historiography of Indian-white relations' falsely position notions of identity that see 'Indian' and 'Christian' as mutually exclusive categories. As Wheeler develops her argument through a comparative study of Puritan and Moravian missions in the New World—a task which we do not have space to review here—she highlights various mechanisms, whether theological or empirical, that both create and exhibit an Indian *and* Christian existence. In regards to Edwards and the Indians at Stockbridge, Wheeler argues that the Puritan pastor's doctrine of original sin acts as a democratizing device that makes such dual or both/and existence possible.

While this essay does not mean to challenge the critical interpretations that highlight Edwards' doctrine on original sin as a socio-theological leveling agency, it does mean to nuance, and, in turn, question the boundaries and/or geography of such interpretation. To do so, it will first consider the shapes of subjectivity initially established through Edwards' sermonic structure of narrative. Next, through questions of interiority and exteriority, this essay will contest the boundaries of such shapes. And, finally, it will posit that just as an examination of subjectivity on the mission frontier cannot be polarised into the 'either/or' dichotomy of colonial and post-colonial interpretation and criticism, it cannot be claimed fully to allow for a 'both/and' Indian and Christian identity. In other words, this essay suggests that the conclusion drawn from Edwards' work at Stockbridge mission, which seemingly escapes the binary of colonial interrelationship through its attention to the democracy of human depravity, itself needs to be complicated, even confused. Ultimately such confusion does posit a 'both/and' inter-subjectivity of Edwards and his Indian congregants, but it is a 'both/and' which necessitates attention to a dialectical relationship not only between culture and religion, and between different persons and cultural groups, but between rhetorical spatial dynamics, and, in turn, the geography of meaning within texts and persons themselves.

Before we proceed any further, however, we should establish that our examination of English-American colonial subjectivity on the mission frontier is primarily one-sided, and, therefore, itself naturally prescriptive to a colonial binary that, in some sense, it cannot escape. Within such a binary, subjectivity is constructed via Edwards' life and thought and writings rather than through any agency and speech of Indian voice and perception. Such one-sidedness largely results from the absence of any significant resources from which the religious lives of the Stockbridge Indians can be reconstructed. True, it can be argued, as Wheeler does, that Edwards' doctrine of original sin results from his experience with his Indian parishioners, and thus holds tracing of how the native 'other' influenced not only the understanding of Edwards' own subjectivity but his understanding of the subjectivity of humankind as a whole. It is difficult, however, to measure such influence. And Edwards' writing itself provides little information about the Indians' lives. He rarely references Indian individuals, and individual Stockbridge Indians are mentioned by name in his manuscripts fewer than twenty times. His silence differs little from other Anglo-Protestant missionaries, so Edwards is not particular in recording how the lives of his Indian flock shaped his own perceptions of selfhood.[5] Therefore, we should be aware of how our examination of subjectivity at the Stockbridge mission is told from the binary position of the coloniser.

Also, we should be critically aware of how our own reading of the colonial binary, as well as anyone can possibly escape from it, necessarily privileges positions of our own interpretations that want to read Christian missions as necessarily 'good' or 'bad'. In other words, just as we mean to examine how Edwards crafted conceptions of his own and Indian subjectivity on the mission frontier, we, in turn, should question how our own interpretations of Edwards' work critically construct or map atextual shapes of identity that we can consciously or consciously relate to our own. In addition, then, to mapping historical narratives of subjectivity, readings of selfhood on the mission frontier conceivably reflect our own attempts to either alleviate our anxiety bound to the implied guilt of colonial projects or to celebrate our connection with the work of missions and the spirituality of Edwards.

Shaping Subjectivity: Narrative

Next, we will explore how Edwards' initially envisioned his identity and his relationship to his new parishioners through the use of narrative and biblical typology. Biblical typology fits well both the translations of his sermons—Edwards could not speak his congregants' language—and the use of narrative that the pastor employed for the better reception of his sermons by his Indian audience.[6] The biblical narrative Edwards choose for his introductory discourse to the Mohawk and Mohican Indians is that of Cornelius the Centurion, which arguably encapsulates Edwards's prospective relationship with his new parishioners, for it establishes the precedent of an inspired 'heathen' coming to Christ's apostle to be instructed in true faith.[7] Within such typology through which Christian events and history are prefigured, Edwards and the Indians continue the process of evangelism and conversion established by Peter.[8] Peter preached the gospel to the Roman Centurion Cornelius. Cornelius was not a Jew; rather, like the Indians, he was of another nation that used to be heathen. Edwards proclaims to his audience:

> Now I am come to preach the true religion to you and to your children,
> as Peter did to Cornelius and his family, that you and all your children
> may be saved.[9]

As Edwards narrates himself and his parishioners into the figures of Peter and Cornelius respectively, he further delineates elements of 'true religion'; and, in doing so, he introduces the dialectic of 'interior' and 'exterior' that marks boundaries not only between localities of the self but between 'self' and 'other' and 'true' and 'false' religion. For instance, through his narrative of Peter and Cornelius, Edwards posits an interior/exterior binary opposition between 'us'—those of the interior who belong to 'true religion'—and 'them'—those of the exterior who pray to the Virgin Mary and to saints and angels, who cross themselves, confess sins to a priest, worship images of Christ and saints, and those who do 'other things that the French do'.[10] Conceivably, through such narrative, Edwards' Indian parishioners are welcomed and included in the 'us'. Nevertheless, Edwards' projected landscape of 'us' and 'them' or of 'interior' and 'exterior' truth and untruth, proves precarious because, at the outset of this sermon, his Indian audience exists not only in possible alliance with the French but as a ubiquitous heathen 'other' that must, so supporters of the mission think, be enveloped within the fold of 'true' religion and thus 'true' interiority. As alluded to earlier, however, 'true' religion and 'true' interiority, are simultaneously linked with implications of 'true' civility: English ways and means of living and interpreting the world. Indians are required to masque the images of themselves as Indians, so that they can 'play' as English Christians. Although this proves to be a reductionistic theory that is complicated by the Mahicans' agency and practice of cultural exchange, for the moment, we should note that at least on one level, the English and even Edwards demanded that the Indians cast off vestiges of their natural exteriors, so that they might 'image' and mirror the vehicle from which 'true' religion comes: English 'whiteness'.[11]

Ironically, as Edwards' language demonstrates, even if the Indians assimilate into English civility through Christianity, the success of the sermon, and, for that matter, of Calvinist theology, depends on the pastor's ability to convince his audience that in relation to God, they are always 'other', always sinful. In other words, the success of Edwards' introductory sermon depends on his ability simultaneously to convince his audience not only of their exterior, transitive, heathen 'otherness'—their cultural particularity that lacks full knowledge of true religion—but their interior permanent otherness, their sinfulness, that separates them from God. As Edwards mirrors the personae of Peter, the Indians, as Cornelius, must discover what the speaker insists is the 'otherness' of human self-hood: sinfulness and the rectification of such 'otherness' by coming to know and understand Christ and the way God saves humankind through him.[12] What is unclear, though, is if Christ necessarily saves them from their cultural particularity as Indians, and thus eliminates or masks their dual 'otherness' as both sinners *and* English.

What is clear, however, is that as Edwards narrates the shift from an exterior geography named as 'otherness'—meaning 'sinful', 'heathen', 'untruth'—to that of interior landscape of true religion and faith, he, in fact, requires the listeners of his audience to 'see' their otherness bound in sin: 'They must see what poor, miserable creatures they be and that they can't help themselves, and [that] they need Christ to pity and help 'em and be their Saviour.'[13] Edwards further insists that they must see that they can never do anything to make satisfaction for their sins, or pay God for the sins they have committed against him, and that they must repent of their sins and be sorry and grieved.[14] Having repented, persons should then spend time praying, going to meeting, and thinking and talking about the things of religion. Edwards further adds that 'all those things must be done with the heart'.[15]

The Geography of Sinfulness

In response to the degrees of otherness sketched above, Wheeler would conceivably argue that, given Edwards' use of sermonic images familiar to Indian culture such as a fishing net or a tree planted by a river, he does not imply that the exterior 'other' of Indian selfhood—Indian cultural particularity—must be abandoned, as the preaching of his contemporary Protestant missionaries might suggest. Rather, it could be concluded, as Wheeler posits, that 'Indian' and 'Christian' are compatible and that the only 'otherness' that separates Indians from English-American colonials is their 'otherness' as non-Christians, for their 'otherness' as sinners binds them to their English neighbours unequivocally. Indeed, Edwards claims in his treatise on *Original Sin* that

> In God's sight no man living can be justified; but all are sinners, and exposed to condemnation. This is true of persons of all circumstances, capacities, conditions, manners, opinions and educations; in all countries, climates, nations and ages; and through all the mighty changes and revolutions, which have come to pass in the habitable world.[16]

Despite Edwards' use of the equalizing language of sin that names all persons as 'other' to God, Edwardsean, or shall we say more generally 'Calvinist' subjectivity, cannot be unequivocally transferred across cultures. It cannot, because a gap exists not only between a sinful self and righteous God but between a 'better opportunity' afforded by Christianity and the cultural particularity of 'poor heathen' groups.

Such a double gap, so to speak, is created and further enlarged by the mechanisms and models of colonial experience, which deem the civility of English colonialism bound-up with Christianity as the proper shape of human existence. Committed to such civility himself, Edwards says to his Mohawk audience, '[Y]ou have a better opportunity than many poor Indians; you have the gospel preached to you and the way of salvation by Christ, when they know nothing of it'.[17] Through such words Edwards reintroduces, albeit unconsciously, the geography of interior and exterior positioning of persons and communities. Here, though, in contrast to the inner–exterior positioning of converted Indian persons and groups, other 'poor Indians'—heathens—remain even more remotely 'outside' of the self of the Calvinist subject than those who are interiorly positioned within Christianity but exteriorly outside of English civility. Although human sinfulness levels any hierarchical structures of race and class and creed, and the grace and salvation of Christian welcomes all in, on one level, the Calvinist, Puritan subject will always be discursively constructed through a binary system of language. Such a system necessarily segregates the world into 'us' and 'them', 'good' and 'bad', and 'inner' and 'exterior' materials. Hence, although the 'other', the 'heathen', the Indian, may be acknowledged and welcomed into the subjecthood of Calvinism, the structure of language through which the Calvinist subject is formed will always keep the 'self' and the 'other'—even the Christianised 'other'— apart. Thus, as discussed earlier, the exterior cultures and groups that are invited into the interior of Edwards' Calvinist Christianity will always remain, to some extent, exterior.

In *Purity and Danger*, Mary Douglas implies that structuring of Calvinist subjectivity on the frontier must operate in this manner, for it is 'only by exaggerating the difference between within and without, above and below, male and female, with and against, that a semblance of order is created'.[18] It could be argued, then, that while the demarcations of sinful 'otherness' unite and democratise all of human kind as one, the 'otherness' and exteriority attributed to cultural difference and ethnicity, must remain, because without it English Christians would not be able to maintain their particular identity that names them as both English and Christian. The colonial Christianity of Edwards, or subjectivity in general, requires that an 'other', whether it be an 'other' of religion or culture or nationality, remain exterior, because definitions of selfhood demand exterior forms of otherness against which selfhood can be defined and comprehended.

True, in the summer of 1756 Edwards does rail at a gathering of the town's English children, saying that he would 'rather go to Sodom and preach to the men of Gomorrah than preach to you and should have a good deal more hopes of success',[19] while he separately advised his Indian congregants to be friends to their souls, perhaps thus indicating that he actually aligned his identity more closely with the Indians than with his English-American compatriots. We could even conclude that Edwards' expression of greater sympathy toward his Indian congregation suggests a reversal of colonial hegemony, inspired on the one hand by the contentions between Edwards and the Williams family that had spilled over from the Northampton controversy into Stockbridge, and on the other by Edwards' expectation that the English should demonstrate greater signs of true religion than their Indian neighbors, since they had the benefit of centuries of gospel learning, while the Indians had been given the light of the gospel only recently.[20] Additionally, we might argue that in constructing subjectivity on the mission frontier, Edwards often understands his own identity and that of the Indians to be more closely aligned than that of himself and the English. Edwards' subjectivity shifts to retain the order of his identity much as how we might say he retained it in his farewell sermon at Northampton in which fracture—sinfulness—within the interiority of the Christian community must be explained. The inclusion of Edwards and his Indian congregants within the same shape of subjectivity, however, does not necessarily result from sin's equalizing nature. Rather, the shape of selfhood shared by Edwards and his Indian flock more closely resembles that of subjects who have been treated objectively—as objects—that have been and can be maligned, oppressed and silenced. Although for Edwards original sin is necessarily an internal condition, he measures sinfulness as being 'outside' and 'exterior' to the interiority of his personal self-fashioning. Images of sinfulness seemingly better owe their existence to the spatial geography of interior and exterior selfhood, and, in turn, to a necessity for an order of comprehension rather than to any theological treatise.

Edwards' sermon 'Warring with the Devil' (April 1754), the Scripture text of which is Luke 11:21–22, 'When a strong man armed keepeth his palace',[21] provides another example of the spatial geography of selfhood and sinfulness. Such geography allows Edwards to shift and reorder patterns of interior and exteriority, so that he explicates or names as understandable the identity of his Indian parishioners, and, in turn, himself. In the sermon Edwards asserts that 'The devil is an enemy like strong man armed' and that 'The devil lives in [a] wicked man as in his house.'[22] Christ, though, is stronger than the devil: 'When a sinner is converted, Christ fights with the devil [and] overcomes [him]'. Furthermore, when a sinner is converted, he 'turns the devil out of his house where he lived and takes possession himself'.[23] Using such images of oppressive occupation and open possession of the self in the Application portion of the sermon, Edwards positions his Indian congregants if not in, at least on the threshold, of the devil's dwelling place:

> I would have you Indians consider how it is with you. Your whole nation was formerly under the power of that strong man armed, and now you are brought under the gospel. Consider how much has been done [for you]. And yet, how is it with you still? How the devil keeps you under his power! What slaves you are![24]

Once again, we could argue that Edwards uses the same type language to admonish and reproach his English audiences. What is important to remember, though, in regards to the pastor's sermons to his Stockbridge Indian congregation, is that his audience—although in Christ's kingdom—still remains a 'whole nation' different than that of the English colonists. In fact, in some sense, the image of the devil as a strong man armed who threatens to occupy the house of all persons mirrors the larger project of the mission that with the strength and cunning of colonials means not only to occupy but to take possession of Indian lands and establish the supremacy of English culture.

Edwards may not have meant to enact the rubric of colonial hierarchy and judgment. Nevertheless, he does. And he does not hesitate to tell the Indians how he thinks their misery—their slavery to the devil—has come to pass. He faults the idleness of young men, he blames the Indians want of good order and government in their families, and he proclaims:

> children rule their parents. Parents don't [really] bring up their chil-
> dren. When they are children, they go to school and are kept orderly;

but as soon as they are grown up, they begin to love drink [and] wander about. [They] serve the devil more and more.[25]

Granted, Edwards does allow a bit of room for rebuttal to his arguments. He says: 'It may be that you will say, "The English are as bad." It may be you will say, "What shall I do?"'[26] Very quickly, however, Edwards returns to insinuated and blatant judgment of his Indian parishioners:

Now, consider, are you not miserable slaves [to the] worst of masters? Consider what must become of you if you thus continue under the power of the devil . . . [There will be] no other pay for your service: none to deliver [you] none to pity [you]. [You] can't run away [from hell, and you] can't die. These things are certain.[27]

This language may echo or even match that which he used to his English congregation, such that, again, sinfulness could be posited as a levelling agent. As we have witnessed, however, there are variances within such levelling, which primarily result from Edwards' necessity to continually renegotiate his own selfhood, whether that means defining what he understands as 'true religion' and practice by aligning it more within his English sensibilities, as expressed through his sermon to the Mohawks, or with feelings of hurt and injustice, through which he aligns himself with the Indians.

Finally, if the continual need to renegotiate selfhood exists for Edwards, why would it not exist for us too—the readers and interpreters of such exchange. Indeed, are not we too bound to maintain our interior geographies so that we map our interpretations of texts by that which is interior and exterior to ourselves in order to maintain our understanding of ourselves as 'historians' or 'theologians' or 'Christian missionaries'? If such is the case, the 'either/or' of the colonial and postcolonial interpretation of Edwards subjectivity and work at Stockbridge, as well as the 'both/and' of the Indian and Christian of Wheeler's argument for the identity of Native persons on the mission frontier, needs to attend to a dialectical relationship not only between culture and religion and between different persons and cultural groups but between rhetorical spatial dynamics and the geography of meaning within texts and persons themselves. Attention to such geography will help us understand and complicate, if not escape, some of the binaries that have created the gaps between coloniser and colonised, oppressor and oppressed, accommodation and resistance.

Notes

1 Marsden, G. (2003) *Jonathan Edwards: A Life*, New Haven: Yale University Press, p. 375.

2 Wheeler, R. (2008) *To Live Upon Hope: Mohicans and Missionaries in the Eighteenth-Century Northeast*, Ithaca, New York: Cornell University Press, p. 213.

3 Marsden, G. (2003) 'Jonathan Edwards, the Missionary', *Journal of Presbyterian History*, 81 (Spring), p. 5.

4 Wheeler, R. (2008), pp. 220, 222. Importantly, though, Wheeler's larger study explored in *To Live Upon Hope* compares the experiences of Mahicans at Stockbridge, Massachusetts, and Shekomeko. New York. The Moravian Christianity practiced at Shekomeko varied greatly from New England Congregationalism practiced at Stockbridge. As we have learned, whereas Puritanism was a religion of the Word and consequently placed great importance on literacy as the means to gain access to God's revealed truths, Moravians emphasized the saving power of Jesus blood. For Congregationalists, Moravians were dangerous because they paid little attention to the social realm. They did not see English civility as a prerequisite to Christianity.

5 Editor's Headnote to 'The Things that Belong to True Religion', in WJE 25, p. 566.

6 *Ibid.*, p. 568; Acts 10.

7 *Ibid.*, p. 568.

8 Edwards, J. 'The Things that Belong to True Religion', in WJE 25, p. 571.

9 *Ibid.*

10 *Ibid.*

11 In addition to nuancing conceptions of Native American or Indian selfhood, categories and definitions of 'Englishness' should rightly be delineated and problematised. That said, as indicated above, since we are already viewing Edwards' understanding of Native and English subjectivity on the Stockbridge mission from the privileged position of the colonizing fraction, and we do not mean this to be an essay contemplating and complicating variations of colonial 'Englishness'. It suffices to note that, arguably, the danger of stereotyping conceptions of existence also exists in discussing notions of the English or 'Englishness' and 'whiteness'.

12 Edwards, J. 'The Things that Belong to True Religion', in WJE 25, p. 572.

13 *Ibid.*

14 *Ibid.*

15 *Ibid.*, p. 573.

16 WJE 3, p. 124.

17 Edwards, J. 'Death and Judgement', in WJE 25, p. 597.

18 Douglas, M. (1966) *Purity and Danger: An Analysis of Concepts of Pollution and Taboo*. London: Routledge & Kegan Paul, p. 4.

19 Edwards, J., MS Sermon on Matthew 13:3–4, 1740, repreached May 1756, Beinecke Rare Book and Manuscript Library, Yale University, Gen. Mss. 151, box 6, folder 463.

20 Wheeler, R. (2003) ' "Friends to Your Souls": Jonathan Edwards' Indian Pastorate and the Doctrine of Original Sin', *Church History*, 72 (December), pp. 736–7.

21 Edwards, J., 'Warring With the Devil', in WJE 25, p. 678.

22 *Ibid.*

23 *Ibid.*

24 *Ibid.*

25 *Ibid.*, p. 679.

26 *Ibid.*

27 *Ibid.*

Philosophy

Chapter 7

Edwards and Hume on Causation

Richard A. S. Hall

> And new Philosophy calls all in doubt, …
> 'Tis all in peeces, all cohaerence gone;
> All just supply, and all Relation.
>
> *John Donne*

In a letter dated December 11, 1755 to his Scottish correspondent, John Erskine, Jonathan Edwards remarks:

> I had before read … that book of Mr. David Hume's which you speak of. I am glad of an opportunity to read such corrupt books; especially when written by men of considerable genius; that I may have an idea of the notions that prevail in our nation.[1]

But why would Edwards condemn Hume's book as 'corrupt', written, as Edwards concedes, by a man of 'considerable genius'? He himself provides an answer in an entry in the 'Miscellanies'. Edwards writes:

> Hume endeavors to subvert all proofs of a particular providence, of a future state, and of an intelligent cause of the universe. He speaks of the doctrine of the being of God as uncertain and useless.[2]

Josiah Royce, in his *The Spirit of Modern Philosophy*, graphically describes the havoc Hume wrought in the philosophical cosmos:

> Has philosophy fallen by its own hands? Is the eternal in which we had trusted really, after all, but the mass of the flying and disconnected impressions of sense? All crumbles at the touch of this criticism of Hume's. All becomes but the aggregate of the disconnected sense-impressions. Nay, if we find the Holy Grail itself, it, too, will fade and crumble into dust.[3]

Hume's reduction of the eternal to the mass of the flying and disconnected impressions of sense is the effect of his thorough-going deconstruction of efficient causality. Edwards seized upon this fact, together with noting the paradox that Hume extols the supreme importance of the causal relation, only to undermine its integrity—what he gives with one hand he takes away with the other:

> Mr. Hume declares that the knowledge of the relation of cause and effect is of the highest importance and necessity, and that all our reasonings concerning matters of fact and experience, and concerning the existence of any being, are founded upon it; yet he sets himself to show that there is no real connection between cause and effect, and that there can be no certain nor even probable reasoning from the one to the other.[4]

Edwards and Hume divided the philosophical world between them. It is regrettable, as well as a mystery, why Edwards did not do Hume the honor of replying to him instead of disparaging him. Had he done so, something like the Copernican Revolution in philosophy might not have had to wait for Kant.

Though Edwards did not reply to Hume directly, he is fundamentally concerned with causation throughout his works. It has been remarked that Edwards' philosophy is essentially a philosophy of causation. Despite his animadversion on Hume's book, he arrives at an understanding of causality precipitously close to Hume's.[5] Edwards, too, denies efficient causation and defines the causal relation in much the same way as Hume, but for quite different reasons, which spell a world of difference between them. Their common rejection of efficient causes and their reasons for doing so is the subject of this chapter.

Hume broaches the issue of causation in *A Treatise of Human Nature* and the later *An Enquiry Concerning Human Understanding*, and his conclusions in both works are roughly the same. ''Tis a general maxim in philosophy, that *whatever begins to exist, must have a cause of existence*', declares Hume in his *Treatise*:

> 'Tis suppos'd to be founded on intuition, and to be one of those maxims, which tho' they may be deny'd with the lips, 'tis impossible for men in their hearts really to doubt of.[6]

One who held this maxim—namely, that every event has a cause— was, of course, Edwards, who avers in 'The Mind':

> When we therefore see anything begin to be, we intuitively know there is a cause of it.... This is an innate principle,..., a necessary fatal propensity so to conclude on every occasion.[7]

He makes the same affirmation later in *Freedom of the Will*:

> That whatsoever begins to be, ... must have a cause why it then begins
> to exist, seems to be the first dictate of the common and natural sense
> which God hath implanted in the minds of all mankind.[8]

Now Edwards' phrase, 'a necessary fatal propensity so to conclude', is especially telling in light of Hume's analysis of causality, since it suggests that the causal principle boils down to an ineluctable volitional disposition or habit.[9]

Hume, expectedly, put paid to this general maxim of universal causality. First, he challenges its supposed certainty. Certainty, for him, is derived from comparing ideas and discovering certain relations between them that are invariable as long as the ideas remain constant. These relations he identifies as '*resemblance, proportions in quantity and number, degrees of any quality, and contrariety*'. Hume finds none of these relations inherent in the causal principle that would certify it as a necessary truth. Second, he disputes the claim, made by Edwards among others, that the denial of this principle is contradictory. Hume lays it down that distinct ideas are separable from one another. Thus the ideas of cause and effect are distinct from the ideas of the *events* themselves that might be associated with them; hence, events are separable from causes and effects. The idea of any event, then, is not necessarily conjoined with the ideas of cause or effect. It is conceivable, Hume points out, that we might have the idea of something's not existing at one moment but doing so at another without conjoining it with the idea of it as an effect of some cause. Further, Hume notes that the disassociation of the idea of an event with the idea of its being a cause or effect is not contradictory:

> The separation, therefore, of the idea of a cause from that of a beginning
> of existence, is plainly possible for the imagination; and consequently
> the actual separation of these objects is so far possible, that it implies
> no contradiction nor absurdity.[10]

The difference between Edwards and Hume over the necessity of universal causation is that Edwards assumes the principle of sufficient reason, Hume does not.

Hume starts out with the *idea* of the causal relation, and looks for the sensory impression, the bit of experience or fact, of which the idea is a copy. This procedure conforms to his empiricist principle that all our ideas (our knowledge of the world) are derived from experience. In his search for the sensory impression that gives rise to the causal relation he looks to any typical causal sequence such as fire causing the sensation of heat, or snow cold. Even after we have observed multiple instances of a causal sequence, such as acid turning litmus paper blue or dry ice burning the skin, so that we believe that the first event in the sequence causes the second, all we ever actually observe is that events of the second kind invariably follow events of the first kind. We witness only a succession of contiguous events, but never any tie or link between them. Every time we approach a fire we feel its heat or touch the snow we feel the cold, and that is it—we do not also observe what, if anything, connects the fire with a sensation of heat or the snow with a sensation of cold. 'All events seem entirely loose and separate', says Hume. 'One event follows another; but we never can observe any tie between them. They seem *conjoined*, but never *connected*.'[11] Furthermore, that events have been previously conjoined within our experience does not imply that they will be so in the future:

> even after experience has inform'd us of their *constant conjunction*, 'tis impossible for us to satisfy ourselves by our reason, why we shou'd extend that experience beyond those particular instances, which have fallen under our observation.[12]

Neither do we detect in a cause any power or potentiality to produce an effect; if we did, we could predict the effect beforehand. Nor can we logically infer its effect by observing the supposed cause by itself:

> From the first appearance of an object, we never can conjecture what effect will result from it. But were the power or energy of any cause discoverable by the mind, we could foresee the effect, even without experience; and might, at first, pronounce with certainty concerning it, by the mere dint of thought and reason.

Thus we cannot tell beforehand by just looking at some unidentified clear liquid what color it will turn litmus paper, unless we had previous knowledge of the fact from our own personal experience or the testimony of others. Only by actually pouring drops of it on the paper shall we be able to determine its color effect—we cannot know it a priori but only a posteriori by observing it. All we empirically know of the causal relation, then, is that events of one kind (fire) are constantly followed by events of another kind (heat). The supposed '*necessary* connection' between cause and effect, notes Hume, is nothing other than a synonym for a 'causal relation' obtaining and a 'causal power' operating between them and so subject to the same reductionism as they. There is no observable necessary connection between a cause and its effect:

> we are never able, in a single instance, to discover any power or necessary connexion, any quality, which binds the effect to the cause, and renders the one an infallible consequence of the other. We only find, that the one does actually, in fact, follow the other.[13]

Hume, then, reduces causation to the constant conjunction of events of certain kinds, and because we have observed that conjunction many times in the past we come to expect its continuance in the future. In the *Enquiry* he juxtaposes two definitions of 'cause': (1) A cause is '*an object, followed by another, and where all the objects, similar to the first, are followed by objects similar to the second*'. This is a definition of the causal relation as 'a *philosophical* relation' or 'a comparison of ideas', as Hume puts it; this amounts to a 'philosophical analysis' of the concept of causality. (2) A cause is '*an object followed by another, and whose appearance always conveys the thought to that other*'.[14] This is a definition of the causal relation as, in Hume's words, 'a *natural* relation' or 'an association' between ideas; this constitutes a definition of causality as 'an empirical law of psychology'.[15] Hume's first definition is about what occurs outside us—those observable events actually conjoined in nature—whereas his second definition concerns what happens inside us—we *imagine* an actual connection between these events we have observed to be conjoined and subsequently *expect* that they will continue so.

Now if all we ever know of the causal relation is this constant conjunction of events of one kind with events of another, then why do we believe in their necessary connection since we see nothing connecting them? Hume explains that having observed two kinds of event or thing constantly conjoined, we *imagine* that they are also necessarily connected or united, so that upon observing a new occurrence of an event of the first kind (the cause) we spontaneously *expect* an occurrence of an event of the second kind (the effect) to follow. Thus having observed multiple times freezing temperatures followed by ice, we come to imagine their necessary connection, so upon feeling the cold we habitually expect ice:

> After a repetition of similar instances, the mind is carried by habit, upon the appearance of one event, to expect its usual attendant, and to

believe, that it will exist. This connexion, therefore, which we *feel* in the mind, this customary transition of the imagination from one object to its usual attendant, is the sentiment or impression, from which we form the idea of power or necessary connexion.[16]

Hume concludes that the idea of the causal relation is not derived from any sensory impression since we have none of a tie or necessary connection between a cause and its effect or of a power in the one to produce the other, nor from a logical inference since there is nothing in the cause that implies its effect; rather, this idea is derived from the *felt* expectation that an event of one kind will be followed by an event of another kind which is based upon their union in the imagination. The causal relation, then, is founded not in reason but in the imagination and feeling. Hume denies that we can empirically know of a necessary and objective connection between any two events in nature, between a cause and its effect; the connection between them is only a contingent and subjective one forged in the crucible of our own minds: 'necessity is something, that exists in the mind, not in objects; . . . 'Tis here that the real power of causes is plac'd.'[17]

Hume, though, does not flatly deny a necessary connection between cause and effect, only our *knowledge* of it. He keeps open the possibility of such an objective connection by saying that the causal sequences of ideas in our minds seem to correspond to the causal sequences of events in nature. In one place, he explains this correspondence by a 'pre-established harmony' between the course of ideas and the course of events:

> Here, then, is a kind of pre-established harmony between the course of nature and the succession of our ideas; and though *the powers and forces, by which the former is governed*, be wholly unknown to us; yet our thoughts and conceptions have still, we find, gone on in the same train with the other works of nature.[18]

Elsewhere, he explains this congruence of mind and nature as the result of a natural instinct: Nature has

> implanted in us an instinct, which carries forward the thought in a correspondent course to that which she has established among external objects; though we are ignorant of those *powers and forces*, on which this regular course and succession of objects totally depends.[19]

By thus referring to 'powers and forces' governing the course of nature and upon which the regular succession of objects in nature absolutely depends, Hume suggests that there may indeed be real, though invisible, connections between events and things in nature, and real, though occult, powers operating upon and through them. Hence, the causal relation is not wholly contingent and subjective after all. It is objective and trustworthy to the extent that it is validated by a pre-established harmony between nature and our minds and by a naturally implanted instinct.

The reason that Hume has knowledge of the causal relation only as constant conjunction is that he limits himself to the parsimonious epistemological principle of 'meaning-empiricism',[20] namely, '*All our simple ideas on their first appearance are deriv'd from simple impressions, which are correspondent to them, and which they exactly represent.*'[21] Thus he looks for the sensory impression, the bit of actual experience, of the causal relation of which the idea is a copy and, of course, he fails to find it. Hume's meaning-empiricism, by the way, is an early form of the positivist verificationist principle.

Edwards discusses causation in several places. His earliest discussion occurs in his youthful essay, 'The Mind'; there are brief discussions of it in entries from the 'Miscellanies'; however, his most sustained treatment of it is found in *Freedom of the Will* and *Original Sin*, though here it is in the context of a larger discussion of other themes. However, Edwards throughout maintains consistency in his discussion of causation. 'It is noteworthy', comments Frank Hugh Foster, 'that the treatise [*Freedom of the Will*] written in mature manhood went no farther than the notes ['The Mind'] of the youth.'[22]

In 'The Mind' no. [27], written in 1725, Edwards gives a definition of cause as constant conjunction that is virtually the same as Hume's first definition of 1739–40, that is, in terms of a philosophical relation: 'Cause is that, after or upon the existence of which, or the existence of it after such a manner, the existence of another thing follows.'[23] He gives substantially the same definition later in *Freedom of the Will*:

> I sometimes use the word 'cause,' in this inquiry, to signify any antecedent . . . , on which an event, either a thing, or the manner and circumstance of a thing, so depends, that it is the ground and reason, either in whole, or in part, why it is, rather than not; or why it is as it is, rather than otherwise.[24]

Though Edwards does not here mention *how* the mind comes to believe in a causal relation—say, through the association of ideas as in Hume's second definition, i.e. in terms of a *natural* relation—he does speculate on how it might be done. In a plan for a projected treatise on the mind, he notes this as a topic for future consideration:

> Concerning the laws by which ideas follow each other or call up one another, in which one thing comes into the mind after another in the course of our thinking. How far this is owing to the association of ideas and how far to any relation of cause and effect or any other relation.[25]

James Dana, who in 1770 published a critique of Edwards' *Freedom of the Will*, early on remarked on the curious similarity between Edwards' and Hume's uses of the words 'cause' and 'effect': 'whenever he [Edwards] uses the former word for any *antecedent*, or the *occasion* of an event or thing, and the latter for the consequence of *another* thing (as he tells us he sometime doth) he so far agrees with Mr. Hume in *words* as well as sense'. Dana goes further, remarking, '[Hume's] essays on some moral subjects are so nearly akin to Mr. Edwards on necessity, that a reader may think the latter copied from the former'.[26] Alexander V. G. Allen, who wrote the first full-length biography of Edwards, concurs with Dana's judgment:

> There is no perceptible difference between Edwards and David Hume on the vital question of the nature of causation. A cause is defined to be, not only that which has a positive tendency to produce a things, but it includes also all antecedents with which consequent events are connected, whether they have any positive influence in producing them or not. He assumes that uniform causes are followed by uniform results.[27]

In some places, though, Edwards implies that there is more to causation than simply constant conjunction. In *Freedom of the Will*, for example, he puts us on notice that he will use the term 'cause' in a broader sense than is usual. A cause need operate not only positively or efficiently to produce something by its presence, but also privatively or negatively by allowing something to occur by its absence:

> The word is often used in so restrained a sense as to signify only that which has a positive efficiency or influence to produce a thing, or bring it to pass. But there are many things which have no such positive productive influence; which yet are causes in that respect, that they have truly the nature of a ground or reason why some things are, rather others; or why they are as they are, rather than otherwise. Thus

the absence of the sun in the night, is not the cause of the falling of the dew at that time, in the same manner as its beams are the cause of the ascending of the vapors in the daytime; and its withdrawment in the winter, is not in the same manner the cause of the freezing of the waters, as its approach in the spring is the cause of their thawing. But yet the withdrawment or absence of the sun is an antecedent, with which these effects in the night and winter are connected, and on which they depend; and is one thing that belongs to the ground and reason why they come to pass at that time, rather than at other times; though the absence of the sun is nothing positive, nor has any positive influence.[28]

Now by acknowledging that a cause may act with such 'a positive efficiency', Edwards seems to be tacitly allowing the operation of efficient causes. And in 'The Mind', he speaks of the causal relation as the power of the cause to produce the effect:

The connection ... between the cause and effect, is what we call power. Thus the sun above the horizon enlightens the atmosphere, so we say the sun has power to enlighten the atmosphere. That is, there is such a connection between the sun being above the horizon after such a manner, and the atmosphere being enlightened, that one always follows the other. So the sun has power to melt wax, that is, the sun and wax so existing, the melting of the wax follows; there is a connection between one and the other.[29]

It is also significant that he here uses the stronger term 'connection' instead of the weaker 'conjunction' to describe the causal relation. Moreover, in attributing power to a cause he appears to be making it an efficient cause. Foster is even of the opinion that Edwards was not that opposed to causal efficiency, and blames his followers for imputing this to him so as to make his thought accord more with the Berkeleian idealism then regnant in the New England school of theology:

Now, in accordance with the Berkeleian idealism which pervaded, whether consciously or unconsciously, the whole New England school at this point of its history, physical causes had no efficient power.[30]

Edwards, then, seems to use 'cause' in two senses, viz. in the Humean sense as constant conjunction and the Aristotelian as efficiency.

Foster, moreover, detects yet another, more fundamental ambiguity in Edwards' use of the term 'cause':

[Edwards] wrapped up in one term both efficient and occasional causes. It was doubtless true that his idealism had much to do with this. If God was the only agent, if, according to the occasionalism of Malebranche, God does everything upon occasion of certain events in the mundane sphere, then there is no essential difference between the occasional, and what seems to us to be the efficient cause. But, however the ambiguity was introduced into his thinking, there it was, at the very foundation of the edifice he was about to rear, and destined to make its whole structure insecure to the highest pinnacle.[31]

Foster is partly right—for Edwards all ostensibly 'efficient' causes are nothing more than occasional causes. And for this reason when Edwards, as in the passages quoted above, describes a physical cause (such as the heat of the sun) as having 'positive efficiency' or 'positive productive influence', and the causal connection as being the same as power, he is not literally imputing efficacy to the cause. These phrases represent nothing more than a *façon de parler*, as when we speak of the sun rising or setting though it is doing neither. Those natural phenomena which are typically thought of as causal agents have no causal efficacy *in themselves*; they are powerless in and of themselves to effect or affect anything—they only *seem* to. For Edwards, though, there is causal efficiency operating in the universe, but it originates solely in God (given metaphysical expression by Edwards as 'being in general'), the only efficient cause.

Why, then, does Edwards deny causal agency or efficacy to natural things and events, and reduce apparently efficient causes to occasional causes? Apart from his theological commitment to God's absolute sovereignty, the reason is to be found in his metaphysical idealism. Like Berkeley, Edwards (by the way, for reasons independent of the Bishop of Cloyne) denies that there is any such thing as a material substance. Physical objects are not materially 'real'. We may think they are because of their solidity; but all we know of their solidity is their resistance to our touch, which is a subjective sensation—we know nothing more, and certainly nothing like a material substance that is doing the resisting. All that is resisting us in that place we perceive a body is a spiritual or mental substance, which is God himself. 'Solidity', concludes Edwards in 'Of Atoms', 'results from the immediate exercise of God's power, causing there to be indefinite resistance in that place where it is.' Hence, 'all body is nothing but what immediately results from the exercise of divine power in such a particular manner.'[32] Now non-substantial things like bodies, which are nothing more than resistance to divine actions, cannot themselves act efficaciously as causal agents since it makes no sense to say that 'resistance resists' or 'actions act'. Physical things and events, then, cannot act as efficient causes but can only be occasions for some other causal agent acting efficiently, which for Edwards is God; hence, so-called efficient causes only appear so because in fact they are occasional causes. In other words, upon the occasion of some natural phenomenon's occurring (itself an effect of God's acting) God has determined in his wisdom and executed through his will that something else should follow. Hence, on the occasion of freezing temperatures God has ordained that ice should form on water. Contrary to Foster, Paul Ramsey asserts:

> [Edwards'] rejection of efficient causation was quite thorough, and he
> speaks only of what 'makes' things to be what they are because of the
> strength of his immediate personal consciousness of God and because
> he believed things have their ground in the sufficiency of the divine
> wisdom. There, but for the grace of God, went Hume![33]

Moreover, Edwards had an ulterior motive for denying material causation. Like Berkeley, he was intent on restoring God to his sovereignty in a world where Deists, inspired by Newton, had made him peripheral. 'His [Edwards'] interpretation of causality and law as the mere mode of God's action was designed to maintain the total dependence of the creature upon God.'[34]

Interestingly, Edwards' doctrine of occasional causes accords well with Hume. For Hume, the distinction between cause *per simpliciter* and cause as occasion is bogus, and so Edwards could not have used 'cause' ambiguously, as Foster suggests. 'If constant conjunction be imply'd in what we call occasion', says Hume, ' 'tis a real cause. If not, 'tis no relation at all.'[35]

Edwards and Hume, then, both agree in rejecting efficient causation, though for different reasons that go to the heart of their more fundamental differences. Hume rejects it on epistemological grounds; his rejection of it depends upon his empiricist criterion of meaning: he can identify no impression or experience of efficacy or power in a cause, nor any necessary connection between a cause and its effect, corresponding to his ideas of them; consequently, he can assign no meaning to the phrase 'efficient cause'. Edwards, on the other hand, rejects efficient causality on meta-physical grounds; his rejection of it follows from his denial of material substance and his occasionalism. Natural phenomena are powerless to effect or produce, or affect anything because they are not real substances; a cause is only the occasion upon which God, the sole efficient cause, acts. Consequently, they both agree on defining the causal relation conceptually considered as constant conjunction.

However, their different reasons for rejecting efficient causes betoken deeper differences in their world-views. Most fundamentally, Edwards and Hume differ over whether the constant conjunction between events implies a real or necessary connection between them. For Hume it does not—events 'seem *conjoined*, but never *connected*'. The causal relation is grounded in the nature of mind. But for Edwards it does: 'with Leibniz, Edwards believes causation to be the ground or reason inherent in the world, because of the principle of sufficient reason in acts of will in God'. The causal relation is grounded ultimately in the nature of things. They also differ over the *constancy* of the constant conjunction of events; Hume had doubts about whether events, though conjoined in the past, would remain conjoined in the future, and whether their conjunction is actually grounded in the nature of things. For Hume, even the principle of induction upon which our expectation of future conjunctions depends is doubtful. Edwards, on the other hand, has no such doubts about conjunctions holding in the future since he adheres to the principles of sufficient reason and pre-established harmony. Notes Ramsey:

> For Hume conjunction was constant only in experience up to the present, while Edwards was sure of it for the future because the connection was a part of God's great system where whatever is has sufficient reason.[36]

Finally, Hume dissents from Edwards' reposing causal efficacy in God, and for the same reason that both he and Edwards refuse to repose it in nature:

> Since these philosophers [Descartes, Edwards, *et al.*], therefore, have concluded, that matter cannot be endow'd with any efficacious principle, because 'tis impossible to discover in it such a principle; the same course of reasoning shou'd determine them to exclude it from the supreme being.[37]

In brief, Hume's theory of causation is that of a rigorous and consistent empiricist. By contrast, Edwards' theory is that of an empiricist *cum* rationalist—Edwards owes as much to the rationalism of Leibniz as he does to the empiricism of Locke.

Now what may account for their similar views on causality? Edwards, of course, did not crib from Hume because Edwards, remarkably, anticipated Hume by several years—Edwards' 'The Mind' was written between 1723 and 1728 (though never published in his life time), 16 years before the publication of Hume's *Treatise* in 1739. We do know from his letter to Erskine that he had read Hume by 1755, though after the publication of *Freedom of the Will* in 1754. Flower and Murphey in their *History of American Philosophy* surmise that Edwards undoubtedly 'learned the meaning of causality from Newton and did not have to wait for Hume', who no doubt learned it from the same source. After all, Hume, Edwards, Locke and Berkeley all came within the orbit of Newton, the brightest star in the philosophical firmament of the eighteenth century—'Nature and Nature's laws lay hid in night: God said, *Let Newton Be!* and all was light.'

Notes

1 WJE 16, p. 679. It is not clear to which of Hume's books Edwards is referring. It would have been either the *Treatise on Human Nature* or the *Inquiry into Human Understanding* where Hume addresses the problem of causality. It is probably the latter since the first had few sales, prompting Hume's rueful remark that it fell still-born from the press.

2 'Miscellanies' no. 1297, in WJE 23, p. 243.

3 Royce, J. (1892) *The Spirit of Modern Philosophy, An Essay in the Form of Lectures*, Boston: Houghton, Mifflin and Company, p. 97.

4 WJE 23, p. 243.

5 Nor is it just between their conceptions of causality that there are significant similarities (as well as significant differences); the same can be said of their positions on personal identity and freedom of the will, and their common elevation of the emotions as a decisive determinant in the economy of human life especially with regard to religion and ethics. Sang Hyun Lee has proposed that 'a comparison and contrast between Edwards and Hume would make an interesting study'. See Lee, H. L. (1988) *The Philosophical Theology of Jonathan Edwards*, Princeton, New Jersey: Princeton University Press, p. 28, n. 33.

6 Hume, D. (1967) *A Treatise of Human Nature*, ed. L. A. Selby-Bigge, Oxford: Oxford University Press, p. 79.

7 Edwards, J. 'The Mind', in WJE 6, p. 370.

8 WJE 1, p. 181.

9 Moreover, Edwards' alternative descriptions of the causal principle as 'an innate principle', or as 'the first dictate of the common and natural sense which God hath implanted in the minds of all mankind', are particularly noteworthy since his admission

here of an innate idea marks a major departure from the Lockean empiricism which he so admired and professed.

10 Hume, D. (1967), pp. 79, 79–80.

11 Hume, D. (1977) *An Enquiry Concerning Human Understanding*, ed. E. Steinberg, Indianapolis, Indiana: Hackett, p. 49.

12 Hume, D. (1967), p. 91.

13 Hume, D. (1977), pp. 41–2, 41.

14 *Ibid.*, p. 51. My emphasis.

15 The phrases 'a *philosophical* relation', 'a comparison of ideas', 'a *natural* relation', and 'an association' are Hume's as found in Hume, D. (1967), p. 170. The phrases 'philosophical analysis' and 'an empirical law of psychology' are taken from Robinson, J. A. (1966) 'Hume's Two Definitions of "Cause"', in Chappell, V. C. (1966) *Hume: A Collection of Critical Essays*, Modern Studies in Philosophy, New York: Doubleday, p. 130.

16 Hume, D. (1967), p. 50.

17 Hume, D. (1977), pp. 165–6.

18 My emphasis.

19 Hume, D. (1977), pp. 36, 37. My emphasis.

20 The phrase 'meaning-empiricism' is from Bennett, J. (1971) *Locke, Berkeley, Hume: Central Themes*, Oxford: Clarendon Press, p. 225.

21 Hume, D. (1967), p. 4.

22 Foster, F. H. (1963) *A Genetic History of the New England Theology*, New York: Russell & Russell, p. 63.

23 Edwards, J. 'The Mind', in WJE 6, p. 350.

24 WJE 1, pp. 180–1.

25 Edwards, J., 'The Mind', in WJE 6, pp. 391–2.

26 Dana, J. (1770) *An Examination of the Late Reverend President Edwards's 'Enquiry on Freedom of Will'*, Boston: Daniel Kneeland, pp. vi, 126, cited in WJE 1, p. 34, n. 3.

27 Allen, A. V. G. (2007) *Jonathan Edwards, The First Critical Biography, 1889*, The Jonathan Edwards Classic Studies Series, Eugene, Oregon: Wipf & Stock, p. 289.

28 WJE 1, p. 180.

29 Edwards, J. 'The Mind', in WJE 6, p. 352.

30 Foster, F. H. (1963), p. 239.

31 *Ibid.*, p. 64.

32 Edwards, J. 'Of Atoms', in WJE 6, p. 215.

33 WJE 1, p. 36, n. 5.

34 Flower, E., and Murphey, M. G. (1977) *A History of Philosophy in America*, Vol. 1, New York: Capricorn Books, p. 167.

35 Hume, D. (1967), p. 171.

36 WJE 1, p. 35.

37 Hume, D. (1967), p. 160.

Chapter 8

Witherspoon, Edwards, and 'Christian Magnanimity'

H. G. Callaway

> On two days, it steads not to run from thy grave,
> The appointed, and the unappointed day;
> On the first, neither balm nor physician can save,
> Nor thee, on the second, the Universe slay.
> *Ali Ibn Abu Talib*

Introduction

'Christian Magnanimity' is a commencement oration that John Witherspoon presented to successive graduating classes of the Presbyterian College of New Jersey—later to become Princeton University. With Witherspoon as President, the institution facilitated the influence and integration of the Scots and Scots-Irish immigrants who arrived in large numbers in the decades before the American Revolution, totaling 10% of the American population by 1790.[1] Many of them came to America through Philadelphia and spread out across south-eastern Pennsylvania, down the Shenandoah Valley, into Virginia and Western North Carolina and then across the mid-south, forming the basis of the U.S. Bible belt.[2] These settlers long maintained their connection to Princeton—which was only seriously interrupted by the American Civil War[3]—and later by the divisions between fundamentalist and mainline denominations and the eventual secularisation of Princeton.

There is serious tension between Witherspoon's theme of Christian magnanimity and Puritan conceptions of original sin and human depravity—that is, Puritan conceptions of humility. Witherspoon, who arrived at Princeton in 1768 at the age of 45 and remained for the rest of his career, was more willing to seek an empirical middle ground of legitimate moral interests between Edward's 'true virtue' of universal benevolence and the particularisms and destructive power of human passions. In this connection, we begin to see the significance of Witherspoon, fresh from Scotland, taking the position earlier held by Jonathan Edwards (1703–58) at Princeton—and greatly diminishing the influence of Edward's philosophy. This, in fact, served the end of American liberty, helping to detach the new nation from imperial claims.

Witherspoon, Magnanimity and Virtue

There was an important influence of the Renaissance upon the Reformation. Renaissance scholars looked back to classical antiquity and found that the ancient world was in some ways better than their own—they romanticised the classical world, as we might say in hindsight. The intellectual stimulation provided by the Renaissance humanists, in particular, helped spark the Reformation.[4] But in reconsidering the ancient world, it was also found that 'greatness of soul' was part of the classical ideal, though it has frequently been set at odds with Christian humility.

If we are saved by 'grace alone', say, and not by our own good 'works', then it may be difficult to see how cultivating the ambition to perform great works in the secular world can constitute a virtue. But, on the other hand, if the classical world of republican virtue was in some ways better than the Roman Empire, or if the Middle Ages and knowledge of it helped point out defects of the church in the high Renaissance, then arguably, it must be possible to improve the world—it can and does change in response to human efforts, even apparently those of non-Christians. That is the problem that Witherspoon took up from a moderate Calvinist perspective in his address on 'Christian Magnanimity'. Doing so, he plausibly encouraged the belief that Americans could improve their world through their own 'greatness of soul'; and arguably, that was a significant influence on the American Revolution and the development of the republic. Of particular importance is Witherspoon's influence upon the American conception of religious freedom.

The Scottish 'common-sense' philosophy Witherspoon advocated was very influential, becoming almost official, in the U.S. between the Revolution and the Civil War; and it was only replaced, first by Transcendentalism and later by pragmatism, because it was eventually judged ineffective—especially regarding the problems of sectionalism and slavery that brought on the American Civil War. Still, Witherspoon's writings embody important elements of what has come to be called 'classical republican' values: extending the conception of grace, envisioned as the ability to build the church, to that involved in building a society in which freedom of conscience is secure. The ability to build the congregation is arguably a matter of grace and not of works, as our 'good works' are usually contrasted with matters of grace. Building the congregation belongs to 'the Lord's work', and, if so, then it may be argued that the establishment of religious freedom—removing official support and patronage from any particular denomination, since this facilitates freedom of conscience as needed in building the congregation—is also a matter of grace. This perspective helps open the door to Witherspoon's 'Christian Magnanimity'.

Witherspoon helped bring the Scottish Enlightenment and moderate Scottish Calvinism to America. He was a signer of the Declaration of Independence. He supported the American Revolution in his sermons and public addresses and helped to draft the Articles of Confederation. He served in the Continental Congress and a good number of his students would eventually serve in the U.S. Congress and other high offices. James Madison, his most famous student, helped draft the Constitution, was the chief author of the Bill of Rights—and later became the 4th President of the United States. Witherspoon's lectures were also an important influence in a multitude of colleges established through the mid-South as a consequence of his work in Princeton.[5]

The word 'magnanimity' came into English as a translation of the Greek and Latin term used by classical philosophers to describe appropriate moral ambitions. Understood in these terms, it means 'greatness of soul', including the aspiration to perform noble acts in public life and a certain generosity of spirit. Speaking on 'Christian Magnanimity', which he paraphrases as a matter of 'spirit, dignity, or greatness of mind',[6] Witherspoon took his biblical text from 1 Thessalonians 2:12: 'That you would walk worthy of God, who hath called you into his kingdom and glory'. In Witherspoon's writings, this glory can and occasionally does shine through human secular endeavors.

According to James McCosh (1811–94), a later Scottish immigrant and president of Princeton, in his book, *The Scottish Philosophy* (1875), Witherspoon 'refers to the theory of his predecessor in office, Edwards, that "virtue consists in the love of being as such," but without approval'.[7]

He held instead a version of the doctrine of moral sense, or conscience, as a form of common sense:

> There is in the nature of things a difference between virtue and vice; and, however much virtue and happiness are connected by the divine law and in the event of things, we are made so as to feel toward them and conceive of them as distinct,—we have the simple perceptions of duty and interest.[8]

In the prior paragraph of his *Lectures on Moral Philosophy* Witherspoon says:

> True virtue certainly promotes the general good, but to make the good of the whole our immediate principle of action is putting ourselves in God's place and actually superseding the necessity and use of the particular principles of duty which he hath impressed upon the conscience.[9]

Witherspoon clearly held that it is proper to act on our particular duties and moral interests, as we have the light to see them. 'The obligations of virtue', he maintains, are of 'two general kinds, duty and interest'.[10] The emphasis on 'distinct perceptions' of duty and interest implies that no generalised human conception of universal benevolence—on the assumption this is a duty—can hope to effectively decide among or always override the claims of our particular moral duties and interests; and our engagement with particular moral interests, and love or benevolence within a narrower circle, is needed as a guide to broader benevolence.

Witherspoon's work is close to the naturalizing, humanizing influence of Francis Hutcheson (1694–1746) in many ways. The point can be illustrated by a quotation from Hutcheson's (1725) *Inquiry Concerning the Original of our Ideas of Virtue or moral Good*:

> The universal benevolence toward all men, we may compare to that principle of gravitation, which perhaps extends to all bodies in the universe; but increase as the distance is diminished, and is strongest when bodies come to touch each other. Now this increase, upon nearer approach, is as necessary as that there should be any attraction at all. For a general attraction, equal in all distances, would by the contrariety of such multitudes of equal forces, put an end to all regular motion, and perhaps stop it altogether. Beside this general attraction, the learned in these subjects show us a great many other attractions among several

sorts of bodies, answering to some particular sorts of passions, from some special causes. And that attraction or force by which the parts of each body cohere, may represent the self-love of each individual.[11]

Witherspoon, in fact, disputes this metaphor from Hutcheson, maintaining that 'the more enlarged affections are intended to be more powerful than the confined'.[12] Yet, in the end, he agrees with its suggestion that universal benevolence may be properly approached *via* particular duties and moral interests. As a general matter, then, the argument is that the particularities of our various situations—moral duties to self and family, community and country—must be consulted and inform the abstract ideal of universal benevolence, if the latter is to have its full meaning; particularities of duty and moral interests must inform the duty of universal benevolence and help bring it into effective action: 'for it is only or chiefly by doing good to those we are particularly related to that we can promote the general happiness'.[13]

In his writings, Jonathan Edwards equated 'true virtue' with universal benevolence, arguing as follows in *The Nature of True Virtue* (1765):

> This is allowed by all with regard to *self-love*, in which good will is confined to one person only. And there are the same reasons why any other private affection or good will, though extended to a society of persons, independent of and insubordinate to benevolence to the universality, should not be esteemed truly virtuous. For, notwithstanding it extends to a number of persons, which taken together are more than a single person, yet the whole falls infinitely short of the universality of existence; and if put in the scales with it, has no greater proportion to it than a single person.[14]

The key idea here is the claimed subordination of local or limited benevolence to universal benevolence. Yet even if we suppose, consistent with all the views consulted here, that a universal wisdom understands exactly how local and particular duties, moral interests and relations must be subordinated to universal benevolence, it by no means follows that we mere mortals will always or normally know how this might best be worked out.

It seems clear that a federative church, for instance, preserving both local autonomy of the congregations and their mutual comity, essentially leaves open the question of the proper relationship between local and universal benevolence; though it is surely recognised as a matter requiring mutual consultation and guidance. In any case, the historical judgment implied by this same democratic and federative character is that the mere claim of catholic interests and universality is not a sufficient basis for direct rule of the congregations by a centralised authority.

Witherspoon's chief differences with the moderate party in his native Scotland concerned their alliance with cosmopolitan interests and their aim to diminish the role of the congregations in the selection of ministers.[15] In that conflict he had sided with the conservatives and their concern for local autonomy of the congregations, but he was not a conservative Calvinist. In the American context, he worked both for independence from the British Empire and for unity of the American cause—and we might certainly see the traditional emphasis on the 'comity of the states' in American constitution thought as a reflection of Witherspoon's view of the federative character of the congregations in the church. Like the Quaker William Penn (1644–1718) and the Congregationalist-Baptist, Roger Williams (1603?–83) of Rhode Island, Witherspoon defended 'liberty of conscience' against politicised centralization of ecclesiastical authority. If we require a contemporary analogy, then we might say that Witherspoon was judged 'politically incorrect' in his native Scotland in view of his emphasis on conscience and the autonomy of the local; yet, this same emphasis, combined with much that he took from the liberalizing tendency of Hutchison and the Moderates, made him a perfect president for Princeton, since in America the power of locality was stronger and imperial patronage weaker.

Witherspoon writes, in traditional terms, that

> the humility of the creature, the abasement and contrition of the sinner, the dependence and self-denial of the believer, and above all, the shame and reproach of the cross itself all conspire in obliging us to renounce magnanimity,[16]

and still he rejects this judgment. For Witherspoon, the virtue of magnanimity belongs to religion, and it is only a purely worldly version which he rejects and criticises:

> magnanimity is an amiable and noble quality—one of the greatest ornaments of nature, so I affirm that it belongs only to true and undefiled religion and that every appearance of one without the other is not only defective but false.[17]

Where we can depend on the independence of the congregations, there is to be no separatist or secessionist-communalist withdrawal from the larger world.

In Witherspoon's hands, magnanimity finally becomes a Christian grace, though it starts as a natural character that we should wear with appropriate esteem:

> To magnanimity it belongeth to attempt (1) great and difficult things; (2) to aspire after great and valuable possessions; (3) to encounter dangers with resolution; (4) to struggle against difficulties with perseverance; and (5) to bear sufferings with fortitude and patience.[18]

However, we are to be wary of the desire for possessions, in particular, because of 'its frequent perversion'.[19]

Human Progress and the Law of Freedom

Witherspoon maintained in his 'Speech to Congress, upon the Confederation', during the Revolutionary War, that 'There have been great improvements, not only in human knowledge, but in human nature, the progress of which can be easily traced in human nature.'[20] This claim is part of his argument for a permanent union of the American states; and a chief element of the progress in human nature, according to Witherspoon, was the establishment of the freedom of religious conscience. In a sense, freedom of conscience was basic to Witherspoon, just as it is basic to the First Amendment of the Constitution, penned by James Madison, where the freedom of religion and the prohibition of the establishment of religion support freedom of religious conscience as a matter of basic public law. Given that Edwards held that 'sermons, sacraments, even the fear of hell' can be 'means of grace',[21] and he justifies the appeal to emotion in this way, it is as though Witherspoon argues that fear of tyranny can equally be a means to the grace of magnanimity, and the prevalence of such magnanimity constitutes an improvement in human nature.

We thus have a spectrum of Calvinistic views, ranging from a Puritan emphasis on love for the divine, religion itself, unrestricted universal benevolence—and the separate congregation—to more liberal varieties which maintain that religion is only secure within a free state which is capable, because of the republican virtue of the citizens, of defending the freedom of conscience, and which therefore turns attention to the defence and configuration of such a state. If we think of the federative church as having two alternative poles or modes, the first involving emphasis on the autonomy of the congregation and its religious and moral mission, and the second emphasizing the interrelation of the congregations in representative bodies, then the first might be thought of as better suited to the formation of religious and personal ideals, and the second mode better suited to their social implementation. These objectives are not mutually exclusive, though one may find room for a preponderance of one mode over another at particular times, and we should recall in this connection that even Calvin in Geneva (whose work was made possible by a Protestant army from Bern[22]) aimed to reconfigure the canton politically.

Given the perceived threat to the autonomy of the local in his native Scotland, Witherspoon resisted attempts of cosmopolitanism to impose a ministry of patronage upon the congregations. But given the relative security of the congregations in the colonial American context, and the remoteness of any pretending political-ecclesiastical imposition, Witherspoon turned the energies of his ideals toward independence of a nation designed to guarantee the freedom of conscience. That is the broader objective of his 'Christian Magnanimity'. The religious and the political positions sketched here seem to be fully parallel, and this is part of the plausibility of seeing the American Revolution as a continuation of the same religious and political contest which divided the Puritans and Cavaliers in the English Civil Wars of the 1640s. Emphasizing the contribution of south-western Scotland in particular, and the need for general religious tolerance, such as we find in the First Amendment, Kevin Phillips has argued that the American Civil War was a further episode of the conflict between Puritans and Cavaliers,[23] with the southern planters playing the role of the oppressive aristocrats.

In Anglo-American history, the tendency toward empire is an expected and repeated result of the excesses of commercial expansion and of the international conflicts that arise in the wake of economic excesses. Recovery, on the other hand, has often involved a history of religious revivals—in reaction to our dizzy history of economic excesses. It belongs to the problem of our present situation in the U.S. that traditional American religion has much declined in its public standing and intellectual authority. It is too easily subjugated by political alignments and too easily disregarded. Magnanimity may become a disguise for the desire for permanent, galloping economic expansion and for the excessive desire for possessions.

The Decline of American Common-Sense Philosophy

Before the American Civil War of 1861–5, there were many signs that the prosperity of the new republic was being purchased at the expense of ignoring deep problems. I would like to evoke the American religious thinker Ralph Waldo Emerson (1803–82). This is appropriate, partly because his thought, like New England Unitarianism, is significantly derivative from the Calvinistic tradition. In his 'Lecture on Slavery' from 1855 Emerson discusses the political compromise concerning slavery in the original Constitution. One might argue, Emerson hypothesises, that the American Revolution would have been impossible without the South, and that action against slavery in 1776 would have been an impediment to independence.

The arguments from the necessities of war do not clearly extend to decisions made in the constitutional convention. Emerson argues, persuasively, that other options existed. Speaking of the Constitutional Convention, Emerson says:

> The fathers, in July 1787, consented to adopt population as the basis of representation, and to count only three-fifths of the slaves, and to concede the reclamation of fugitive slaves;—for the consideration, that there should be no slavery in the Northwestern Territory. They agreed to this false basis of representation and to this criminal complicity of restoring fugitives: and the splendour of the bribe, namely, the magnificent prosperity of America from 1787, is their excuse for the crime. They should have refused it at the risk of making no Union.[24]

The view is that the decisions on slavery at the Constitutional Convention were short-sighted. Emerson sees them as primarily motivated by economics. Or, as it might also be put, there was a misguided, generalised benevolence toward the interests of the slaveholders. The Northwest Ordinance, forbidding slavery north of the Ohio and east of the Mississippi, was adopted on 13 July of the same year, one of the last acts of Congress under the Articles of Confederation, and Emerson suggests there was a *quid pro quo*.

Expediency and high political compromise, neglecting moral deliberation, were the order of the day. Emerson thought the expressed ideals of the American Revolution, understood to include the slaves, should have overruled even the imperative of Union. A central point in his argument is the need for moral deliberation in political decisions. Ignoring great moral crimes, by and by, he says, we will produce 'great disaster'.

In spite of a quite significant tradition directed against slavery, it is not difficult to illustrate complicity in support of the slaveholding South in the series of 'great compromises' between the sections before the Civil War. One might first think of antislavery, New England Whig Daniel Webster's role in the Compromise of 1850, facilitating the Fugitive Slave Act of that year and 'The Devil and Daniel Webster',[25] but I briefly turn to Francis Wayland (1796–1865), who was a Baptist minister, the president of Brown University, and also a defender of Scottish common sense.

Wayland wrote a popular nineteenth-century college text book, *The Elements of Moral Science*.[26] Beginning with its first publication in 1835 and through many subsequent editions, Wayland maintained under the heading of 'Personal Liberty', that though it was the duty of the slaveholder to free his slaves, it was at the same time the duty of the slaves to obey their masters and be faithful to them.[27] In effect he left the problem of slavery to the conscience of the individual slaveholder, when, as seems clear, nothing short of large-scale state action could have resolved this outstanding contradiction to American ideals or avoided the national catastrophe which arrived in 1861.

It belonged to the meaning of the 'transcendentalism' which Emerson represented for many, that there is occasional need to 'transcend' common sense—of the sort represented by the compromise between North and South embodied in the Constitution of 1787; and arguably, it is just such transcendence which we find in the post-Civil-War Amendments to the Constitution. Yet, things were soon to turn in an opposite direction, and the end of Reconstruction in the mid-1870s eventuated in a further compromise including a free reign for Northern industrial and commercial interests, on the one hand, and the Jim Crow regime in the South on the other. The subsequent judgment of American history has been that Emersonian transcendence was ineffective in preventing the evils of the Gilded Age—from the end of Reconstruction leading up to the Spanish-American War of 1898. There are signs that Emerson's conception of freedom, a sophisticated compatibilist position, was lost from sight during that period, or became an esoteric doctrine. There was also a significant revolt against Puritanism and Calvinism in the U.S. after the Civil War, and none of this says much in favor of the Puritan emphasis on Predestination and Divine foreknowledge in the formation of congregations. Following Witherspoon, we do better to emphasise particular moral duties and human interests, as contrasted with raw passions, as possible indications of the better course to follow—always wary of the excesses.

I want to close with a couplet from the Persian poet Hafiz—a favorite of Emerson's. He quoted the lines in contrast to the opening quotation above, from Imam Ali—as America stood on the verge of the American Civil War in 1860:

> 'Tis written on the gates of paradise,
> 'Woe upon him who suffers himself to be betrayed by Fate'.

That we may allow ourselves to so suffer, or instead resist and conspire to adapt the laws, is part of the doctrine of freedom that Witherspoon helped make explicit to his contemporaries—as matters of tolerance, magnanimity, and the freedom of conscience. In contemporary American intellectual life, the corresponding defect, all too prevalent, often takes the form of the conviction that discussion and intellect are to no avail, since people will only listen to what serves the pre-ordained patronage of large-scale institutions, media, and markets. We can either go along with such demands, putting the eventual outcomes substantially beyond our control and submitting ourselves to fate, or take seriously the freedom implicit in propinquity, locality, and the pluralism of our closer affinities. As Witherspoon helped make clear to the generation that founded the American republic, we are not obligated to follow the greatest, most comprehensive set of human interests and powers in evidence—least of all, not in conflict with conscience.

Notes

1 See Miller, T. (1990) 'Introduction', in *The Selected Writings of John Witherspoon*, Carbondale and Edwardsville, Illinois: Southern Illinois University Press, p. 14.

2 There was also a significant Scots-Irish flow into the Carolinas through Charleston. See Boyer, P. S. *et al.* (1993) *The Enduring Vision: A History of the American People*, Lexington, Massachusetts: D.C. Heath, pp. 106–7.

3 Flower, E., and Murphey, M. G. (1977) *History of Philosophy in America*, Vol. I, p. 240: 'As feelings rose in the country, they were mirrored in microcosm in the college. Northern and Southern Presbyterians broke apart and the faculty, generally Union in feeling, lost the support of the Southerners but never worked up sufficient moral indignation to woo

the abolitionists. The tragedy was capped by the war itself.'

4   See 'Renaissance', *Encyclopaedia Britannica* (1999).

5   See Flower, E., and Murphey, M. G. (1977), p. 236, on the influence of Witherspoon's *Lectures on Moral Philosophy*. 'Although not published until 1800…, they were carried as manuscript notes southward to Virginia and the Carolinas, and westward through Pennsylvania and Kentucky. They were used in courses taught by his students and then by students of their students. They were bearers of Presbyterian influence in the enormous network of Presbyterian-dominated colleges that sprang up in the next four decades.'

6   Witherspoon, J. (1775–87) 'Christian Magnanimity', in Stroh, G. W., and Callaway, H. G. (2000) *American Ethics: A Source Book from Edwards to Dewey*, Lanham, Maryland: University Press of America, p. 48. Webster's defines 'magnanimity' as meaning 'loftiness of spirit enabling one to bear trouble calmly, to disdain meanness and pettiness, and to display a noble generosity'.

7   McCosh, J. (1875) *The Scottish Philosophy*, London: Macmillan, p. 188.

8   Witherspoon, quoted in McCosh, J. (1875), p. 188; see Witherspoon's *Lectures on Moral Philosophy*, in Miller, T. (ed.) (1990), p. 168.

9   Witherspoon, J., *Lectures on Moral Philosophy*, in Miller, T. (ed.) (1990), pp. 167–8.

10 *Ibid.*, p. 168.

11 Hutcheson, F. (1725) *An Inquiry Concerning the Original of our Ideas of Virtue or Moral Good*; reprinted in Hutcheson (1994) *Philosophical Writings*, Vermont: Charles E. Tuttle, p. 101.

12 Witherspoon, J., *Lectures on Moral Philosophy*, in Miller, T. (ed.) (1990), p. 180.

13 *Ibid.*

14 Edwards, J. (1756) *The Nature of True Virtue*, in Smith, J. E. *et al.* (eds) (1995) *A Jonathan Edwards Reader*, New Haven: Yale University Press, p. 254.

15 See Miller, T. (1990) 'Introduction', pp. 11–12; Noll, M. A. (1989) 'Witherspoon Comes to Princeton', in *Princeton and the Republic, 1768–1822*, Princeton, New Jersey: Princeton University Press, p. 23.

16 Witherspoon, J. (1775–87) 'Christian Magnanimity', pp. 48–9.

17 *Ibid.*, p. 49.

18 *Ibid.*, p. 50.

19 *Ibid.*

20 Witherspoon, J. 'Part of a Speech in Congress, upon the Confederation', in Miller, T. (ed.) (1990), p. 151.

21 See Schafer, T. A. (2009) 'Jonathan Edwards', in *Encyclopaedia Britannica*; Edwards, J. (1746) *A Treatise Concerning Religious Affections*, in Smith, J. E. *et al.* (eds) (1995), p. 162.

22 See Fahrni, D. (2003) *An Outline History of Switzerland*, Pro-Helvita: Zurich, pp. 36–41.

23 See Phillips, K. (1999) *The Cousins' Wars, Religion, Politics and the Triumph of Anglo-America*, New York: Basic Books, especially pp. 263–4.

24 Emerson, R. W. (1855) 'Lecture on slavery', in Gougeon, L., and Myerson, J. (eds) (1995) *Emerson's Antislavery Writings*, New Haven: Yale University Press, pp. 99–100.

25 See Benêt, S. V. (1999) *The Devil and Daniel Webster and other Writings*, New York: Penguin Books.

26 Wayland, F. (1963) *The Elements of Moral Science*, ed. Blau, J., Cambridge, Massachusetts: Harvard University Press.

27 *Ibid.*, pp. 188–209 and especially p. 195.

Chapter 9

Human Will, Divine Grace, and Virtue:
Jonathan Edwards Tangos with Immanuel Kant

Natalia Marandiuc

Jonathan Edwards' view of virtue arises from at least two intuitions that seem strikingly similar to the thought trajectory of a central European Enlightenment figure—Immanuel Kant. Iimportant dissimilarities notwithstanding, both Edwards and Kant assume that reason is the locus of human volition, which operates under two major constraints: immersion in finitude and bondage to evil. Both thinkers suggest that a self-determining human will cannot be logically accommodated in a finite universe without absurdity. They both further intuit that the will is comprised of two ingredients, or more simply, two loves, which are always ranked, one conditioning the other. I will show that for both of them these loves amount to self-love and love of God, that human beings are born with self-love ranking over the other love, and that the reversal of this ranking is achievable only with the supernatural aid of divine assistance. My argument is that in a carefully defined sense Edwards' thought mirrors Kant's logic on the relationship between human will and divine grace, and that they invoke grace similarly as the condition of the possibility of genuine virtue.[1]

Causality, Freedom, and the Determination of the Will

Edwards understands the will to be the dimension of human interiority by virtue of which 'the mind chooses anything'.[2] The will itself is passive, while the mind is the active agent behind it and the proper residence of choice making. The will simply functions as a bridge between apprehension and action, yet it remains fully determined by reason and its faculty of knowing.

Furthermore, what the will wants is always immediate and produces action. We are constituted so that *choosing* to move one's body in a certain way is instantly followed by the respective gesture. Human preference is not for a remote goal towards which one can make a variety of movements, but rather for the immediate move in which our body or reasoning engages.[3] For example, if I say that my preference is for good health, it would be too remote of a *telos* to count as a proper object of the will in this Edwardian scheme; if I reach out for a glass of water rather than one of Coca-Cola, I engage my will directly.

Edwards claims that every time there is an act of the will, it is preceded by a 'preponderation of the mind',[4] which is inclined towards one option more than others. If there is no such inclination and all options are aligning themselves with equal appeal, willing is simply impossible. The will cannot proceed out of a state of perfect equilibrium, devoid of desire. Instead, it proceeds in the same direction as the strongest inclination.

Kant differs from Edwards in one significant aspect here. He suggests that reason is not the *sole* determiner of the will. Human beings are creatures of need, who experience inclinations that can and often do run contrary to reason, particularly to moral reason. Whereas the moral good may be discerned through the employment of reason, which represents the moral law objectively to all people, inclinations are subjective feelings about what seems agreeable yet is not universal.[5] And since it is not universal, it cannot be declared morally good according to Kant. The will 'stands . . . as at a crossroads'[6] between the a priori duty to the moral good, which reason perceives objectively, and some a posteriori incentive that lures the subjective inclinations. Thus the will is conflicted between knowing the moral good and being inclined towards subjective ends that contradict it. Kant assumes the knowledge of the good and renders the will actively productive of the choice of such good. The will is pulled in opposite directions by these two determinants—objective reason and subjective inclinations—which both compete, albeit unequally, to cause a choice. I will later return to the ranking of these two contributors to the determination of the will.

While Kant places the conflict between possible choices at the level of the will and its ingredients, Edwards posits the disequilibrium among the possible targets of the will *in the mind*. For Edwards the will is determined by a *motive*,[7] which is what causes it to choose water over Coke. Now the motive is in the faculty of perception or understanding, which Edwards understands broadly, not reduced to reason or judgment.[8] His key argument here is that the mind includes the capacity to be attracted by various things and is not a merely neutral computer-like intelligence pantry. The mind provides material for volition to go for a choice. The will is determined by the kind of perception the mind has with respect to an object, which leads to judgment, which in turn triggers the will, which issues itself right away into action without resistance.

Edwards insists at great length that unless the first piece in this domino-like causal chain is free, none of the subsequent steps is free. However, it is impossible to have a free first act of choice, or a purely voluntary first act, because positing the self-determination of the will only leads to a logical impasse. How so? If the will were to freely determine its own acts, it would do so in virtue of an act of freely choosing or willing. Then every free act of the will would be determined by a preceding act of the will, which would be the basis for the logically subsequent one. In order for the choice to be free, this preceding act must itself be free. Simply put, this entails an infinite regression of choices attempting to lead to a free first act of willing, which Edwards finds absurd.[9] The whole logical chain presupposes a contradiction: 'it supposes an act of the will preceding the first act in the whole train, or a free act of the will before the first free act of the will.'[10] Since this is logically impossible according to Edwards, none of the acts in the causal chain is free.

> From whence it follows, that *no liberty consists in the will's power to determine its own acts:* or, which is the same thing, that there is no such thing as liberty consisting in a self-determining power of the will.[11]

The will is causally determined through the inherent biases linked to the faculty of knowing, which operates in such a way that inclinations and affections are always connected with it. The causal chain may *appear* to reach asymptotically towards a first free cause, but in reality freedom eludes the causal empirical world and its finitude.

This is where Edwards and Kant agree. For Kant, causality is also one of the categories of finitude. Whatever happens on the plane of finite existence is caused *within* the finite realm. The principle of cause can be sustained only when applied to the domain of finite possible experience—what he calls the realm of phenomena. With respect to the world of things as they are in themselves—the noumena—we cannot conceptualise how they can work as causes to others 'or be in community with others'.[12] The concept of cause is not associable with things in themselves, but only with experience and its sequence in time, whereby 'antecedent cognition can be connected with the subsequent one according to the rule of hypothetical judgments'.[13] Yet objects that make up the world of phenomena where causal connections exist also transcend it and are located in the noumenal reality of things in themselves, where they enjoy freedom. Most significantly for my argument, human beings are also bi-located in the phenomenal and noumenal spheres. Kant's distinction between the categories of phenomena and noumena allows him to affirm that the same person can be both causally determined and autonomously free without contradiction. All actions of rational beings are subject to natural necessity and causality insofar as they are experienced. But the very same actions are free with respect to the noumenal pure reason of each individual.[14] The human will may appear to be causally determined, but it is noumenally free. Its freedom just cannot be contained in the finite universe.

Neither can it be for Edwards. He claims that the will can only be free if in perfect neutrality, with no inclination and no affection, but that is precisely what renders it inoperative. The freedom of the will is nothing less than the death of the will, and with it the death of any action and of life itself. '[T]ake away all [inclinations and affections] and the world would be, in great measure, motionless and dead'.[15] Freedom and volition are each other's contradiction: 'one excludes and destroys the other, as much as motion and rest, light and darkness, or life and death'.[16] To posit that human beings have a will at all is thus identical in Edwards' view with abolishing its freedom.

The Edwardsean will is determined by the faculty of knowing in the mind. What appears to be most agreeable to the mind springs the will into motion.[17] Consequently, the *kind* of knowing in which the mind engages is what determines the *kind* of willing that follows suit. A morally good will able to give rise to virtuous action depends then on some morally good kind of knowing and related affective inclinations that determine it. So, how can we know what we know?

Edwards' Notion of Spiritual Principle

Edwards thinks that human beings operate with a two-tiered epistemology. Simply put, at one level people have a mediated knowledge of the world, the self and God, while at another level there is an immediate knowledge that God imparts directly to the human psyche. The first kind of knowledge is universally available to all. Although God is ultimately its author, 'flesh and blood is made use of as the mediate or second cause of it'.[18] In other words, both creaturely efforts and divine import synergistically contribute to the production of this type of knowing. The second kind of knowledge is reserved for a subset of humanity, the regenerated. Edwards calls this 'spiritual knowledge', or 'spiritual and divine light',[19] which does not make its way to the human mind through any intermediate natural causes, but is obtained from the Holy Spirit directly.

The difference between these two kinds of knowledge is not in their content. The new spiritual light adds nothing to which the rest of human beings do not have informational access. In fact, both kinds of knowledge proceed from the same first cause or origin: the Spirit of God. When the Spirit imparts to the human mind the immediate kind of knowledge, the Spirit does not infuse a new morality into the conscience, give new material for the imagination, reveal new propositions such as new doctrine, or induce emotions stemming out of one's views of religious things. All such dimensions of the human interiority are the product of natural principles. Even though they, too, proceed from a divine ultimate source, they are nonetheless part and parcel of the created order with its own laws of operation and creaturely powers. The Spirit assists them without adding anything new to them.

What the Spirit does do when God imparts immediate divine knowledge to the human creature is to communicate a new 'indwelling vital principle ... of life and action'[20] to the mind. *The Spirit is being united with the human mind permanently.* It takes anthropological residence. Consequently, the human empirical world is indelibly linked with the transcendental domain. Edwards argues that only God's volition is both self-moved and free.[21] Freedom can be predicated on the human person only insofar as he or she is in union with the Spirit of God. Thus both Kant and Edwards provide a link between the causal chain contained exclusively in the empirical reality and the world of freedom. Whereas Kant extends the will into the noumena, Edwards brings his own noumena so to speak, that is, God's Spirit, into union with the human heart. The key difference between mediated and unmediated knowledge is that in the former case the Spirit of God may act upon the natural operations of the soul occasionally and extrinsically, without altering either their kind or their ranking, whereas in the latter case the Spirit unites itself with the human interiority though a self-communication 'peculiar'[22] to itself and, as I will show, changing the ranking of the soul's desires. In the first case, the Spirit assists human knowing through the mediation of the natural principles of apprehension and volition, while in the second the Spirit intervenes such that

> those things are wrought in the soul that are *above nature*, and of which there is nothing of the like kind in the soul by nature: and they are caused to exist in the soul *habitually* […] The mind thenceforth *habitually* exerts those acts that the dominion of sin had made it as wholly destitute of.[23]

The Spirit does not restore the fallen human condition when the Spirit's activity remains at the mediated level. Yet when the Spirit communicates itself to the human mind directly, regeneration ineluctably occurs and is irreversible. Hence, the new principle that works in the soul does so 'habitually'. Once lit in the heart, the 'spiritual and divine light' remains on.[24] Its concrete effect is a new weight that the revelation contained in the Scripture has for the human mind. Edwards describes the phenomenology of the Spirit's immediate presence as follows:

> There is not only a rational belief that God is holy, and that holiness is a good thing: but there is a sense of the loveliness of God's holiness. There is not only a speculatively judging that God is gracious, but a sense [of] how amiable God is on account; or a sense of the beauty of this divine attribute.[25]

The human person is thus able not only to reason about God and God's engagement with the world, but also have a sense of delight in this knowledge. The mediated knowledge of God involves the faculty of understanding without moving the will to love God, at least not more than any other apparent good that competes for the mind's apprehension. In the direct knowledge of God the will, or the 'disposition of the soul', is changed and becomes inclined towards God.[26] The Spirit's union with human nature enables the mind to perceive God as the greatest good. The love of God becomes its foremost principle of action. Moreover, because of this union, as the Spirit unites itself with the human interiority, the human interiority becomes more like the Spirit:

> This light . . . assimilates the nature to the divine nature, and changes the soul into an image of the same glory that is beheld: [. . .] it reaches the bottom of the heart, and changes the nature, so it will effectually dispose to an universal obedience . [. . .] It draws forth the heart in a sincere love to God, which is the only principle of true, gracious, and universal obedience.[27]

Such obedience counts as virtue for Edwards. Virtue then is the result of the human person becoming deified, increasingly resembling God's own nature, which is united to the soul through the Holy Spirit. This union, which results in virtue, enables the heart to have as its first principle the love of God, on which virtue rests.[28] Thus divine grace, which takes the form of this union, is the source of the possibility of human virtue and of the will's inclination to it.

Effects of Grace: Reversal of the Ranking of Loves

How exactly is the will affected by grace, and how is virtue generated? In this section, I will follow both Kant and Edwards' thought trajectories side by side and argue that both of them see grace as a lever which reverses the fallen ranking of loves and enables the human person to live virtuously.

Kant portrays human beings as morally defined by what he calls a fundamental 'disposition',[29] or ground on which we adopt logically ulterior principles of action or maxims. In Kant's structure of the self, this disposition resides in the noumenal, rather than phenomenal realm,[30] and it has two significant traits. First, it is singular, which means that it is the ultimate and only ground for adopting moral principles. In this sense, Kant maintains an exclusive disjunction: every action and character issue from a singular moral disposition, which is theoretically either good or evil. A mix is excluded. Secondly, human beings adhere to this moral disposition in genuine freedom.[31]

Although singular and ultimate, a moral disposition is not structurally pure. Rather, each one of the two possible dispositions, good or evil, is comprised of the same two elements: the moral law, and the sensuous nature. We love them both, although in different ways. The moral law residing in our reason calls us irresistibly to exercise our moral duty without any ulterior motive, whereas our sensuous nature provides the subjective principle of self-love, by which we are inclined to achieve our own happiness. Both loves determine the will, and both are necessary characteristics of being human.

These two ingredients that are being incorporated in the moral maxim are never ranked equally. One is always subordinated to the other. Then the nature of the moral disposition is given by the one love that becomes the supreme condition for the satisfaction of the other. In a good disposition, the love for the moral law conditions the self-love oriented to achieve happiness, whereas in an evil disposition desire for happiness ranks higher than the bent towards moral duty. Thus, human beings are not morally evil because they repudiate the moral law, which 'imposes itself irresistibly', but because they reverse the moral order and make self-love the condition of their compliance with the moral law.[32] Kant's notion of love for the moral law roughly corresponds to the Christian (and Edwardsean) notion of love of God. As Kant translates Christian doctrines within the boundaries of reason, the moral law stands for God the Father.[33] Loving the law is loving the first person of the Trinity, and by extension, loving God.

The good and evil moral maxims do not rank equally in the human nature either. In fact, throughout *Religion within the Boundaries of Mere Reason* Kant is careful to consistently characterise the good in us as a *predisposition*, and the evil as a *propensity*. Translating the theological doctrines of creation and fall into the philosophical language of reason, Kant refers to the predisposition to good as a necessary condition of being human, and to the propensity to evil as contingent for humanity.[34] Nonetheless, evil is 'woven into human nature' universally,[35] so that even the very best of human beings are not exempt from this propensity. Although we are all fallen, it is not the original state in which we find ourselves. In the same way in which creation precedes the fall, the predisposition to good is more basic than the propensity to evil. Although universally present, the latter is not conceptually necessary for being human.[36]

Now this propensity towards evil is, however, '*radical*, since it corrupts the ground of all maxims' from which every trait and action stem out.[37] This radical character of evil is the hinge on which Kant's discussion of grace stands. Since it corrupts the ground of all maxims, it cannot be extirpated by human forces. In order to uproot it we would need to reverse the highest maxim from which all others derive. But that would require that we would be outside this fundamental maxim, which is logically impossible. The very ultimate ground of choice is corrupted in us. We cannot place ourselves outside ourselves in order to reverse the evil maxim. We need extra-human help. Kant admits that such help is nothing less than divine grace.

Similar to Kant, Edwards makes the claim that there are two operative principles that give shape to the heart's disposition. One is the 'inferior' or 'natural' principle of self-love, which entices one's inclination towards goods such as 'liberty, honor and pleasure'.[38] The other is the 'superior', 'supernatural' principle of 'divine love',[39] depending on the heart's union with the Holy Spirit that results in a qualitatively higher knowledge of God. These two principles do not sit side by side within human interiority; they do not have an equal influence upon the soul. Mirroring Kant's logic, Edwards sees them as ranked: one is always subordinate to the other. Although by virtue of creation the principle of divine love is 'given to possess the throne, and maintain an absolute dominion in the heart', while the principle of self-love is destined 'to be wholly subordinate and subservient',[40] the present human condition is altered by sin, and the principles do not operate according to their original ranking. They are upside down.

Although it may seem that in the postlapsarian state the human person is left with the principle of self-love alone, I would like to suggest that in Edwards' scheme we are still inhabited by both principles, albeit with the love of God radically shadowed by the egotistic affection. I base my claim on Edwards' theory of knowledge, which entails an intrinsic connection between knowing and the affections. I argued earlier that the faculty of knowing by its nature generates inclinations towards what seems to be good among the known objects. Edwards calls the stronger inclinations affections, thus arguably loves. Causally speaking, they are the spring of actions.[41] In particular, both morally good and morally evil acts stem out of the heart's inclinations: 'all moral qualities, all principles, either of virtue or of vice, lie in the disposition of the heart'.[42]

On the surface it may seem that Edwards suggests that only one principle, that of self-love, dwells in the human heart after its plunge in the sinful condition. He states that when sin entered the human race God left God's communion with it:

that communion with God, on which these principles depended, entirely ceased; the Holy Spirit, that divine inhabitant, forsook the house … Therefore immediately the superior divine principles wholly ceased.[43]

The inferior principle instead ascended from its proper role of a servant to the principle of divine love, to an inflated position of supremacy:

The inferior principles of self-love and natural appetite, which were given only to serve, being alone, and left to themselves, of course became reigning principles; having no superior principles to regulate or control them, they became absolute masters of the heart. The immediate consequence of which was a *fatal catastrophe*, a turning of all things upside down … Man did immediately set up himself, and the objects of his private affections and appetites, as supreme; and so they took the place of God.[44]

The consequence of the fall is the withdrawing of God from God's union with the human interiority, and leaving human persons on their own. However, as I showed earlier, the communion of the Spirit of God with the human person *only* accounts for the *immediate* knowledge of God, directly imparted from divinity to humanity, and *not* for the other, indirect of knowledge of God which Edwards claims that all human beings have. The mediated knowledge of God remains operative *in spite of the fall*. As I already conveyed, this is a mere notional kind of knowledge. It does not have enough strength to determine the will to incline itself towards God *as the greatest good*. However, it need not be devoid of *any* inclination, as knowing inherently generates inclinations and preferences for Edwards. Self-love instead is perceived as the highest good in this case, even if deceptively. Any inclination towards God stemming out of mediated knowledge can only have a subordinate status to the natural principles of the heart that seek self-pleasure. The superior principle departs *as* superior, and metamorphoses into a caricature of its former status.

For Edwards, knowing and loving are inherently connected. I showed earlier that after the Edwardsean mind apprehends certain objects, it tries to see whether and to what degree they are wanted or not. Then the heart follows the judgment of the mind and is inclined towards the most desirable object. The love for this object in turn activates the will and triggers some action. The mind is intrinsically connected with love, because it can never remain simply neutral but judges and bends into either inclination or disinclination, or into love or the opposite of it.

The unmediated knowledge of God goes then hand in hand with a love of God ranked first and conditioning the love of the self. Conversely, the mediated knowledge of God, when operating alone in the unregenerate mind, arguably corresponds to a love of God that is subordinated to and overshadowed by self-love. For Edwards, the former ranking can be predicated only on the prelapsarian human condition and that of regenerated humanity. The latter ranking, however, universally describes human beings after the fall. Regeneration, which results from grace, is the unique and effectual lever that reverses the ranking of the two loves to their original state. Edwards writes:

> Particularly, if there be anything in the nature of man, whereby he has a universal, unfailing tendency to that moral evil [which] implies his utter ruin, that must be looked upon as an *evil tendency or propensity*; however divine grace may interpose . . . to overrule things to an issue contrary to that which they tend to of themselves. Grace is a sovereign thing . . . introduced to oppose the natural tendency, and reverse the course of things.[45]

Edwards insists both that creation is good and that evil pervades it as a universal tendency. However, creation's goodness is more fundamental than its infection with evil, even though the tendency to moral ruin is inescapable and human efforts are ineffectual in reversing this tendency. Hence, the propensity towards evil leads to 'utter ruin' and 'a fatal catastrophe' that would follow its course to the very end of total destruction without an intervening extraneous agency, which for Edwards, as for Kant, is divine grace.[46]

Yet in spite of the insufficiency of any human endeavor to reverse the ranking of loves in the heart, Edwards advises his readers to engage in works preparatory for grace.[47] As Noah engaged in the large undertaking of building the ark in obedience and preparation for the salvation of his family from the flood, so are the rest of us called to 'engage in and go through great undertakings, in order to [seek] our own salvation'. Specifically, we are to strive to observe God's moral commandments with utmost devotion. Although salvation and therefore the love of God reinstated as a supreme principle of life are not achieved through this observance, it is nonetheless a 'prerequisite to salvation'. Salvation is of too great value to be obtained without 'great labor and diligence'. By virtue of creation human beings are endowed with creaturely powers and capacities for action. While we are not to presume that our own efforts would trigger divine mercy as a recompense, we are to make use of these creaturely good gifts as we knock at the door of God's grace.

Kant proposes a strikingly similar solution. In his view, the condition of the possibility of any moral advance is the reversal of the evil maxim via divine assistance. We cannot step outside our own selves to reverse the ultimate ground of our decision making. Yet it is also Kant's view that before we qualify for any divine aid, we must make ourselves worthy of receiving it:

> Granted that some supernatural cooperation is also needed to his becoming good or better, whether this cooperation only consist in the diminution of obstacles or be also a positive assistance, the human being must nonetheless make himself *antecedently* worthy of receiving it.[48]

> [T]he right way to advance is not from grace to virtue but rather from virtue to grace.[49]

In what way can we make ourselves worthy if we are under the evil maxim, and all of our principles and actions are inherently corrupt? Kant resolves this apparent contradiction by reminding his readers that the predisposition to good is more fundamental in us than the propensity to evil. Although the radical evil that indwells us is a 'foul stain' on our race and 'hinders the germ of good from developing as it otherwise would',[50] it still does not annihilate the good. Now if Kant is to be internally coherent, this must mean that the seed of good be not merely passive, but capable of being *somewhat* active. Its potency is arguably too weak to achieve the reversal of the ranking of loves, but it must nonetheless be able to produce some fruit, as experience often shows that non-Christians (or non-religious people for that matter) can exhibit astonishing degrees of moral uprightness. Kant suggests that one must 'not bury [one's] innate talent (Luke 19:12–16) [and] make use of the original predisposition to the good in order to become a better human being'.[51] On this basis one may hope that what is beyond human power God will supply. God sees our seed of goodness as the *original* predisposition of the possibility of being human, and on this basis works on our behalf to accomplish what Kant calls a moral *revolution*, making true, lasting virtue possible.

Both for Edwards and for Kant, grace alone is the source of the reversal of the loves. In Edwards' thought grace is the enabler of the holy affections in the believer's heart. The Spirit of God provides the external, divine agency as an aid to the human heart by uniting itself with the soul and bringing an import of power that gives birth to a new nature:

> The Spirit of God is given to the true saints to dwell in them, as his proper lasting abode; and to influence their hearts, as a principle of new nature, or as a divine supernatural spring of life and action ... not only as moving, and occasionally influencing the saints, but as dwelling in them as his temple, his proper abode, and everlasting dwelling place. And he is represented as being there so united to the faculties of the soul, that he becomes there a principle or spring of new nature and life.[52]

As the Spirit of God starts dwelling in the 'human temple', or human interiority, it produces 'those effects wherein he exerts and communicates himself in his own proper nature. Holiness is the nature of the Spirit of God.'[53] Because the Spirit of God generates this intimate communion with the human heart, and due to the Spirit's indestructible communion with the other two persons of the Trinity, the human person is enabled to enter the intra-trinitarian world of love.[54] The Spirit's union with the soul generates a supernatural influence upon the human knowing, loving, willing, and acting, respectively. Direct knowledge of God paired with supreme love of God leads to willing virtuously and acting morally.[55] The Spirit implants a 'new spiritual sense'[56] entirely different from the resources of an unregenerate person. Still, its newness is qualified:

> This new spiritual sense, and the new dispositions that attend it, are no new faculties, but are new principles of nature ... So this new spiritual sense is not a new faculty of understanding, but is a new foundation laid in the nature of the soul, for a new kind of exercise of the *same* faculty of understanding. So that new holy disposition of heart that attends this new sense, is not a new faculty of will, but a foundation laid in the nature of the soul, for a new kind of exercises of the *same* faculty of will.[57]

The newness does not consist in any alteration of the ingredients that enter the composition of the human psychology. Before the Spirit unites itself with the heart as much as after it, the same faculty of understanding and will are operative. However, what is new is the different 'foundation' in their operation. This new foundation consists of a new, reversed ranking of the affections, with the love of God becoming supreme and the love of self taking a subordinate role to it. The unmediated knowledge of God correspondingly takes precedence over the mediated one. This reversal produces new effects, or fruits, that are recognizable at the level of morally good behavior, persisting until the end of one's life.[58]

Whereas the determination of the unregenerate will rests in inclinations related to reigning self-love, the determination of the regenerate will is given by the love of God. The Holy Spirit unites itself with the human heart and supernaturally achieves the reversal of the ranking of affections. The causal chain of determination arches from the inscrutable influence of God to human virtue. The union of God's Spirit with the human soul opens up one's access to an unmediated knowledge of God and a consequent love of God as the highest principle of life. This activates the will towards morally good choices, which counts as virtue. Therefore divine grace, or the Spirit's aid, is the lever that reverses the ranking of loves and fires the causal domino chain that passes through the will and makes virtue possible.

Kant follows a parallel logic, minus the idea of the union of the heart with the Spirit. However, he invokes divine grace as directly assisting the humanly insufficient efforts of reversing the ranking of loves. He claims that the moral law calls us to comply with it with a loud enough voice that we are bound to hear it.[59] Furthermore, human beings are engaged in a project of ultimate moral self-assertion. We must make ourselves into whatever we should become, in a moral sense, good or evil.[60] Clearly, we are confronted with a dilemma. We are under the dual constraint that we ought to be able to overcome our evil disposition and revert the moral order back to the dominance of moral law, and *also* that our own resources are so radically flawed that this is impossible.

Kant resolves this antinomy by positing that supernatural cooperation, or more simply grace, is both needed and available for this transformation. It consists in a 'positive increase of force', which must be accepted by human persons and incorporated into their highest maxims. God's grace is the source of the reversal of the ranking of loves, such that the love of moral law becomes the first love, while self-love takes a subordinate role.

The moral law has indeed an irresistible capacity to command us that we 'ought' to obey it.[61] It is our universal human duty to elevate ourselves to moral perfection and thus seek virtue.[62] The very fact that we experience this command entails that it must somehow be possible for us to do it. *But* we can only do this with divine assistance, which remains 'higher' and 'inscrutable':

> [I]n spite of [the] fall, the command that we ought to become better
> human beings resounds unabated in our souls; consequently, we must
> also be capable of it, even if what we can do is of itself insufficient and,
> by virtue of it, we only make ourselves receptive to a higher assistance
> inscrutable to us.[63]

The change of the heart's disposition does not constitute a recovery of something that has been lost. We *never* lose the predisposition towards good, even though the evil maxim that universally enslaves us has the self-love ranked above the love for moral duty. This is particularly significant for Kant's understanding of how divine grace works, and it entails, as I already argued, a parallel logic with that of Edwards regarding the preparatory works in anticipation of salvific grace. Since we never lose the moral law as an ingredient in our highest maxim, but only subjugate it to self-love, the restoration Kant suggests consists in merely regaining the *purity* of the moral law. This way the law becomes the supreme ground of all our maxims, or the '*self-sufficient* incentive' of our power of choice, whereas all other inclinations become subservient to it.[64] A human being ought to become morally good and therefore pleasing to God for no other reason except the character of the moral law, 'and thus in need of no other incentive.'[65]

This has a key consequence in Kant's argument. No incremental change in the human heart would suffice to effect the transition from moral evil to moral goodness. True moral goodness requires a *revolution* in the moral disposition, replacing the evil maxim with a maxim of holiness, which is only achievable by grace. True virtue can emerge from here alone. While Kant attempts to translate the theological ideas of regeneration and a new creation into the philosophical language of Enlightenment and of reason,[66] some notions remain untranslatable. The notion of grace is a case in point. It stems from outside human reason and the human domain entirely, flowing from the world of God's own love, yet reaching us as the condition of the possibility of genuine virtue. Staying squarely within the language of theology, Edwards concurs.

Conclusion

I tried to argue in this essay that in spite of notorious differences, the two thinkers are surprising allies. They both uphold a clear conceptual distinction between empirical causality and transcendent freedom, although they use different specific terms to develop their logic. Edwards and Kant are especially allies with respect to their position on grace: divine assistance is the sole effectual lever that reverses the ranking of the heart's loves and reinstantiates the love of God above the love of the self.

In Edwards' view the causal chain that produces human action, which passes from apprehension through will, does not regressively extend to a first free cause. Freedom is simply outside the phenomena of the world. Similar to Kant, Edwards intuits that the freedom of the will cannot be posited in the realm of experience and causal connections, but can only be thought of in the realm of the transcendent. While Kant locates the human will itself in the noumenal domain of freedom, Edwards situates freedom in the soul's union with God's Spirit, who does incline the heart and influences human affections. Both for Edwards and for Kant the engine that ultimately produces virtue is only in a provisional sense causal and contained in the world of experience. It ultimately issues from a transcendent source: Edwards connects humanity with this domain through the Holy Spirit's union with the regenerate heart, while Kant affirms that the human will itself is not simply trapped in the world of causal determinations but also resides autonomously free in noumenal transcendence.

Both Edwards and Kant understand human will as entailing two operative principles that are confined to a wrong ranking in the postlapsarian condition of the human race. Egotistic love trumps any higher love, which Edwards calls love of God while Kant refers to it as love for the moral law. Yet they both invoke divine grace as the only kind of assistance that reverses the ranking of the two loves and constitutes the effectual resource for the generation of true virtue.

Does this reconcile two otherwise quite different thought worlds? My argument was not to propose a holistic congruence, but to show a strikingly similar intuition of Kant and Edwards about the root cause of a virtuous, good life, perhaps anchored in the spirit of their time. After all, their common intellectual ethos is that of Enlightenment. One may object that Kant's idea of a graced autonomy remains different from Edwards' concept of a divine causality. However, as Enlightenment thinkers, they both intuit that morality is connected with reason, yet there is a precipice of *need* in us, and the call to love and do the good outruns our ability to honor it. We *need* grace. At the very least, the common merit of Kant and Edwards is a compelling account of how divine assistance takes the form of *divine presence*, entering the structure of human interiority to both supplement creaturely powers and restore the disordered ranking of loves so as to connect finite, fallen human creatures with a realistic possibility of virtue.

Notes

1 I am indebted to John E. Hare of Yale University for my interpretation of Kant, including his discussion of the Kantian notion of grace in Hare, J. E. (1996) *The Moral Gap: Kantian Ethics, Human Limits, and God's Assistance*, Oxford: Oxford University Press.

2 WJE 1, p. 137 (1.1).

3 *Ibid.*, p. 138 (1.1).

4 *Ibid.*, p. 140 (1.1).

5 Kant, I. (1997) *Groundwork of the Metaphysics of Morals*, Cambridge: Cambridge University Press, p. 25 (4:413).

6 *Ibid.*, p. 13 (4:400).

7 WJE 1, p. 141 (1.2).

8 *Ibid.*, p. 148 (1.2).

9 *Ibid.*, pp. 172, 188-9, 194, among many other places (2.1, 2.4, 2.5).

10 *Ibid.*, p. 172 (2.1).

11 *Ibid.*, p. 176 (2.2); emphasis mine.

12 Kant, I. (1997) *Prolegomena to Any Future Metaphysics*, trans. Gary Hatfield, Cambridge: Cambridge University Press, p. 64.

13 *Ibid.*, p. 66.

14 *Ibid.*, pp. 97–101.

15 Edwards, J., *A Treatise Concerning Religious Affections* in Smith, J. E. *et al.* (eds) (1995) *A Jonathan Edwards Reader*, New Haven: Yale University Press, p. 145.

16 WJE 1, p. 207 (2.7).

17 *Ibid.*, p. 217 (2.9).

18 Edwards, J. 'A Divine and Supernatural Light', in WJE 17, p. 409.

19 *Ibid.*

20 *Ibid.*, p. 411.

21 WJE 1, pp. 25–6.

22 WJE 17, p. 411.

23 *Ibid.*, p. 413; emphasis mine.

24 *Ibid.*, p. 413.

25 *Ibid.*

26 *Ibid.*, p. 414.

27 *Ibid.*

28 Edwards, J., *The Nature of True Virtue*, in Smith, J. E. *et al.* (eds) (1995), pp. 257–8.

29 Kant, I. (1998) *Religion within the Boundaries of Mere Reason and Other Writings*, trans. A. Wood and G. DiGiovanni, Cambridge: Cambridge University Press, p. 50 (6:25).

30 *Ibid.*

31 *Ibid.*, pp. 48–50 (6:24–5).

32 *Ibid.*, pp. 57–9 (6:35–6).

33 *Ibid.*, pp. 143–6 (6:142–6).

34 *Ibid.*, p. 52 (6:28).

35 *Ibid.*, p. 54 (6:30).

36 *Ibid.*, p. 64 (6:43).

37 *Ibid.*, p. 59 (6:37).

38 Edwards, J., *The Great Christian Doctrine of Original Sin Defended*, in Smith, J. E. *et al.* (eds) (1995), p. 233.

39 *Ibid.*

40 *Ibid.*

41 Edwards, J., *Religious Affections*, in Smith, J. E. *et al.* (eds) (1995), p. 144.

42 Edwards, J., *Original Sin*, in *ibid.*, p. 255.

43 *Ibid.*, p. 234.

44 *Ibid.*

45 *Ibid.*, pp. 225–6.

46 *Ibid.*, pp. 225, 234.

47 Edwards, J. (1742) 'The Manner in Which the Salvation of the Soul is to Be Sought' (online source), available at http://www.biblebb.com/files/edwards/je-manner.htm (accessed 30 Oct. 2010).

48 Kant, I. (1998), p. 65 (6:44); emphasis mine.

49 *Ibid.*, p. 191 (6:202).

50 *Ibid.*, p. 61 (6:38).

51 *Ibid.*, p. 71 (6:52).

52 Edwards, J., *Religious Affections*, in Smith, J. E. *et al.* (eds) (1995), p. 157.

53 *Ibid.*, p.158.

54 *Ibid.*

55 Edwards, J., *The Nature of True Virtue*, in Smith, J. E. *et al.* (eds) (1995), pp. 257–8.

56 Edwards, J., *Religious Affections*, in *ibid.*, pp. 160, 161.

57 *Ibid.*, p. 161; emphasis mine.

58 *Ibid.*, p. 164.

59 Kant, I. (1998), p. 66 (6:45).

60 *Ibid.*, p. 65 (6:44).

61 *Ibid.*, pp. 65–6 (6:44).

62 *Ibid.*, p. 80 (6:61).

63 *Ibid.*, p. 66 (6:45).

64 *Ibid.*, p. 67 (6:46).

65 *Ibid.*, p. 68 (6:47).

66 *Ibid.*

Aesthetics

Chapter 10

Beauty is truth, truth beauty:
Jonathan Edwards and John Keats

Susan Miller*

Framework for Comparison and Historical Background
According to the late philosophical historian Roland Delattre,

> the aesthetic aspect of Jonathan Edwards' thought and vision, which
> finds its definitive formulation in his concepts of beauty and sensibility,
> provides a larger purchase upon the essential and distinctive features
> of his thought than does any other aspect.[1]

While one cannot say that Jonathan Edwards influenced Keats, they
do share a common perception of the fact that beauty is at the heart of the
mystical or transcendental experience. In her essay in this volume, Natalia
Marandiuc notes that she is not proposing a holistic congruence between
Kant and Edwards, but rather similar intuitions based on the age. Similarly,
Richard Hall, comparing Edwards and Hume, mentions affinities versus
continuities. This essay will attempt to explore Edwards and Keats' conceptions of beauty, and to determine what common linguistic ground they
share. While Edwards was a theologian, revivalist and philosopher, and
Keats a poet, nevertheless Edwards felt that beauty on earth provides a
glimpse of divine beauty, and Keats echoes that sentiment:

> Heard melodies are sweet, but those unheard
>
> Are sweeter; therefore, ye soft pipes, play on;
>
> Not to the sensual ear, but, more endear'd,
>
> Pipe to the spirit ditties of no tone.[2]

Jonathan Edwards, hailed as America's Milton as well as America's
Augustine,[3] lived on the American frontier in the eighteenth century, and
thus did not experience certain aspects of European culture that would
have been natural to John Keats. Edwards 'never saw a cathedral or an art

gallery, never heard a symphony or an opera', and the world in which he lived was 'ignorant of Shakespeare and the stage and of sculpture'.[4] Keats, on the other hand, was taken by Benjamin Robert Hayden to see the Elgin Marbles from the Pantheon when they first arrived in London, and could explore St. Paul's Cathedral, designed by Sir Christopher Wren, at his liberty. He attended the Drury Lane Theater and particularly enjoyed Shakespeare's *Hamlet* and *Richard III* performed by 'the diminutive but mercurial Edmund Kean'.[5] Edwards was a preacher and philosopher for whom God was as central to his writing as it was to his existence, while Keats was a poet who 'had little time for Christianity' (although this will be discussed in greater length later).[6] Edwards appreciated the arguments of Locke, Newton and Berkeley, and adapted them to his theology:

> Newton's universal laws confirmed to Edwards the wisdom and benevolence of the Creator; Locke's psychology, how God communicated to 'perceiving being'; and Berkeley's philosophy, the immanence of God in all reality.[7]

Keats, on the other hand, felt the precision of scientific inquiry in Sir Isaac Newton's *Optics* robbed nature of her divine mystery.[8] In *Lamia* he laments:

> Do not all charms fly
> At the mere touch of cold philosophy?
> There was an awful rainbow once in heaven:
> We know her woof, her texture; she is given
> In the dull catalogue of common things.[9]

Given all of these contradictions, is it possible to find a source of continuity between these two distinct and disparate figures? Although it appears at first glance that the two men shared few things in common, a deeper look reveals a striking similarity in at least one particular. John Keats lost his mother to consumption in 1810 when he was just 15, and he nursed his brother, Tom, who died of the same disease in 1818. David Brainerd, a missionary whom Edwards greatly admired, succumbed to consumption in Edwards' home on October 9, 1747, at 30 years of age.[10] Edwards' second daughter, Jerusha, nursed him on his deathbed, and died herself at 18 the following February. No one had known at the time what the disease was, nor that it was contagious; however, Edwards 'described the symptoms so accurately that the modern physician can make the diagnosis at once'.[11] Thus, consumption and its consequences on loved ones was a factor for each man. Both shared an intense awareness of the presence of death, so much so that when W. A. Oldfather was translating Epictetus in the 1920s, he immediately thought of John Keats. In the following passage, Epictetus is describing Socrates' final hours:

> For he did not care, he says, to save his paltry body, but only that which is increased and preserved by right conduct, and is diminished and destroyed by evil conduct.... What, then, will the children do? 'If I had gone to Thessaly, you would have looked after them; but when I have gone down to the house of Hades, will there be no one to look after them?' See how he calls death soft names, and jests at it.[12]

Oldfather connects this final line to Keats' *Ode to a Nightingale:*

> Darkling, I listen; and, for many a time
>> I have been half in love with easeful Death,
> Call'd him soft names in many a musèd rime.[13]

Edwards' keen awareness of death is clear in several of his 'Resolutions' written in 1722 at 19 years of age. Resolution 9 states, 'Resolved, to think much on all occasions of my own dying, and of the common circumstances which attend death'; Resolution 17, 'Resolved, that I will live so as I shall wish I had done when I come to die'; and Resolution 19, 'Resolved, never to do anything, which I should be afraid to do, if I expected it would not be above an hour, before I should hear the last trump.'[14]

In addition, both men exhibited a single-handed dedication and commitment, with complete and unerring focus, on what they felt they needed to do, and neither would deviate from their course though both suffered severe criticisms and setbacks. Edwards' aforementioned Resolutions provide an example of this, with Resolution 1 stating:

> Resolved, that I will do whatsoever I think to be most to God's glory, and my own good, profit and pleasure, in the whole of my duration, without any consideration of the time, whether now, or never so many myriads of ages hence. Resolved to do whatever I think to be my duty, and most for the good and advantage of mankind in general.

And Resolution 5: 'Resolved, never to lose one moment of time; but improve it the most profitable way I possibly can'; and 6: 'Resolved, to live with all my might, while I do live.'[15] These are powerful statements that convey Edwards' determination, drive, and unwillingness to wallow in self-pity or other emotions which would not propel him forward. Keats' commitment, on the other hand, is manifested in his pursuit of poetry. When Keats was a boy, his 'passion at times was almost ungovernable', though he learned to harness it as he matured. He had been an apprentice to a surgeon for several years, he passed his examinations in July 1816, but he abandoned this career shortly after completing his training in order to pursue poetry full time. Here is the exchange between Keats and his guardian:

> Not intend to be a Surgeon! why what do you mean to be? I mean to rely upon my Abilities as a Poet—John, you are either Mad or a Fool, to talk in so absurd a Manner. My Mind is made up, said the youngster very quietly. I know that I possess Abilities greater than most Men, and therefore I am determined to gain my Living by exercising them.

This cannot be considered a practical decision, but to the great benefit of posterity, is one from which Keats would not be deterred. As the devout Haydon noted, 'Keats was the only man I ever met with who seemed and looked conscious of high calling, except Wordsworth'.[16] Perhaps Keats had a prescient sense of his own battle with tuberculosis that was to come, for in late 1817 or early 1818, prior to Tom's decline in health, he penned the following sonnet:

> When I have fears that I may cease to be
>   Before my pen has glean'd my teeming brain,
> Before high piled books, in charactry,
>   Hold like rich garners the full ripen'd grain;
> When I behold, upon the night's starr'd face,
>   Huge cloudy symbols of a high romance,
> And think that I may never live to trace
>   Their shadows, with the magic hand of chance;
> And when I feel, fair creature of an hour,
>   That I shall never look upon thee more,
> Never have relish in the fairy power
>   Of unreflecting love; —then on the shore
> Of the wide world I stand alone, and think
>   Till love and fame to nothingness do sink.[17]

For Edwards, this quality of pure concentration manifested through a sense of urgency in his writings, particularly in his sermons, which were Edwards' 'essential literary form'.[18] Sermons functioned as an intermediary 'between the present moment and eternity, between the secular and the sacred, and between humans and their God'.[19] As Kimnach points out, it is a blessing that all of Edwards' works have survived: 'Although the complete working papers of a colonial preacher are rarely found today, the methodicalness of Jonathan Edwards and the filial piety of his family have made it possible to amass what is undoubtedly the bulk of his sermon manuscripts and related papers.'[20] One famous example of an Edwards sermon, albeit surrounded by controversy, is 'Sinners in the Hands of an Angry God', preached on July 8, 1741 in Enfield, Connecticut. In this sermon:

> Edwards finally achieved an absolutely sustained tone, a sharply delimited range of imagery, and a syntactical structure tightly meshed through both small and large patterns of repetition. As a matter of fact, had Edgar Allan Poe been so inclined he might have used this sermon more plausibly than Hawthorne's tales to illustrate his theory of the 'single effect'. The sheer centripetal force of mediation upon the governing idea of the sermon—a quality apparent in many of Edwards' writings—is unequalled in intensity anywhere.[21]

For Edwards, a Puritan and a revivalist, there was no time to waste in making a commitment to following one's conscience and changing for the better, as this sermon demonstrates:

> The bow of God's wrath is bent, and the arrow made ready on the string, and justice bends the arrow at your heart, and strains the bow, and it is nothing but the mere pleasure of God, and that of an angry God, without any promise or obligation at all, that keeps the arrow one moment from being made drunk with your blood.[22]

Both men also attempted to foster positive human relations and to be of service, or to manifest what Edwards termed, 'Consent to being'. This can be seen when Edwards dropped important projects in order to devote himself to publishing David Brainerd's private diary, which would influence John Wesley, among others. As Edwards explained in a letter to a minister in Scotland, the Reverend John Erskine:

> I have for the present, been diverted from the design I hinted to you, of publishing something against some of the Arminian Tenets, by something else that divine providence unexpectedly laid in my way, and seemed to render unavoidable, viz. publishing Mr. Brainerd's Life, of which the enclosed papers of proposals gives some account.[23]

Edwards describes in his preface to the volume that Brainerd was persuaded 'with difficulty' to entrust these very personal papers to Edwards for publication 'for God's glory and the interest of religion'. Although the writings are Brainerd's, Edwards put a shape to them, and therefore, 'the volume as Edwards conceived it belongs to him'. Perhaps because Brainerd never intended to publish his account, he was able to write freely and with complete honesty. This gave the text a freshness and a sense of integrity which was greatly appreciated; however, it does not paint a glorious picture, according to the editor of the Yale series, Norman Pettit:

> But the reader should not expect to find romance. One looks in vain for an heroic frontiersman, a noble sachem, or an inspired woodland scene. The settlers, mainly Scots-Irish, are depicted as slovenly and mean. The Indians are resentful, hounded by the Dutch, and the forest is a 'howling wilderness' greatly to be feared. There is nothing here of the forest that James Fenimore Cooper later described.[24]

Interestingly, Keats' brother, George, emigrated to America in 1818, leaving John in some sense bereft, particularly after Tom died later that same year on December 1. One of Keats' last poems, *Lines to Fanny* or *What can I do to drive away*, was written after he had traveled to Italy for the benefit of the climate in order to improve his chances of surviving consumption. This poem expresses, in part, his sentiments concerning America, which perhaps were similar to Brainerd's in terms of the danger and discomfort of the wild:

> Where shall I learn to get my peace again?
> To banish thoughts of that most hateful land,
> Dungeoner of my friends, that wicked strand
> Where they were wrecked and live a wreckèd life;
> That monstrous region, whose dull rivers pour,
> Ever from their sordid urns into the shore,
> Unowned of any weedy-hairèd gods;
> Whose winds, all zephyrless, hold scourging rods,
> Iced in the great lakes, to afflict mankind;
> Whose rank-grown forests, frosted, black and blind,
> Would fright a Dryad; whose harsh-herbaged meads
> Make lean and lank the starved ox while he feeds;

There flowers have no scent, birds no sweet song,

And great unerring Nature once seems wrong.[25]

Keats, for his part, evinced 'Consent to being' with kindness. According to his friend, John Hamilton Reynolds, Keats was 'the most loveable associate,—the deepest Listener to the griefs & disappointments of all around him', and one who possessed 'the greatest power of poetry in him, of any one since Shakespere'. To show how sincerely Reynolds felt this, when he died he had placed in large letters on his tombstone the words, 'THE FRIEND OF KEATS'.[26] Keats' desire for harmony filters through his letters:

> Things have happen'd lately of great Perplexity—You must have heard of them—Reynolds and Haydon retorting and recriminating—and parting for ever—the same thing has happened between Haydon and Hunt—It is unfortunate—Men should bear with each other—there lives not the Man who may not be cut up, aye hashed to pieces on his weakest side.[27]

Moreover, Keats' tenderness can be observed in the careful attention to detail he paid in letters to his younger sister, Fanny:

> Tell me also if you want any particular Book; or Pencils, or drawing paper – any thing but live Stock—Though I will not now be very severe on it, remembering how fond I used to be of Goldfinches, Tomtits, Minnows, Mice, Ticklebacks, Dace, Cock salmons and all the whole tribe of the Bushes and the Brooks: but verily they are better in the Trees and the water—though I must confess even now a partiality for a handsome Globe of goldfish—then I would have it hold 10 pails of water and be fed continually fresh through a cool pipe with another pipe to let through the floor—well ventilated they would preserve all their beautiful silver and Crimson—Then I would put it before a handsome painted window and shade it all round with myrtles and Japonicas. I should like the window to open onto the Lake of Geneva—and there I'd sit and read all day like the picture of somebody reading.[28]

In addition, neither man favored taking revenge, instead opting to control their anger. This can be seen in Edwards' Resolutions (nos. 14–16),[29] and in Keats' lines from *Hyperion*:

'O ye, whom wrath consumes! who, passion-stung,

'Writhe at defeat, and nurse your agonies

'Shut up your senses, stifle up your ears,

'My voice is not a bellows unto ire…'[30]

In the *Nature of True Virtue*, Edwards insists that 'Beauty does not consist in discord and dissent, but in consent and agreement',[31] a statement with which John Keats would surely agree.

The Divine Nature of Beauty and the Divine Beauty of Nature

Upon the death of his grandmother in December 1814, when he was 19, Keats wrote one of his earliest sonnets. He did not tell a soul about it until years later when he mentioned it to a friend, Rich Woodhouse, in 1819.[32] This sonnet, first published in 1876, indicates that Keats was perhaps not as hostile to the spiritual life as critics claim:

As from the darkening gloom a silver dove

Upsoars, and darts into the Eastern light,

On pinions that naught moves but pure delight,

So fled thy soul into the realms above,

Regions of peace and everlasting love;

Where happy spirits, crown'd with circlets bright

Of starry beam, and gloriously bedight,

Taste the high joy none but the blest can prove.

There thou or joinest the immortal quire

In melodies that even Heaven fair

Fill with superior bliss, or, at desire

Of the omnipotent Father, cleavest the air

On holy message sent—What pleasures higher?

Wherefore does any grief our joy impair?[33]

It is a Petrarchan sonnet, a very difficult form in English, and Gorell finds the poem to be 'characteristic' of Keats' later work, possessing 'a singular charm: it is pure Keats, however young, and could have come from no other mint'.[34] Thus, this early poem exposes a dichotomy in Keats' thought: his deep-seated detachment from the world and acceptance of the perfection and eternity of the human soul, as contrasted with the sensuous language he employs to describe the perfection he sees. For Keats:

Poetry should be great & unobtrusive, a thing which enters into one's soul, and does not startle it or amaze it with itself, but with its subject.

– How beautiful are the retired flowers! how would they lose their beauty were they to throng into the highway crying out, 'admire me I am a violet! dote upon me I am a primrose'!³⁵

Here Keats' humility in his approach to poetry is evident. He elaborates: 'we need not be teazed with grandeur & merit—when we can have them uncontaminated & unobtrusive'.³⁶ Although these statements are difficult to discern—how does one separate the poetry from the language in which it is contained? How can a poem be both great and unobtrusive?— examples of what Keats meant can be found in his poems.

As a young man, Keats cried when his friend, Charles Cowden Clarke, read the scene from Shakespeare's *Cymbeline* to him, in which Imogen watches her lover, Posthumus, departing:

> Till the diminution
> Of space had pointed him sharp as my needle:
> Nay, followed him, till he had melted from
> The smallness of a gnat, to air: and then
> Have turn'd mine eye, and wept.³⁷

In the *Ode to a Nightingale*, Keats employs a metaphor similar to the one Shakespeare used in *Cymbeline*, though he draws upon biblical imagery to do so. When Naomi's two sons die, she encourages her daughters-in-law to return to the land of Moab, start a new life and remarry. Orpah obeys, but Ruth does not:

> And Ruth said, Intreat me not to leave thee, or to return from following
> after thee: for whither thou goest, I will go; and where thou lodgest,
> I will lodge: thy people shall be my people, and thy God, my God.
> Where thou diest, will I die, and there will I be buried: the LORD do so
> to me, and more also, if ought but death part thee and me.³⁸

In Stanza VII of *Ode to a Nightingale*, Keats touches upon this loyalty, which cannot be broken:

> Thou wast not born for death, immortal Bird!
> No hungry generations tread thee down;
> The voice I hear this passing night was heard
> In ancient days by emperor and clown:
> Perhaps the self-same song that found a path
> Through the sad heart of Ruth, when, sick for home,
> She stood in tears amid the alien corn;
> The same that oft-times hath

Charmed magic casements, opening on the foam

Of perilous seas, in faery lands forlorn.[39]

Yet how Keats presents Ruth is noteworthy. In spite of her role as a tow-ering Biblical figure, she appears as a sad and dejected foreigner weeping in a field. There, she is not comforted by her husband, her mother-in-law or a friend, but by the song of the nightingale. It is understood that she was not vain or self-serving, and yet in spite of her loyalty and dedication to duty, her humanness is paramount—she weeps, she aches, she longs for home. It is a touch of sheer Keatsean genius, manifesting all of the qualities that he held so dear in poetry.

The timelessness of human relations is expressed in this ode through the song of the nightingale. From boyhood onward, music was an integral part of Keats' life. Charles Cowden Clarke introduced him to both poetry and music, when they would read and discuss Spenser's *The Fairie Queen* together, and then Clarke would play the piano.[40] Music deeply touched Edwards as well. He was an avid singer; he

> introduced hymnody at Northampton (hiring singing teachers to instruct in congregational harmony), there were violins and lutes about the house that his children played, and one acquaintance men-tioned that the family sang so much that the house was like an 'aviary'.[41]

In addition, 'From the beginning of his career, Keats had been trying to find insight in nature—recall the sonnets "On the Grasshopper and the Cricket" and "On the Sea".'[42] Keats wrote to a friend:

> 1st I think Poetry should surprise by a fine excess, and not by Singularity; it should strike the Reader as a wording of his own highest thoughts, and appear almost a Remembrance—2nd Its touches of Beauty should never be half way, thereby making the reader breathless, instead of content.[43]

Edwards would have appreciated these sentiments, and expressed them with exactitude in his writings, as can be seen from the following excerpt found in 'Miscellanies' no. 108 (1722), entitled the 'Excellency of Christ':

> when we behold the fragrant rose and lily, we see his love and purity. So the green trees and fields, and singing of birds, are the emanations of his infinite joy and benignity; the easiness and naturalness of trees and vines [are] shadows of his infinite beauty and loveliness; the crystal

rivers and murmuring streams have the footsteps of his sweet grace and bounty. When we behold the light and brightness of the sun, the golden edges of an evening cloud, or the beauteous bow, we behold the adumbrations of his glory and goodness; and the blue skies, of his mildness and gentleness.[44]

Interestingly, Keats offers a similar description in a letter to Jane Reynolds, written on September 14, 1817 in Oxford:

Believe me, my dear Jane it is a great Happiness to me that you are in this finest part of the year, winning a little enjoyment from the hard World—in truth the great Elements we know of are no mean Comforters—the open Sky sits upon our senses like a sapphire Crown—the Air is our Robe of State—the Earth is our throne and the sea a mighty Minstrell playing before it[.][45]

Memorably, both Edwards and Keats apply the word 'ravishing' to wonderful effect. Keats' opening lines to *Ode on a Grecian Urn* need no introduction:

Thou still unravish'd bride of quietness,
Thou foster-child of silence and slow time.[46]

Edwards uses a similar expression in his hymn to Sarah Pierpont when he describes her union with God in heaven: 'There she is to dwell with him, and to be ravished with his love and delight forever.'[47] Keats is describing a bride on a Grecian vase, Edwards his own future bride, and yet they both are speaking of a mystical union between lover and beloved.

Ultimately, Jonathan Edwards and John Keats were unique individuals who each possessed a 'brilliant and versatile intelligence', though it manifested in different ways. Today, Edwards is being studied more than ever before, and Keats is cherished as a poet with 'extraordinary inventive resources'.[48] Perry Miller considers Edwards' life to be a life of the mind, and Keats felt that that was true of himself too: '[Lord Byron] describes what he sees—I describe what I imagine—Mine is the hardest task.'[49] Both attempted to use their writings to express the sacredness of life, and each used the metaphor of beauty to do so. Music figures prominently in Edwards' thought as well as in Keats' imagery. Although Keats' letters are prized today, being described by T. S. Eliot as 'the most important ever written by any English poet',[50] they were written for a private audience. According to Barnard[51] (1988, p. xiv), the poetry Keats published in his lifetime was 'uniformly "poetic" and serious. His high conception of "Poesy" and of "Fame" has its constrictions', because it does not allow for his more human side, the side that is revealed in the letters.

In *The Nature of True Virtue*, Edwards notes that 'True virtue most essentially consists in benevolence to Being in general. Or perhaps to speak more accurately, it is that consent, propensity and union of heart to Being in general, that is immediately exercised in a general good will'.[52] For Keats, 'benevolence to Being' came in the form of poetry; according to Paul de Man, Keats had 'a dream about poetry as a redeeming force'.[53] Many people become doctors to help others; Keats gave up medicine in order to inspire others via poetry. In *Endymion*, he echoes Edwards' formulation for true virtue:

> Wherein lies happiness? In that which becks
> Our ready minds to fellowship divine,
> A fellowship with essence; till we shine,
> Full alchemiz'd, and free of space. Behold
> The clear religion of heaven![54]

It goes without saying that Edwards considered the task of the preacher to be a noble endeavor, as did Keats that of the poet.

Notes

* The author would like to express her thanks to the Keats-Shelley Memorial Association for support in the form of a Sheila Birkenhead Bursary, which enabled her to attend the conference on 'Edwards and Scotland'.

1 Delattre, R. A. (1968) *Beauty and Sensibility in the Thought of Jonathan Edwards: An Essay in Aesthetic and Theological Ethics*, New Haven: Yale University Press, p. vii.

2 *Ode on a Grecian Urn*, Stanza II, ll. 11–14, in Keats, J. (1927) *The Poetical Works of John Keats*, London: Oxford University Press, p. 223.

3 Smith, J. E. *et al.* (eds) (1995) 'Editors' Introduction', in *A Jonathan Edwards Reader*, New Haven: Yale University Press, p. vii.

4 Miller, P. (1949) *Jonathan Edwards*, New York: William Sloane, pp. 292, 110.

5 Watts, C. (1985) *A Preface to Keats*, London: Longman, pp. 31, 36–7.

6 Barnard, J. (1988) 'Introduction', in *John Keats, a New Selection*, London: Penguin Books, p. ix.

7 Minkema, K. P. (2005) 'Jonathan Edwards: A Theological Life', in Lee, S. H. (ed.) (2005) *The Princeton Companion to Jonathan Edwards*, Princeton: Princeton University Press, p. 3.

8 Minahan, J. A. (1992) *Word Like a Bell: John Keats, Music and the Romantic Poet*, Kent, Ohio: Kent State University Press, pp. 123–4.

9 *Lamia*, Pt. II, ll. 229–33, in Keats, J. (1927), p. 187.

10 WJE 7, 'Editor's Introduction', p. 2.

11 Miller, P. (1949) pp. 198, 202.

12 Bk. IV, ll. 164–7, in Epictetus (1928), *The Discourses, Books III–IV, Fragments, Encheiridion*, trans. W. A. Oldfather, Cambridge, Massachusetts: Harvard University Press, pp. 300–301.

13 *Ode to a Nightingale*, Stanza VI, ll. 51–3, in Keats, J. (1927), p. 221.

14 Smith, J. E. *et al.* (eds) (2003), p. 275.

15 *Ibid.*, pp. 274–5.

16 Watts, C. (1985) pp. 6, 7–8, 14, 27, 19.

17 Keats, J. (1927), p. 281.

18 Kimnach, W. H. (2005) 'The Sermons: Concept and Execution', in Lee, S. H. (ed.) (2005), p. 256.

19 Kimnach, W. H. *et al.* (eds) (1999) 'Editors' Introduction', in *The Sermons of Jonathan Edwards, A Reader*, New Haven: Yale University Press, pp. xii–xiii.

20 Kimnach, W. H. (2005), p. 244.

21 *Ibid.*, pp. 253–5.

22 Kimnach, W. H. *et al.* (eds) (1999), p. 57.

23 WJE 7, pp. 3, 10.

24 *Ibid.*, p. 96, 1, 2.

25 *Lines to Fanny*, ll. 30–43, in Keats, J. (1927), p. 417.

26 Watts, C. (1985), p. 23.

27 Letter 55 to Benjamin Bailey, in Keats, J. (1958) *The Letters of John Keats, In Two Volumes*, ed. Hyder Edward Rollins, Cambridge, Massachusetts: Harvard University Press, vol. 1, p. 210.

28 Letter 151 to Fanny Keats, in Keats, J. (1958), vol. 2, p. 46.

29 Smith, J. E. *et al.* (eds) (2003), p. 275.

30 *Hyperion*, bk. II, ll. 173–6, in Keats, J. (1927), p. 249.

31 *Ibid.*, p. 245.

32 Gorell, L. (1970) *John Keats: The Principle of Beauty*, New York: Haskell House Publishers p. 37.

33 Keats, J. (1927), p. 266.

34 Gorell, L. (1970), p. 38.

35 Letter 59 to John Hamilton Reynolds, in Keats, J. (1958), vol. 1, p. 224.

36 *Ibid.*, pp. 224–5.

37 Shakespeare, *Cymbeline*, Act I, scene iv, ll. 18–22; as quoted in Watts, C. (1985), p. 9.

38 Ruth 1:16–17 (KJV).

39 *Ode to a Nightingale*, ll. 61–70, in Keats, J. (1927), p. 222.

40 Minahan, J. A. (1992), pp. vii–ix.

41 Marsden, G. M. (2003), pp. 79, 106, and correspondence from Kenneth P. Minkema, 7 Oct. 2010.

42 Minahan, J. A. (1992), p. 179.

43 Letter 65 to John Taylor, in Keats, J. (1958), vol. 1, p. 238.

44 WJE 13, p. 279.

45 Letter 34 to Jane Reynolds, in Keats, J. (1958), vol. 1, p. 158.

46 *Ode on a Grecian Urn*, ll. 1–2, in Keats, J. (1927), p. 223.

47 Miller, P. (1949), p. 201.

48 Lee, S. H. (2005), p. xi; Matthews, G. M. (ed.) (1971, 1995) *John Keats, The Critical Heritage*. London: Routledge, p. 36.

49 Miller, P. (1949), p. xi; Letter 199 to the George Keatses, in Keats, J. (1958), vol. 2, p. 200.

50 Matthews, G. M. (ed.) (1971, 1995), p. 36.

51 Barnard, J. (1988), p. xiv.

52 Smith, J. E. *et al.* (eds) (2003), p. 245.

53 de Man, P. (ed.) (1966) 'Introduction', in *John Keats' Selected Poetry*, New York: Signet, p. xiv.

54 *Endymion*, bk. I, ll. 777–81, in Keats, J. (1927), p. 78.

Chapter 11

Jonathan Edwards' Reformed Doctrine of the Beatific Vision

Kyle Strobel

In many theological circles, particularly Protestant, the beatific vision has fallen out of theological favour. Yet it would be a mistake to assume it had no place in Protestant theology. Historically, Protestant theologians

> largely neglected the notion [of the beatific vision]; but in doing so they neglected an important element in the eschatological hope of the New Testament and lost some of the valuable insights of medieval theology and spirituality.[1]

Contrary to this view, we can argue that Protestant theologians were far from ignoring the beatific vision. Many, in fact, advanced theologically creative and biblically astute observations about life in glory. We provide proof by tracing key Reformed proposals concerning the beatific vision, culminating in Jonathan Edwards' trinitarian depiction of the heavenly vision of God.

It could be Edwards' fascination with the beatific that explains commentators' talk of the mystical strain in Edwards' thought, or even suggestions that his personal life was something of an existential struggle within the bonds of an over-binding Calvinism. Rarely, however, is his understanding of the beatific addressed, either in *his* thought specifically, or in the immediate context in which he worked. In light of this, I work closely with Suzanne McDonald's work on John Owen and the 'Reforming' of the beatific vision.[2] I argue that Edwards commandeers Owen's idiosyncratic view, and, as Edwards tended to elsewhere, advances his position beyond Owen's own. This 'advancement', I suggest, answers McDonald's critique of Owen's position: that his understanding of the beatific vision fails to be truly trinitarian.

In order to accomplish this task, I exposit Edwards' view of the beatific vision with a particular focus on two of his favorite theologians: John Owen on the one hand, and Francis Turretin on the other. In brief, John Owen argues for a strictly christological reading of the heavenly vision, where the Father is only known in Christ, as Christ is the image of the invisible God.[3] Turretin, by contrast, is concerned with the nature of the vision more than the object of the vision. In effect, Turretin's God becomes monadic in the beatific vision, a deity abstracted away from the divine persons. By contrast, Edwards follows Owen's christological mediation, moving beyond it to invoke a true vision of the Father and the Son by the Spirit.[4]

By looking at Owen and Turretin, I briefly chart the theological questions and debates leading up to Edwards' own exposition. This is in contrast to Paul Ramsey's erudite discussion on the beatific, which focuses on Aquinas and Dante as Edwards' theological precursors, rather than charting Edwards' own theological resources.[5] In engaging Edwards' immediate sources, his somewhat idiosyncratic position will be grounded within the larger context concerning the nature of spiritual sight in glory. In each of these brief expositions of the beatific vision, our focus is on the doctrinal decisions made in reference to the vision itself. In other words, our overarching questions concern what doctrinal resources are wielded *by these* Reformed thinkers in their development of the beatific vision.

John Owen and the Beatific

McDonald suggests that Owen reformed Aquinas' view of the beatific vision. This reworking was specifically christological.[6] Owen, in his work on Christ's glory, states:

> That which at present I design to demonstrate is, that the beholding of the *glory of Christ* is one of the greatest privileges and advancements that believers are capable of in this world, or that which is to come.[7]

Owen defines this 'beatifical' vision as 'such an intellectual present view, apprehension, and sight of God and his glory, especially as manifested in Christ, as will make us blessed unto eternity'.[8] Owen delineates two ways or degrees of beholding Christ's glory: first, by faith, which is the 'sight' given in this world; and second, by sight, which is the immediate vision in eternity.[9] The beatific vision, Owen states, is christologically focused: as 'it is the Lord Christ and his glory which are the immediate object both of this faith and sight'.[10] Therefore, the sight that saints behold in heaven is the result of their beholding Christ by faith during life on earth. This connection is important: just as seeing Christ in heaven is the perfection of faith on earth, so seeing Christ immediately in heaven is the perfection of seeing through a glass darkly in this world. As Owen describes it,

> The enjoyment of God by sight is commonly called the BEATIFICAL VISION; and it is the sole fountain of all the actings of our souls in the state of blessedness . . . Howbeit, this we know, that God in his immense essence is invisible unto our corporeal eyes, and will be so to eternity; as also incomprehensible unto our minds. For nothing can perfectly comprehend that which is infinite, but what is itself infinite. *Wherefore the blessed and blessing sight which we shall have of God will be always 'in the face of Jesus Christ'.*[11]

The means, in other words, are perfected, but the object remains the same. It is still Christ, even in glory, who is the image of the invisible God.

Therefore, knowledge of God on the earthly side of glory is a pilgrim knowledge, mediated by the person and work of Christ. Owen states:

> Nothing is more fully and clearly revealed in the Gospel, than that unto us Jesus Christ is 'the image of the invisible God'; that he is the character of the person of the Father, so as that in seeing him we see the Father also; that we have 'the light of the knowledge of the glory of God in his face alone', as hath been proved.[12]

Unlike the vision of Christ available to believers on earth, which is either by faith or through bodily sight in the case of the apostles, the vision of him in heaven is immediate, direct and intuitive.[13] What is mediated by *faith* and the *gospel* on earth—the object of the sight, *Christ*, and the faculty of seeing through bodily eyes—are both perfected by *immediacy* in heaven. Therefore, in Owen's words,

> principally, as we shall see immediately, this vision is intellectual. It is not, therefore, the mere human nature of Christ that is the object of it, but his divine person, as that nature subsisteth therein.[14]

Owen's understanding of the beatific vision is governed by his unmistakable christocentric focus. McDonald summarizes:

> For Owen the content of the beatific vision *is* primarily Jesus Christ, fully God, fully man, acknowledged by faith now, apprehended in its fullness in eternity. Beholding the glory of God is beholding the

glory of the person of Christ in the mystery of the union of the two
natures.[15]

In other words, Christ is, and will always be, the visible image of the invisible God.[16] Owen invokes Christology to do the doctrinal 'heavy lifting' in
his doctrine of the beatific vision. Christ, far more than being a functional
aspect of the vision, whether of the Father or the divine 'essence', is central
to the vision itself. This move brings a certain biblical emphasis to the discussion with specific attention on Christ's role as the image of the invisible
God. Furthermore, Owen can focus on Christ's eternal mediation without
diminishing his 'imaging' role established in the economy. Therefore, 'This
union of his human nature unto God is *immediate*, in the person of the
Son; ours is *mediate*, by the Son, as clothed with our nature.'[17]

By focusing his doctrine of the beatific vision on Christ, Owen connects the vision in glory with the vision had through faith. Faith perfected,
as it were, is sight. This necessitates anthropological perfection—the addition of new *faculties* of sight—as well as the immediacy only available in
glory. Furthermore, heaven is, in a sense, tethered to what has already been
revealed on earth: 'No man ought to look for anything in heaven', Owen
evinces, 'but what one way or other he hath some experience of in this
life'.[18] Owen's account is grounded in Christ's eternal mediation and the
faculties available to truly *see* Christ in his divinity (and not only see him
as the disciples did).

Francis Turretin and the Beatific

As a foil to the theological creativity of Owen, Francis Turretin stands as
one of Edwards' other main theological resources. Although we argue that
Edwards follows and expands Owen, Turretin's insights are important for
their radical difference from Owen's, as well as the certainty that Turretin's
view would have been known by Edwards.[19] In one such instance, sound-
ing very much like the New England divine, Turretin states:

> This perfection of the intellect by the beatific vision will be followed by
> no less a consummation of the will by absolute holiness and by a most
> pure and intense love to arise from that infinite light and the celestial
> intuition of it.[20]

Turretin, in volume three of his elenctic theology, addresses the
concept of the beatific vision within the question concerning eternal life.

Claiming that Aquinas holds to a vision of Christ located in the intellect, while Scotus holds to love through the will, Turretin suggests that these are not mutually exclusive and must be understood as united in the beatific vision.[21] Specifically, what is united in the vision of God is: sight, love and joy.[22] Turretin explains:

> Sight contemplates God as the supreme good; love is carried out towards him, and is most closely united with him; and joy enjoys and acquiesces in him. Sight perfects the intellect, love the will, joy the conscience.[23]

Turretin's focus in his exposition is on seeing God *qua* deity.[24] In doing so, he makes it clear that while it is possible to talk about 'sight' prior to glory—quoting 1 Corinthians 13:12, 'For now we see through a glass, darkly; but then face to face'—this sight is qualitatively different than that had in glory. In comparing these two kinds of sight, he states:

> (1) one vision is ocular, sensible and external, another mental, intellectual and internal; (2) one is the natural of reason, another the supernatural and spiritual of faith; (3) one symbolic and enigmatic, the other intuitive and beatific; (4) one apprehensive and inadequate, the other adequate and comprehensive.[25]

God cannot be seen naturally with bodily eyes; rather, a vision of God necessitates a mental, spiritual and intellectual vision. For Turretin, the overriding issues are God's invisibility, God's infinity, and the human possibility for true knowledge of God. For the same reasons Owen puts Christology to work for him in explaining the invisibility and incomprehensibility of God, Turretin focuses instead on the *kind of vision* necessary, and in so doing, focuses on issues of anthropology rather than theology proper. Therefore, while Owen offers a christological recasting of the beatific vision, Turretin ignores Christ's role entirely. As McDonald describes Turretin's view:

> Christ is literally almost invisible throughout his entire discussion of the vision of God in glory. He is mentioned only a few times in passing, and only because references to the book of Revelation require it.[26]

Turretin therefore, advances his argument based upon attributes abstracted from God *qua* deity, and posits a glory where Christ's 'imaging' has become irrelevant.

Admittedly, Turretin is undertaking a certain kind of polemical task.[27] What we have from him, in other words, is not a constructive theology of the beatific vision, but a polemical argument concerning how, in his mind, Protestants should conceive of the vision of God. It is not surprising then to find Turretin holding his position against Aquinas and Scotus. That being said, his polemical tactics may be just as telling as a robust analysis would be. Owen, it would seem, would have engaged his opposition on the beatific vision with a robust Christology, wielding specifically dogmatic decisions against his opponents. Turretin does not do so. Instead, Turretin focuses on anthropology (as noted above) as well as soteriological doctrines in an attempt to outline the specific contours of the beatific. This proves instructive.

Turretin understands heavenly glory to entail a perfection of faith, hope and love. Faith finds its consummation in sight, he argues, just as the love begun on earth is consummated in union with God in eternity.[28] Hope, furthermore, is replaced in the heavenly realm by joy: 'God cannot be seen without being loved; love draws joy after it because he cannot be possessed without filling with joy.'[29] Furthermore, Turretin continues to draw links, not only abstracting virtue to its perfection, but contrasting the blessings of the saints with the damnation of unbelievers. Turretin highlights the contrasting ends:

> Vision is opposed to the banishing of the damned from his face and to the most dense darkness of ignorance in which they lie; love to the most furious hatred which they cherish towards him; joy to the dreadful despair and wailing which will arise from the multiplicity and continuity of the torments they will feel.[30]

His development of his doctrine is based on a threefold delineation of faith, hope, and love, attending to their nature in perfection. He moves into a discussion of anthropology, virtue, and, more generically, God's attributes and essence to sketch his position. Therefore, the primary foundation of his account is his discussion of God as infinite and invisible, and his exposition of soteriological virtues and anthropology, rather than, in the case of Owen, Christology.

Commentating on Owen and Turretin, McDonald addresses a critique that I wish to pick up here in mapping Edwards' background. She notes that just as Turretin's discussion of the beatific negated the role of Christ, so Owen's discussion occurs without real reference to the Holy Spirit. I suggest, in response, that Edwards utilized and expanded Owen's

christological insights, developing a trinitarian understanding of the beatific vision, which addresses McDonald's concerns in a way in which Owen
and Turretin failed to. For the remainder of this essay, I focus my attention on Edwards' sermon on Romans 2:10, which is a major source for
his understanding of the beatific vision. Though the theme of the beatific
is ubiquitous in Edwards' work, this sermon is his only focused discussion on the nature, manner, and object of the vision.[31] I will then conclude
with general observations and further inquiries concerning a distinctively
Reformed account of the vision of God.

Edwards and the Beatific: Exposition of Romans 2:10

Edwards preached on Romans 2:10 in 1735, claiming '[t]o give a description of the consummate and eternal glory and blessedness of the saints,'[32]
showing first, its nature and wherein it consists, and second, its circumstances. Edwards provides six major points under his first emphasis: first,
heaven is more glorious than any other aspect of created reality (God is the
builder, and there is 'no want of skill in this architect');[33] second, as glorious as the heavenly realms are, they pale in comparison to the glorified
bodies of the saints; third, as glorious as the saints' bodies will be, those
will be overshadowed by the glory of the saints' souls; fourth, the saints
in heaven will commune in perfect harmony and union with one another;
and fifth, the saints will converse and see Christ in a twofold sense. Before
moving on to the sixth point, we must pause to look at Edwards' twofold
delineation of conversing *with* and *seeing* Christ. First, the saints 'shall see
him as appearing in his glorified human nature with their bodily eyes'; and
second, '[t]hey shall see him with the eye of the soul.'[34]

In this sight of Christ, glorified humanity will come to understand
Christ's mediatorial role, the eternal covenant of redemption, Christ's love
to them before the foundation of the world, the mystery of the incarnation,
the glorious way of salvation by Christ, and a full understanding of the infinite wisdom of God in contriving the way of salvation.[35] There, the heart
will no longer be 'dull' concerning these things, but will be fully enlightened. Everything in the work of redemption, Edwards claims, will appear
in its true glory, 'like the clear hemisphere with the sun in the meridian,
and there shall never come even one cloud to darken the mind.'[36] Christ's
exalted and glorified human state will, furthermore, appear without a veil,

and the saints will have full access to converse with Christ. These conversations will be, first, most free and intimate, and second, they will be with the greatest endearments and love from Christ to his spouse: 'the soul shall, as it were, all dissolve in love in the arms of the glorious Son of God and breath itself wholly in ecstasies of divine love into his bosom'.[37]

Edwards' sixth point is that the saints in heaven shall see God, which Edwards calls the *beatifical* vision. In seeing the divine nature, they will 'behold that bright and perfect image of God that the Father beheld and was infinitely happy in beholding from all eternity'. Edwards qualifies his remarks by focusing the beatific vision specifically on a 'sight of the glory of Christ in his divine nature'. Edwards, in this sense, takes on something of the christological emphasis of Owen. Christ, rather than simply being a functional aspect of the vision, serves as the object of the vision as well. Edwards claims that '[t]he sight of Christ . . . is not here to be excluded because he is a divine person. The sight of him in his divine nature therefore belongs to the beatifical vision.'[38] As christological as Edwards' focus is, he is clear that the embodied Christ is not the object of the vision as such, that is, as *embodied*.[39] The vision of God had by the glorified saints is primarily spiritual. It is not beholding forms or representations, shapes or colours that make the soul 'happified'; rather, ''tis in seeing God, who is a spirit, spiritually with the eye of the soul'. In explaining this 'eye of the soul', Edwards states:

> The soul has in itself those powers, whereby 'tis sufficiently capable of apprehending spiritual objects, without looking through the window of the outward senses. The soul is capable of seeing God more immediately and more certainly, and more fully and gloriously, than the eye of the body is.[40]

This 'intellectual' sight, as Edwards goes on to call it, this sight of the soul, is immediate.[41] 'They shall see God as we immediately behold the sun after it is risen above the horizon, and no cloud or vapour in the heavens to hinder its light', Edwards continues.[42] The nature of this 'immediacy' becomes clear when Edwards qualifies what he means by contrasting immediate sight with a mediated sight. This sight will not necessitate an argument from words or the making use of ordinances; in other words, immediacy highlights the nature of *receiving* the sight, and does not delineate how direct the access is to God (namely, an immediacy to God's soul, which Edwards was concerned to protect against). Importantly, he does argue that this sight is perfect, but only perfect *in its kind*.

> It shall not be a comprehensive sight because 'tis impossible that a finite mind should comprehend God, but yet it shall be perfect in its kind. It shall be perfectly certain without any doubt or possibility of doubt. There shall be such a view of God in his being and in his power and holiness and goodness and love and all sufficiency that shall be attended with an intuitive certainty without any mixture of unbelief.[43]

Here, Edwards seems to be working within the same broad sphere as Turretin and Owen, leaning more towards the latter than the former. The focus is on an intellectual vision, following both Turretin and Owen, but includes both the divine nature of Christ, as well as that of the Father. Again, following both, Edwards is sensitive to the anthropological issues of finitude. On the other hand, *contra* Turretin, the vision is not viewing God as a passive object, or God as an abstracted deity. Instead, as we turn our attention to now, Edwards offers a vision to glorified humanity *as a vision of love pro nobis*.

Edwards continues by offering a twofold analysis of the vision itself: first, the saints shall see everything in God that tends to excite and inflame love; and second, they shall see everything in him that gratifies love. In the latter of the two, Edwards declares:

> This very manifestation that God will make of himself that will cause the beatifical vision will be an act of love in God. It will be from the exceeding love of God to them that he will give them this vision which will add an immense sweetness to it … They shall see that he is their Father and that they are his children … therefore they shall see God as their own God, when they behold this transcendent glory.[44]

What the saints enjoy in the beatific vision therefore is a vision of God *pro nobis*. God is not passive in the vision, nor is he merely an object to be beheld. God is all act, and the vision is made manifest by God through an act of love, the love which binds the elect to Christ, the beloved. 'Love desires the love of the beloved', Edwards claims, 'so the saints in glory shall see God's transcendent love to them.'[45] Following upon the insights of Turretin, that the perfection of love reveals something of its nature in glory, Edwards advances his insights concerning the vision by noting that love desires love in return, which can only find fulfilment in perfection.

Furthermore, as noted above, it is God's love that *causes* the beatific vision. This insight, and the trinitarian theology which undergirds it, is what forms Edwards' understanding of both the manner and means of the vision.

Turning our attention to the manner in which the elect shall see God, Edwards states:

> The saints shall enjoy God as partaking with Christ of his enjoyment of God, for they are united to him and are glorified and made happy in the enjoyment of God as his members.

The saints' access to God is through the person of Christ alone:

> They being in Christ shall partake of the love God the Father [has] to Christ, and as the Son knows the Father so they shall partake with him in his sight of God, as being as it were parts of him as he is in the bosom of the Father.[46]

The saints come to participate, according to their capacity, in God's own self-joy and delight.

Edwards' view of christological participation, as both *object* and *manner* of the vision, anticipates the *means by which* God grants this vision to his saints. This, particularly in response to Owen's view, is a relevant point. In uniting the elect to Christ in the work of redemption, it is the Spirit who acts as the bond of union. Likewise, he states:

> By the Holy Ghost a spiritual sight of God is given in this world, so 'tis the same Holy Spirit by which a beatifical vision is given of God in heaven.[47]

In heaven, the saints are as dependent upon God as on earth for grace, holiness and light. Thus, Edwards says, 'They shall have this beatifical vision of God because they will be full of God, filled with the Holy Spirit of God.'[48]

Edwards ends the discussion by addressing the effects of the vision, stating that 'the soul hereby shall be inflamed with love':

> The soul shall not be an inactive spectator but shall be most active, shall be in the most ardent exercise of love towards the object seen. The soul shall be, as it were, all eye to behold, and yet all act to love.[49]

The effect of the beatific vision, Edwards says elsewhere, is 'happifying'.[50] God is pure act, we could say *infinite* act, and brings the soul to a perfect though finite act of love through a vision of himself. The vision is not passive beholding, in other words, but purely active; uniting the elect to himself *through* Christ and *by* the Spirit for eternity.

Edwards' development of the beatific vision takes its theological cues from his doctrine of the immanent and economic Trinity. The elect come to participate, in a real way, in the immanent life of God, but this participation is mediated christologically. In the economy, Christ took on human nature and redeemed the elect, binding them to his own person by the Holy Spirit of God. Through the cross the 'purchase' of the Spirit was made for the elect, from the Father by Christ, and it is by the Spirit that they truly do partake in the divine nature (2 Peter 1:4). Rather than employing Christology, with Owen, to do the bulk of his theological 'heavy lifting', Edwards turns to his understanding of the Trinity. Furthermore, *contra* Turretin, who triangulates the vision based on faculties of seeing, virtues and God's nature as infinite and invisible, Edwards turns to doctrines more central to God's nature, refusing to settle for depictions of God based on attributes abstracted from the persons.

Edwards' view follows the 'Reforming' nature of Owen's, but refuses to stop with a christological re-working of the vision of God and moves on to a trinitarian recasting with Christ and his redeeming work at its center. The union the elect have with Christ, which is their mediating point to the inner-triune life, grows closer asymptotically for eternity. As the elect continue to see and be seen, and know as they are known, they do not somehow exhaust God's depth, but only come to desire and find satisfaction in his perfection. This perfection of Christ's mediation provides an immediate view of God, with the qualifications on 'immediate' noted above, and follows Calvin himself in regards to Christ's eternal mediation. Richard Muller notes that Calvin refers to the conclusion of Christ's earthly mediation, but qualifies this by noting that *conclusion* 'speaks literally not of the *termination* of the office (*munus*) but of the *perfecting* of the mediatorial work (*officium*)'.[51] By focusing on the perfection of Christ's mediation as that by which an eternal increase of the beatific vision is obtained and provided, Edwards offers a creatively reworked but nonetheless 'Reformed' account of the beatific vision.[52]

Conclusion

Richard Bauckham, in his essay on eschatology in *The Oxford Handbook of Systematic Theology*, provides a terse overview of the vision of God. He states:

> The vision of God … offers a symbol of human destiny that highlights its theocentricity. It combines a sense of being in the immediate presence of God with the idea of knowing God in his true identity, as it were 'face to face'. It has sometimes been understood in a rather intellectualized and individualized way, but need not be. It is the whole person that is engaged in immediate relationship with God.[53]

Edwards' account of the beatific vision provides a distinctive exposition of theocentricity, immediacy and relationality based on his doctrine of the Trinity and Christ's eternal role as mediator. It seems possible that Edwards adapted Owen's insights by positing a christologically robust understanding of the beatific vision. Edwards, however, does not stop with a christocentric emphasis, but addresses the vision through *participation* in the inner-trinitarian vision of love. Christ's role is both object of the vision, as well as a twofold mediation: one concerning the reality of salvation (the hypostatic union, the eternal decrees, etc.), clearly building upon Owen's insights; the other, as mediation by union, uniting the elect to Christ as his spouse for participation in the inner-life of the Trinity. In so doing, Edwards jettisons Turretin's focus of seeing God as such, focusing instead on seeing God *pro nobis*—seeing God as he who unites us to his own life. Edwards' view also addresses the lacuna McDonald laments concerning Owen's normally robust pneumatology, which disappears in his account of the beatific. By placing the vision in the context of the triune life, Edwards incorporates his Augustinian insights of the Spirit as the bond of union, therefore uniting believers mystically into Christ's person and mediating the vision itself.

A distinctively *Reformed* account of the beatific vision, it would seem, is hard to delineate. Owen, Turretin, and Edwards each provide a different doctrinal focus to account for the vision of God, with Owen and Edwards turning to the nature of the triune God, in one way or another, and Turretin turning to aspects of anthropology and soteriology as his primary doctrinal import. Each thinker avoids a discussion of the divine essence, other than noting that God's essence is infinite and invisible, and therefore, unknowable.[54] An emphasis on the persons over the essence, even considering Turretin's lack of development, seems to be the constituting factor for any *Reformed* account of the beatific vision. While Turretin does not develop his argument positively along these lines, by focusing away from the essence, his account would have to advance with an emphasis on the persons, in some way or another.

Furthermore, in the constructive accounts of Owen and Edwards, the vision of God is delineated as a vision *pro nobis*. For Owen, the vision of God is translated through Christ's mediatorial office; the God who is *for us* in Christ is only known *in* Christ. Edwards, in a broadly similar fashion, outlines Christ's work *pro nobis*, but advances his pneumatology to outline the implications; God being *for us* is God's love uniting us to his life through Christ by his Spirit. The beatific vision is had *in* God's love, and the focus of the vision is on God's personal union—his work to unite the elect to his own life of love. Knowing God in glory is parsed through grace, a vision given of God himself, in Christ, through the enlightening and binding work of the Spirit of God. Creatures remain creatures, but are now fully actualized as glorified persons in communion with the God of glory. In the words of 2 Peter 1:4, believers are now 'partakers of the divine nature'.[55] This focus on the vision *pro nobis*, tied to the economic action of God in redemption—known now as the *God who has redeemed*—provides more adequate contours for a Reformed account of the beatific vision. The primary focus, for both Owen and Edwards, is on the God who *gives*, rather than the vision that is *received*.

Notes

1 Bauckham, R. J. (1988) 'Vision of God', in *A New Dictionary of Theology*, ed. S. B. Ferguson, D. F. Wright, and J. I. Packer, Downers Grove: InterVarsity Press, p. 711.

2 McDonald, S. (2008) 'Beholding the Glory of God in the Face of Jesus Christ: John Owen and the "Reforming" of the Beatific Vision', unpub. paper delivered at the 'John Owen Today' Conference, Westminster College, Cambridge, 2008, pp. 1–17; quoted by permission.

3 Charles Hodge follows Owen when he states, 'This vision of God is in the face of Jesus Christ, in whom dwells the plenitude of the divine glory bodily. God is seen in fashion as a man; and it is this manifestation of God in the person of Christ that is inconceivably and intolerably ravishing.' Hodge, C. (1960) *Systematic Theology*, London: James Clarke & Co., vol. 3, p. 860.

4 For the sake of the space allotted, I have focused the discussion on the nature of the beatific vision itself, including the object, means and manner, rather than focusing on the prolegomenal issues of archetypal and ectypal knowledge. For a full-blown account of the beatific one would have to address these issues as well.

5 'Heaven is a Progressive State', in WJE 8, pp. 706–38.

6 I follow McDonald's analysis closely and focus on Owen's work, 'Meditations and Discourses on the Glory of Christ in his Person, Office, and Grace: with The Differences Between Faith and Sight; Applied Unto the Use of Them that Believe', in Goold, W. H.

(ed.) (1850–5) *The Works of John Owen*, 24 vols., London: Johnstone and Hunter, vol. 1, pp. 273–415. McDonald argues that Aquinas' christological approach to the beatific is an 'essentially functionalist approach to the role of the person of Christ in relation to the beatific vision'. She states, 'In the Thomistic tradition, the emphasis seems to be upon Christ as instrumental for our participation in the beatific vision, but not upon presenting Christ as being intrinsic for our participation in the beatific vision itself'. Likewise, 'For Aquinas, the person of Christ is pivotal to the possibility of the beatific vision for us. Owen agrees wholeheartedly with the christological and pneumatological dynamic by which we come to partake in the beatific vision, but in addition, insists upon placing Jesus Christ at the heart of the vision itself.' McDonald summarizes Aquinas' view: 'The beatific vision is wholly intellectual for Aquinas. The language of sight is metaphorical, to indicate the clarity with which we understand, in contrast to seeing through a mirror dimly by faith.' McDonald, S. (2008), pp. 11, 14. Aquinas' discussion of the beatific is beyond the bounds of our exposition here (see *Summa Theologia, Supplementum Tertiae Partis* Q. 92, *Summa Contra Gentiles*, bk. III, Q. 49–63, and, as noted by Paul Ramsey, *Com. Sent.* I, 1, 2, ad 3; *Com. Sent.* III, I, 1, 3 ad 6). In short, Thomas understands the beatific vision to be of the divine essence, whereas Reformed thinkers focus the vision elsewhere. Admittedly, there is some debate concerning Aquinas' use of 'essence'. See Smith, T. L. (2003) *Thomas Aquinas' Trinitarian Theology: A Study in Theological Method*, Washington, D.C.: Catholic University of America Press, pp. 24, 50–2, 60. Joseph Wawrykow notes: 'Yet while the vision provides a knowledge of God in God's essence, Aquinas is insistent that the knowledge granted the human is not total, in the sense of utterly comprehensive. The light of glory is a created light, and the human remains human even in this rising to God; the finite is unable to totally grasp God as God is . . . beatific vision is but a sharing, a participation in the manner set by God for the creature in God's own life.' Wawrykow, J. P. (2005) *The SCM Press A–Z of Thomas Aquinas*, London: SCM Press, p. 18.

7   Goold, W. H. (ed.) (1850–5), vol. 1, p. 287; my emphasis.

8   *Ibid.*, p. 240.

9   *Ibid.*, p. 288.

10 *Ibid.*, p. 288. This distinction does not entirely separate the two for Owen. For Owen, there is a sense where sight is the perfection of faith, and therefore without faith, sight will never occur. He states (*ibid.*), 'No man shall ever behold the glory of Christ by *sight* hereafter, who doth not in some measure behold it by *faith* here in this world. Grace is a necessary preparation for glory, and faith for sight.'

11 *Ibid.*, pp. 292–3; my emphasis.

12 *Ibid.*, p. 305. For Owen, this is connected with the renewal of the image of God: 'This is that whereby the image of God is renewed in us, and we are made like unto the first-born.'

13 *Ibid.*, p. 378.

14 *Ibid.*, p. 379.

15 McDonald, S. (2008), p. 7.

16 There are points where Owen's own understanding of this seems to digress, but in the broader context it is clear that his view is solidified. At one of these points, Owen states, 'This beholding of the glory of Christ given him by his Father, is, indeed, subordinate unto the ultimate vision of the essence of God.' This comment, at face value, seems to run contrary to all that Owen has stated until this point in his discourse. In an attempt to clarify, however ambiguously, he continues by adding, 'For he is, and shall be to eternity,

the only means of communication between God and the church'. By demarcating the glory as that 'given him by his Father', Owen seems to be referring to Christ's glory in the Father's exalting him in his mediatory office, rather than that a beholding of the divine person by spiritual sight. Owen is clear in his explanation that the only true sight of God is a christological sight. Goold, W. H. (ed.) (1850–5) vol. 1, pp. 385–6.

17 *Ibid.*, p. 240.

18 *Ibid.*, p. 290.

19 I am making a minimalist assertion concerning Edwards' use of sources here. I do not propose to show that Edwards did, in fact, have these texts on hand, though it is clear that he knew and owned both of these works. My particular point is simply to empha-size that these were the ideas floating around his chosen theological moorings.

20 Turretin, F. (1992) *Institutes of Elenctic Theology*, ed. James T. Dennison, trans. George Musgrave Giger, Phillipsburg: P&R Publishing, vol. 3, p. 611.

21 Bavinck follows this same line of thought but does so by invoking Bonaventure. He states, 'In theology, theologians have disputed whether this blessedness in the hereafter formally had its seat in the intellect or in the will and hence consisted in knowledge or love. Thomas claimed the former, Duns Scotus the latter, but Bonaventure combined the two, observing that the enjoyment of God (*fruitio Dei*) was the fruit not only of the knowledge of God (*cognitio Dei*) but also of the love of God (*amor Dei*) and resulted from the union and cooperation of the two.' Bavinck, H. (2003) *Reformed Dogmatics: Holy Spirit, Church, and New Creation*, ed. J. Bolt and J. Vriend, Grand Rapids: Baker Academic, vol. 4, p. 722.

22 Turretin, F. (1992), p. 609.

23 *Ibid.*

24 This is not to say that Turretin's doctrine of the trinity does not continue fully into eternity. Instead, it is noteworthy that Turretin's doctrine of the trinity is not employed in his discussion of the beatific. Michael Horton claims that 'Turretin, summarizing the Reformed consensus, refused to consider God merely as "deity" (*in abstracto*)–a view he attributes to Thomas–but rather as the triune God who has "covenanted in Christ" (*in concreto*)'. Horton, M. S. (2007) *Covenant and Salvation: Union with Christ*, Louisville: Westminster John Knox Press, p. 282. This is, overall, true of Turretin's the-ology, but Horton seems to be reading his own emphases and concerns into Turretin's account of the beatific vision here. In Turretin's account, we are not confronted with the triune God of glory, but with 'God' abstractly considered.

25 Turretin, F. (1992), p. 610.

26 McDonald, S. (2008), p. 13.

27 Admittedly, 'elenctic' and 'polemical' are not strictly synonymous. 'Whereas *polemic* indicates simple attack, *elenctic* implies refutation leading toward positive statement'. Muller, R. A. (1985) 'Elenchticus', in *Dictionary of Latin and Greek Theological Terms: Drawn Principally from Protestant Scholastic Theology*, Grand Rapids: Baker Academic, p. 101.

28 Johannis Wollebius makes a similar move, contemplating humanity prior to the fall and applying a conception of perfection to that reality: 'The soul will be given much greater perfection than existed in man before the fall. There will be understanding without error, light without shadow, wisdom without ignorance, reason without obscurity, memory without forgetfulness. There will also be will without depravity, joy without sorrow, and pleasure without pain. In the state of innocence man was able not to sin; in the state of glory he will not be able to sin.' Wollebius, J. (1965) *Compendium Theologiae*

Christianae in *Reformed Dogmatics: Seventeenth-Century Reformed Theology Through the Writings of Wollebius, Voetius, and Turretin*, trans. John W. Beardslee III, Grand Rapids: Baker Book House, p. 189.

29 Turretin, F. (1992), p. 609.

30 *Ibid.*

31 While Romans 2:10 is, without question, Edwards' most sustained treatment of the beatific vision, there is some question as to whether or not he changes his position. Approximately three years after Edwards preached this sermon, he wrote 'Miscellanies' no. 777, arguing, 'Therefore a spiritual, created being can't have an immediate view of another mind without some union of personality'. WJE 18, p. 427. As shown below, this does not change Edwards' view. First, this union of personality is impossible with God because humanity cannot fully comprehend an infinite God. Edwards' established creature-Creator distinction would not allow this kind of union. Second, God *qua* God can fully comprehend other persons, but no creature can comprehend God other than Jesus Christ. Edwards continues on to add, 'Therefore, there is no creature can thus have an immediate sight of God, but only Jesus Christ, who is in the bosom of God: for no creature can have such an immediate view of another *created spirit*, for if they could they could search the heart and try the reins. But to see and SEARCH THE HEART is often spoken of as GOD'S PREROGATIVE, and as one thing God's divinity and infinite exaltation above all creatures appears.' *Ibid.*, p. 428; my emphasis. Note that Edwards immediately shifts to *created spirits* rather than God, since God is, by definition, unable to be fully grasped by finite minds. Third, as is shown fully below, creatures never reach a sight of God that is not mediated, in some sense, by Christ. Here, again, Edwards states, 'And Jesus Christ, who alone sees immediately, [is] the grand medium of the knowledge of all others; they know no otherwise than by the exhibitions held forth in and by him, as the Scripture is express'. *Ibid.* There is nothing about his exposition here that contradicts his statements in the sermon on Romans 2:10, which are simply fleshed out more fully.

32 Edwards, J., MS Sermon on Rom. 2:10 (1735), [L. 31r.], transcript supplied by Jonathan Edwards Center, Yale University. All quotations from this sermon are edited for readability. The leaf number from the transcript appears in brackets.

33 *Ibid.*, [L. 31v.–L.32r.].

34 *Ibid.*, [Ll. 37v.–38r.].

35 *Ibid.*, [L. 38r.].

36 *Ibid.*, [L. 38v.].

37 *Ibid.*, [L. 40v.].

38 *Ibid.*, [Ll. 39r., 41r.].

39 We could say that the bodily sight of Christ's glorified body perfects the body while the spiritual sight of God and Christ perfects the soul, but Edwards does not make that specific distinction himself. One of Edwards' reasons for not allowing the highest sight of God to be an embodied sight is that the angels, who do not have bodily faculties, share in the vision as well. This is an interesting employment of angelology. *Ibid.*, [L. 41v.].

40 *Ibid.*, [Ll. 41v., 42v.–L.43r.]. Edwards also says that 'The soul is capable of apprehending God in a thousand times more perfect and glorious manner than the eye of the body is'. *Ibid.*, [L.42r].

41 The 'immediacy' of the sight, which Edwards focuses on here, is not in contradiction to his comments in 'Miscellanies' no. 777, where he claims that an immediate sight of

God is not possible. There, he is referencing the immediacy of God as such, whereas here he references anthropology, with specific reference to the faculty of sight—mediated through the bodily eyes or immediate (in other words, not mediated) with the soul. Edwards' point is similar to Bavinck's when he states, 'The redeemed see God, not—to be sure—with physical eyes, but still in a way that far outstrips all revelation in this dispensation via nature and Scripture. And thus they will all know him, each in the measure of his mental capacity, with a knowledge that has its image and likeness in God's knowledge—directly, immediately, unambiguously, and purely. Then they will receive and possess everything they expected here only in hope'. Bavinck, H. (2003), p. 722.

42 Edwards, J., MS Sermon on Rom. 2:10, [L. 43r.].

43 *Ibid.*, [L.43r–L.43v].

44 *Ibid.*, [L.44r–L.44v].

45 *Ibid.*, [L.44r].

46 *Ibid.*, [L.44v–L.45r].

47 *Ibid.*, [L.45r]. See Caldwell, R. W. (2006) *Communion in the Spirit: The Holy Spirit as the Bond of Union in the Theology of Jonathan Edwards*, Milton Keynes, Great Britain: Paternoster.

48 *Ibid.*, [L.45r]. Notice that the issue for Edwards is a participation in the *relational* life of the Trinity through sight, and not, as with Aquinas, a sight of the divine essence. This kind of exposition puts Edwards closer to an Eastern view of the vision of God. Vladimir Lossky states: 'the idea of beatitude has acquired in the West a slightly intellectual emphasis, presenting itself in the guise of a vision of the essence of God ... In the tradition of the Eastern Church there is no place for a theology ... of the divine essence. The goal of Orthodox spirituality, the blessedness of the Kingdom of Heaven, is not the vision of the essence, but, above all, a participation in the divine life of the Holy Trinity'. Lossky, L. (1957) *The Mystical Theology of the Eastern Church*, Cambridge: James Clarke & Co., pp. 64–5. On resonances between Edwards and the Eastern tradition, see also McClymond, M. J. (2003) 'Salvation as Divinization: Jonathan Edwards, Gregory Palamas and the Theological Uses of Neoplatonism', in Helm, P., and Crisp, O. D. (2003) *Jonathan Edwards: Philosophical Theologian*, Burlington, Vermont: Ashgate, pp. 139–59.

49 Edwards, J., MS Sermon on Rom. 2:10, [L. 45v.].

50 Edwards, J., 'The Pure in Heart Blessed', in WJE 17, p. 63.

51 Muller, R. A. (1981) 'Christ in the Eschaton: Calvin and Moltmann on the Duration of the *Munus Regium*', *Harvard Theological Review*, 74, no. 1(January), p. 45. It is not fully clear from the *Institutes* how Calvin understands the beatific vision. His discussions are terse and ambiguous but are nonetheless ripe with theologically insight. Under a major heading on the two natures of Christ in a single person, Calvin makes several comments about the beatific vision, stating that 'Christ is said to be seated at the right hand of the Father [Mark 16:19, Rom. 8:34]. Yet this is but for a time, until we enjoy the direct vision of the Godhead'. Calvin, like Edwards, seems to be focusing on a vision of the trinitarian God as such, rather than focusing solely on Christ as the image. He continues: 'But when as partakers in heavenly glory we shall see God as he is, Christ, having then discharged the office of Mediator, will cease to be the ambassador of his Father, and will be satisfied with that glory which he enjoyed before the creation of the world.' Therefore, in a sense, Christ's office as mediator is 'discharged' with his office as ambassador. Furthermore, Calvin notes: 'That is, to him [Christ] was lordship committed by

the Father, until such a time as we should see his divine majesty face to face ... Then, also, God shall cease to be the Head of Christ, for Christ's own deity will shine of itself, although as yet it is covered by a veil' (Calvin, *Institutes*, 2.14.3). Like Edwards' depiction of the beatific vision, Christ's divine nature is included in the consummate vision, and, it would seem, Christ's role as mediator is perfected in some real sense, so that believers are no longer *veiled* by his humanity. Todd Billings offers an overview of Calvin's understanding of the union with God in eternity, which follows remarkably similar contours as Edwards': In their union with Christ, believers are 'participants not only in all his benefits but also in himself'. Indeed, 'day by day, he grows more and more into one body with us, until he becomes completely one with us . . . Yet this union with Christ is impossible without a participation in the Spirit, who unites the believer to Christ.' Billings, T. (2007) *Calvin, Participation, and the Gift: The Activity of Believers in Union with Christ*, Oxford: Oxford University Press, p. 52.

52 'Reformed' in the sense that Edwards' focus is on Christ's work in the *historia salutis* and his eternal role as mediator, followed by a refusal to move beyond God's inherent personhood.

53 Bauckham, R. J. (2007) 'Eschatology', in *The Oxford Handbook of Systematic Theology* ed. J. Webster, K. Tanner, and I. Torrance, Oxford: Oxford University Press, p. 320.

54 Lewis Bayly seems to undermine this when he writes, 'For as soon as the soul is admitted into the actual fruition of the *beatifical* essence of God.' Yet Bayly goes on to qualify this by noting that 'this joy shall arise chiefly from the vision of God . . . But especially from the blissful sight of Jesus, the Mediator of the New Testament, our Emmanuel, God made Man. His sight will be the chief cause of our bliss and joy.' Bayly, L. (1719) *The Practice of Piety: Directing a Christian How to Walke that he May Please God*, London: Printed for Daniel Mindwinter, pp. 95–6; editing mine.

55 Thomas Watson puts it well: 'Not that the saints shall partake of God's essence; for as the iron in the fire is made fiery, yet remains iron still, so the saints, by beholding God's majesty, shall be made glorious creatures, yet creatures still.' Watson, T. (1838) *A Body of Practical Divinity, in a Series of Sermons on the Shorter Catechism*, Aberdeen: D. Chalmers and Co., p. 270.

Bibliography

1. Works by Edwards

a. Works of Jonathan Edwards (Yale Series)

WJE 1   Ramsey P. (ed.) (1957) *The Works of Jonathan Edwards, vol. 1, Freedom of the Will*, New Haven: Yale University Press.

WJE 2   Smith, J. E. (ed.) (1959) *The Works of Jonathan Edwards, vol. 2, Religious Affections*, New Haven: Yale University Press.

WJE 3   Holbrook, C. A. (ed.) (1970) *The Works of Jonathan Edwards, vol. 3, Original Sin*, New Haven: Yale University Press.

WJE 4   Goen, C. C. (ed.) (1972) *The Works of Jonathan Edwards, vol. 4, The Great Awakening*, New Haven: Yale University Press.

WJE 5   Stein, S. J. (ed.) (1977) *The Works of Jonathan Edwards, vol. 5, Apocalyptic Writings*, New Haven: Yale University Press.

WJE 6   Anderson, W. A. (ed.) (1970) *The Works of Jonathan Edwards, vol. 6, Scientific and Philosophical Writings*, New Haven: Yale University Press.

WJE 7   Pettit, N. (ed.) (1985) *The Works of Jonathan Edwards, vol. 7, The Life of David Brainerd*, New Haven: Yale University Press.

WJE 8   Ramsey, P. (ed.) (1989) *The Works of Jonathan Edwards, vol. 8, Ethical Writings*, New Haven: Yale University Press.

WJE 9   Wilson, J. F. (ed.) (1989) *The Works of Jonathan Edwards, vol. 9, A History of the Work of Redemption*, New Haven: Yale University Press.

WJE 10   Kimnach, W. H. (ed.) (1992) *The Works of Jonathan Edwards, vol. 10, Sermons and Discourses, 1720–1723*, New Haven: Yale University Press.

WJE 12   Hall, D. D. (ed.) (1994) *The Works of Jonathan Edwards, vol. 12, Ecclesiastical Writings*, New Haven: Yale University Press.

WJE 13   Schafer, T. A. (ed.) (1994) *The Works of Jonathan Edwards, vol. 13, The 'Miscellanies': Entry Nos. a–500*, New Haven: Yale University Press.

WJE 14   Minkema, K. P. (ed.) (1997) *The Works of Jonathan Edwards, vol. 14, Sermons and Discourses, 1723–1729*, New Haven: Yale University Press.

WJE 15   Stein, S. J. (ed.) (1998) *Works of Jonathan Edwards, vol. 15, 'Notes on Scripture'*, New Haven: Yale University Press.

WJE 16   Claghorn, G. S. (ed.) (1994) The Works of Jonathan Edwards, vol. 16, Letters and Personal Writings, New Haven: Yale University Press.

WJE 17   Valeri, M. (ed.) (1999) *The Works of Jonathan Edwards, vol. 17, Sermons and Discourses, 1730–1733*, New Haven: Yale University Press.

WJE 18   Chamberlain, A. (ed.) (2000) *The Works of Jonathan Edwards, vol. 18, The 'Miscellanies', Entry Nos. 501–832*, New Haven, Yale University Press.

WJE 19   Lesser, M. X. (ed.) (2001) *The Works of Jonathan Edwards, vol. 19, Sermons and Discourses, 1734–1738*, New Haven: Yale University Press.

WJE 22   Stout, H. S. *et al.* (eds) (2003) *The Works of Jonathan Edwards, vol. 22, Sermons and Discourses, 1739–1742*, New Haven: Yale University Press.

WJE 23   Sweeney, D. A. (ed.) (2004) *The Works of Jonathan Edwards, vol. 23, The 'Miscellanies', Nos. 1156–1360*, New Haven: Yale University Press.

WJE 25   Kimnach, W. H. (ed.) (2006) *The Works of Jonathan Edwards, vol. 25, Sermons and Discourses, 1743–1758*, New Haven: Yale University Press.

WJE 26   Thuesen, P. J. (ed.) (2008) *The Works of Jonathan Edwards, vol. 26, Catalogues of Reading*, New Haven: Yale University Press.

The Works of Jonathan Edwards Online, 73 vols., Jonathan Edwards Center, Yale University, 2010, http://edwards.yale.edu.

b. Other Works by Edwards

Edwards, J. (1742) *The Distinguishing Marks of the Work of the Spirit of God*, London: Samuel Mason.

Edwards, J. (1742) 'The Manner in Which the Salvation of the Soul is to Be Sought' (online source), available at http://www.biblebb.com/files/edwards/je-manner.htm (accessed 30 Oct. 2010).

2. Secondary works

(1836) *Album studiosorum Academiae rheno-traiectinae MDCXXXVI–MDCCCLXXXVI*, Utrecht: J. Beijers en J. van Boekhoven.

Allen, A. V. G. (2007) *Jonathan Edwards, The First Critical Biography, 1889*, The Jonathan Edwards Classic Studies Series, Eugene, Oregon: Wipf & Stock.

Baker, Frank (ed.) (1982) *The Works of John Wesley, vol. 26: Letters II: 1740–1755*, Oxford: Oxford University Press.

Barnard, J. (1988) *John Keats, a New Selection*, London: Penguin Books.

Bauckham, R. J. (1988) 'Vision of God', in *A New Dictionary of Theology*, ed. S. B. Ferguson, D. F. Wright, and J. I. Packer, Downers Grove: InterVarsity Press, pp. 710–11.

Bauckham, R. J. (2007) 'Eschatology', in *The Oxford Handbook of Systematic Theology*, ed. J. Webster, K. Tanner, and I. Torrance, Oxford: Oxford University Press, pp. 306–24.

Bavinck, H. (2003) *Reformed Dogmatics: Holy Spirit, Church, and New Creation*, ed. J. Bolt and J. Vriend, Grand Rapids: Baker Academic.

Bayly, L. (1719) *The Practice of Piety: Directing a Christian How to Walke that he May Please God*, London: Printed for Daniel Mindwinter.

Bebbington, D. W. (1989) *Evangelicalism in Modern Britain: A History from the 1730s to the 1980s*, London: Unwin Hyman.

Bebbington, D. W. (2003) 'Remembered around the World: The International Scope of Edwards's Legacy', in Kling, D. W., and Sweeney, D. A. (eds) *Jonathan Edwards at Home and Abroad: Historical Memories, Cultural Movements, Global Horizons*, Columbia, South Carolina: University of South Carolina Press, pp. 177–200.

Bellamy, J. (1853) *The Works of Joseph Bellamy, D.D.*, Boston: Doctrinal Tract and Book Society.

Benêt, S. V. (1999) *The Devil and Daniel Webster and other Writings*, New York: Penguin Books.

Bennett, J. (1971) *Locke, Berkeley, Hume: Central Themes*, Oxford: Clarendon Press.

Billings, T. (2007) *Calvin, Participation, and the Gift: The Activity of Believers in Union with Christ*, Oxford: Oxford University Press.

Bogue, C. W. (1975) *Jonathan Edwards and the Covenant of Grace*, Cherry Hill, New Jersey: Mack Publishing.

Boston, T. (1776) *Memoirs of the Life, Time, and Writings of the Reverend and Learned Thomas Boston*, Edinburgh: A. Murray.

Boyer, P. S. et al. (1993) *The Enduring Vision: A History of the American People*, Lexington, Massachusetts: D. C. Heath.

Brand, D. C. (1991) *Profile of the Last Puritan: Jonathan Edwards, Self-Love, and the Dawn of the Beatific*, Atlanta, Georgia: Scholars Press.

Brewster, P. (2010) *Andrew Fuller: Model Pastor-Theologian, Studies in Baptist Life and Thought*, B & H Academic.

Brown, J. (2002) *The Systematic Theology*, introduced by Joel R. Beeke and Randall J. Pederson, Grand Rapids: Reformation Heritage Books.

Caldwell, R. W. (2006) *Communion in the Spirit: The Holy Spirit as the Bond of Union in the Theology of Jonathan Edwards*, Milton Keynes: Paternoster.

Chun, C. (2006) 'A Mainspring of Missionary Thought: Andrew Fuller on Natural and Moral Inability', *American Baptist Quarterly*, 25, no. 4, pp. 335–55.

Colman, B. (1736) *A Dissertation on the Image of God wherein Man was created*, Boston: S. Kneeland and T. Green.

Conforti, J. A. (1985) 'David Brainerd and the Nineteenth-Century Missionary Movement', *Journal of the Early Republic*, 5, pp. 309–29.

Conforti, J. A. (1985) 'Jonathan Edwards' Most Popular Work: 'The Life of David Brainerd and Nineteen-Century Evangelical Culture', *Church History*, 54, pp. 188–201.

Conforti, J. A. (1995) *Jonathan Edwards, Religious Tradition, and American Culture*, Chapel Hill, North Carolina: University of North Carolina Press.

Cooper, T., and Murray, D. B. (2004) 'McLean, Archibald (1733–1812)', in *Oxford Dictionary of National Biography*, Oxford University Press, [www.oxforddnb.com/view/article/17648, accessed 10 Nov. 2006].

Crawford, M. J. (1991) *Seasons of Grace: Colonial New England's Revival Tradition in Its British Context*, New York: Oxford University Press.

Dana, J. (1770) *An Examination of the Late Reverend President Edwards's 'Enquiry on Freedom of Will'*, Boston: Daniel Kneeland.

Danaher, W. J. (2007) 'Beauty, Benevolence, and Virtue in Jonathan Edwards's *The Nature of True Virtue*', *Journal of Religion*, 87, no. 3 (July), pp. 386–410.

Davies, R. E. (2006) 'Missionary Benefactor and Strange Bedfellow: Isaac Hollis, Jonathan Edwards' English Correspondent', *Baptist Quarterly*, 41, no. 5, pp. 263–80.

de Man, P. (ed.) (1966) *John Keats Selected Poetry*, New York: Signet.

Delattre, R. A. (1968) *Beauty and Sensibility in the Thought of Jonathan Edwards: An Essay in Aesthetic and Theological Ethics*, New Haven: Yale University Press.

Douglas, M. (1966) *Purity and Danger: An Analysis of Concepts of Pollution and Taboo*, London: Routledge & Kegan Paul.

du Rieu, W. N. (1875) *Album studiosorum Academiae Lugduno Batavae MDLXXV–MDCCCLXXV*, The Hague: n.p.

Durden, S. (1976) 'A Study of the First Evangelical Magazines, 1740–1748', *Journal of Ecclesiastical History*, 27 (July), pp. 255–75.

Elwood, D. J. (1960) *The Philosophical Theology of Jonathan Edwards*, New York: Columbia University Press.

Elwyn, T. (1997) 'Particular Baptists of the Northamptonshire Baptist Association as Reflected in the Circular Letters', *Baptist Quarterly*, 37, no. 1, pp. 376–81.

Emerson, R. W. (1855) 'Lecture on slavery', in Gougeon, L., and Myerson, J. (eds) (1995) *Emerson's Antislavery Writings*, New Haven: Yale University Press, pp. 91–106.

Emmons, N. (1842) 'Man's Activity and Dependence Illustrated and Reconciled' and Burton, Asa 'Essay XXX' (1824) in Sweeney, D. A., and Guelzo, A. C. (eds) (2006) *The New England Theology: From Jonathan Edwards to Edwards Amasa Park*, Grand Rapids: Baker Academic, pp. 171–86.

Epictetus (1928) *The Discourses, Books III–IV, Fragments, Encheiridion*, trans. W. A. Oldfather, Cambridge, Massachusetts: Harvard University Press.

Erskine, E. (1805) *Faith no fancy, or, A treatise of mental images: discovering the vain philosophy and vile divinity of a late pamphlet entitled [sic] Mr. Robe's fourth letter to Mr. Fisher, and showing that an imaginary idea of Christ as man (when supposed to belong to saving faith, whether in its act or object), imports nothing but ignorance, atheism, idolatry, great falsehood, and gross delusion*, Philadelphia: William M'Culloch.

Erskine, R. (1725, 1770) *Christ the people's covenant*, Edinburgh?: n.p., Boston: Wiliam M'Alpine, 1770.

Evans, E. (1985) *Daniel Rowland and the Great Evangelical Awakening in Wales*, Edinburgh: Banner of Truth Trust.

Evans, E. (2011) *Bread of Heaven: The Life and Work of William Williams, Pantycelyn*, Bridgend: Bryntirion Press.

Fahrni, D. (2003) *An Outline History of Switzerland*, Pro-Helvita: Zurich.

Fawcett, A. (1971) *The Cambuslang Revival: The Scottish Evangelical Revival of the Eighteenth Century*, London: Banner of Truth Trust.

Fiering, N. (1981) *Jonathan Edwards's Moral Thought and Its British Context*, Chapel Hill, North Carolina: University of North Carolina Press.

Fisher, E. (12th edn, 1726) *The Marrow of Modern Divinity*, with notes by Thomas Boston, Edinburgh[?]: n.p.

Flower, E., and Murphey, M. G. (1977) *A History of Philosophy in America*, Vol. 1, New York: Capricorn Books.

Foster, F. H. (1963) *A Genetic History of the New England Theology*, New York: Russell & Russell.

Fuller, A. (1785) *The Gospel of Christ Worthy of All Acceptation*, Northampton: T. Dicey.

Fuller, A. (1988) *The Complete Works of the Rev Andrew Fuller: With a Memoir of his Life by the Rev. Andrew Gunton Fuller*, Harrisonburg: Sprinkle Publications.

George, T. (1991) *Faithful Witness: The Life and Mission of William Carey*, Birmingham: New Hope.

Gillies, J. (1945) *Historical Collections Relating to Remarkable Periods of the Success of the Gospel*, Kelso: John Rutherfurd.

Gorell, Lord (1948, 1970) *John Keats: The Principle of Beauty*, New York: Haskell House Publishers.

Goold, W. H. (ed.) (1850–5) *The Works of John Owen*, 24 vols., London: Johnstone and Hunter.

Goold, W. H. (ed.) (1860) *Works of the Rev. John MacLaurin*, Glasgow: J. Maclaren.

Hare, J. E. (1996) *The Moral Gap: Kantian Ethics, Human Limits, and God's Assistance*, Oxford: Oxford University Press.

Harris, J. A. (2005) *Of Liberty and Necessity: The Free Will Debate in Eighteenth-Century British Philosophy*, Oxford: Oxford University Press.

Haykin, M. A. G. (1994) *One Heart and One Soul: John Sutcliff of Olney, his Friends and his Times*, Durham: Evangelical Press.

Haykin, M. A. G. (ed.) (2004) '*At the Pure Fountain of Thy Word*': Andrew Fuller as an *Apologist*, Studies in Baptist History and Thought, 6, Carlisle: Paternoster Press.

Haykin, M. A. G. (ed.) (2007) *A Sweet Flame: Piety in the Letters of Jonathan Edwards*, Grand Rapids: Reformation Heritage Books.

Henderson, G. D. (1955) 'The Idea of the Covenant in Scotland', *The Evangelical Quarterly*, 27, pp. 2–14.

Hindmarsh, D. B. (2003) 'The Reception of Jonathan Edwards by Early Evangelicals in England', in Kling, D. W., and Sweeney, D. A. (eds) *Jonathan Edwards at Home and Abroad: Historical Memories, Cultural Movements, Global Horizons*, Columbia, South Carolina: University of South Carolina Press, pp. 201–21.

Hodge, C. (1960) *Systematic Theology*, 3 vols., London: James Clarke & Co.

Hog, J. (1947), *Wet en Evangelie*, trans. E. Kuyk, Amsterdam: Kuyk.

Holmes, A. R. (2006) 'The Protestant Clergies in the European World', in Brown, S. J., and Tackett, T. (eds) *The Cambridge History of Christianity: Enlightenment, Reawakening and Revolution, 1660-1815*, Cambridge: Cambridge University Press, pp. 109–27.

Hopkins, S. (1793) *The system of doctrines: contained in divine revelation, explained and defended: showing their consistence and connection with each other: to which is added, A treatise on the millennium*, Boston: Isaiah Thomas and Ebenezer T. Andrews.

Horton, M. S. (2007) *Covenant and Salvation: Union with Christ*, Louisville: Westminster John Knox Press.

House, R., and Coakly, J. (eds) (1999) *Patterns and Portraits: Women in the History of the Reformed Church in America*, Grand Rapids: Eerdmans.

Hughes, D. A. (1986) 'William Williams Pantycelyn's Eschatology as seen especially in his *Aurora Borealis* of 1774', *The Scottish Bulletin of Evangelical Theology*, 4, pp. 49–63.

Hughes, G. H. (ed.) (1967), *Gweithiau William Williams Pantycelyn*, cyfrol II, Cardiff: University of Wales Press.

Hughes, G. T. (1983) *Williams Pantycelyn*, Cardiff: University of Wales Press.

Hume, D. (1967) *A Treatise of Human Nature*, ed. L. A., Selby-Bigge, Oxford: Oxford University Press.

Hume, D. (1977) *An Enquiry Concerning Human Understanding*, ed. E. Steinberg, Indianapolis, Indiana: Hackett.

Hutcheson, F. (1725) *An Inquiry Concerning the Original of our Ideas of Virtue or Moral Good*; repr. in Hutcheson (1994) *Philosophical Writings*, Vermont: Charles E. Tuttle.

Irving, D. (1804) *Lives of the Scottish Poets*, Edinburgh: Alex. Lawrie & Co.

Jones, D. C. (2003) '"The Lord did give me a particular honour to make [me] a peacemaker": Howel Harris, John Wesley and Methodist Infighting, 1739–1750', *Bulletin of the John Rylands University Library of Manchester*, vol. 85, nos. 2 and 3, pp. 73–98.

Jones, D. C. (2004) '*A Glorious Work in the World': Welsh Methodism and the International Evangelical Revival, 1735-1750*, Cardiff: University of Wales Press.

Kant, I. (1997) *Groundwork of the Metaphysics of Morals*, Cambridge: Cambridge University Press.

Kant, I. (1997) *Prolegomena to Any Future Metaphysics*, trans. Gary Hatfield, Cambridge: Cambridge University Press.

Kant, I. (1998) *Religion within the Boundaries of Mere Reason and Other Writings*, trans. A. Wood and G. DiGiovanni, Cambridge: Cambridge University Press.

Keats, J. (1927) *The Poetical Works of John Keats*, London: Oxford University Press.

Keats, J. (1958) *The Letters of John Keats, In Two Volumes*, ed. Hyder Edward Rollins, Cambridge, Massachusetts: Harvard University Press.

Kennedy, J. (1979) *The Days of the Fathers in Ross-shire*, Inverness: Christian Focus Publications.

Kernkamp, G. W. (1936) *De Utrechtsche Universiteit 1637–1936*, Utrecht: A. Oosterhoek's Uitgevers Maatschappij.

Kernkamp, G. W. (ed.) (1938) *Acta et Decrata Senatus Vroedschapsresolutiën en andere bescheiden betreffende de Utrechtse Academie*, Utrecht: Broekhoff N.V.

Kidd, T. S. (2007) *The Great Awakening: The Roots of Evangelical Christianity in Colonial America*, New Haven: Yale University Press.

Kimnach, W. H. *et al.* (eds) (1999) *The Sermons of Jonathan Edwards, A Reader*, New Haven: Yale University Press.

Kling, D. W., and Sweeney, D. A. (eds) (2003) *Jonathan Edwards at Home and Abroad: Historical Memories, Cultural Movements, Global Horizons*, Columbia, South Carolina: University of South Carolina Press.

Krull, A. F. (1901) *Jacobus Koelman. Eene Kerkhistorische Studie*, Sneek: J. Campen.

La Shell, J. (1985) 'Imaginary Ideas of Christ: A Scottish–American Debate', Ph.D. diss., Westminster Theological Seminary.

Lachman, D. C. (1988) *The Marrow Controversy*, Edinburgh: Rutherford House.

Lambert, F. (1999) *Inventing the 'Great Awakening'*, Princeton: Princeton University Press.

Landsman, N. C. (2004) 'Erskine, John (1721–1803)', *Oxford Dictionary of National Biography*, Oxford: Oxford University Press. Available from: www.oxforddnb.com/view/article/8870 (accessed 20 Sept. 2010).

Lee, H. L. (1988) *The Philosophical Theology of Jonathan Edwards*, Princeton, New Jersey: Princeton University Press.

Lee, S. H. (2005) *The Princeton Companion to Jonathan Edwards*, Princeton: Princeton University Press.

Lesser, M. X. (2008) *Reading Jonathan Edwards: An Annotated Bibliography in Three Parts, 1729–2005*, Grand Rapids: Eerdmans.

Lewis, John (ed.) (1742) *The Weekly History*, no. 53 (10 April).

Lloyd-Jones, D. M. (1996) 'Sandemanianism', in *The Puritans: Their Origins and Successors: Address Delivered at the Puritan and Westminster Conference, 1959–1978*, Edinburgh: Banner of Truth, pp. 170–90.

Lossky, L. (1957) *The Mystical Theology of the Eastern Church*, Cambridge: James Clarke & Co.

Macleod, J. (1974) *Scottish Theology: In Relation to Church History*, Edinburgh: Knox Press.

Macleod, W. (ed.) (1893) *Journal of the Hon. John Erskine of Carnock*, Edinburgh: University Press for the Scottish Historical Society

Marsden, G. A. (2003) *Jonathan Edwards: A Life*, New Haven: Yale University Press.

Marsden, G. A. (2003) 'Jonathan Edwards, the Missionary', *Journal of Presbyterian History*, 81 (Spring), pp. 5–17.

Mather, C. (1726) *Manuductio ad Ministerium. Directions for a candidate of the ministry: Wherein, first, a right foundation is laid for his future improvement; and, then, rules are offered for such a management of his academical & preparatory studies; and thereupon, for such a conduct after his appearance in the world; as may render him a skilful and useful minister of the Gospel*, Boston: Thomas Hancock.

Matthews, G. M. (ed.) (1971, 1995) *John Keats, The Critical Heritage*, London: Routledge.

McClymond, M. J. (1998) *Encounters with God: An Approach to the Theology of Jonathan Edwards*, New York: Oxford University Press.

McClymond, M. J. (2003) 'Salvation as Divinization: Jonathan Edwards, Gregory Palamas and the Theological Uses of Neoplatonism', in Helm, P., and Crisp, O. D. (2003) *Jonathan Edwards: Philosophical Theologian*, Burlington, Vermont: Ashgate, pp. 139–59.

McCosh, J. (1875) *The Scottish Philosophy*, London: Macmillan.

McDermott, G. R. (1999) 'A Possibility of Reconciliation: Jonathan Edwards and the Salvation of Non-Christians', in Lee, S. H., and Guelzo, A. C. (eds) *Edwards in our Time: Jonathan Edwards and the Shaping of American Religion*, Grand Rapids: Eerdmans, pp. 173–202.

McDermott, G. R. (ed.) (2009) *Understanding Jonathan Edwards: An Introduction to America's Theologian*, New York: Oxford University Press.

McDonald, S. (2008) 'Beholding the Glory of God in the Face of Jesus Christ: John Owen and the "Reforming" of the Beatific Vision', unpub. paper delivered at the 'John Owen Today' Conference, Westminster College, Cambridge, 2008.

McFadden, I. D. (2008) '"Amidst the Great Darkness": The Practical Missiology of Jonathan Edwards at Stockbridge, 1751–1758', STM Thesis, Yale Divinity School.

McLaurin, J. (1830) *Works of the Rev. John McLaurin*, Glasgow: Printed for William Collins.

McLaurin, J. (1854) *Glorying in the Cross of Christ*, New York: Anson D.F. Rudolph.

Mclean, A. (1786) *The Commission Given by Jesus Christ to his Apostles Illustrated*, Edinburgh: Printed for W. Gray, Paternoster Row.

Miller, P. (1938) *The New England Mind: The Seventeenth Century*, Cambridge, Massachusetts: Harvard University Press.

Miller, P. (1949) *Jonathan Edwards*, New York: William Sloane.

Miller, T. (1990) 'Introduction', in *The Selected Writings of John Witherspoon*, Carbondale and Edwardsville, Illinois: Southern Illinois University Press.

Minahan, J. A. (1992) *Word Like a Bell: John Keats, Music and the Romantic Poet*, Kent, Ohio: Kent State University Press.

Minkema, K. P. (2004) 'Jonathan Edwards in the Twentieth Century', *Journal of the Evangelical Theological Society*, 47 (December), pp. 659–87.

Mitchell, C. W. (1997) 'Jonathan Edwards's Scottish Connection and the Eighteenth-Century Scottish Evangelical Revival, 1735–1750', Ph.D. diss., St. Mary's College, University of St. Andrews.

Mitchell, C. W. (2003) 'Jonathan Edwards' Scottish Connection', in Kling, D. W., and Sweeney, D. A. (eds) (2003) *Jonathan Edwards at Home and Abroad: Historical Memories, Cultural Movements, Global Horizons*, Columbia, South Carolina: University of South Carolina Press, pp. 222–47.

Mitchell, L. J. (2003) *Jonathan Edwards on the Experience of Beauty*, Studies in Reformed Theology and History, 9, Princeton: Princeton University Press.

Morden, P. (2003) *Offering Christ to the World: Andrew Fuller (1754–1815) and the Revival of Eighteenth Century Particular Baptist Life*, Studies in Baptist History and Thought, 8, Carlisle: Paternoster Press.

Morgan, D. L. (1988) *The Great Awakening in Wales*, London: Epworth Press.

Morris, W. S. (1991) *The Young Jonathan Edwards: A Reconstruction*, Chicago: University of Chicago Press; repr. Eugene, Oregon: Wipf & Stock, 2005.

Muller, R. A. (1981) 'Christ in the Eschaton: Calvin and Moltmann on the Duration of the *Munus Regium*', *Harvard Theological Review*, 74, no. 1 (January), pp. 31–59.

Muller, R. A. (1985) *Dictionary of Latin and Greek Theological Terms: Drawn Principally from Protestant Scholastic Theology*, Grand Rapids: Baker Academic.

Muller, R. A. (2003) *After Calvin: Studies in the Development of a Theological Tradition*, Oxford: Oxford University Press.

Muller, R. A. (2003) *Post-Reformation Reformed Dogmatics: The Rise and Development of Reformed Orthodoxy, ca. 1520 to ca. 1725*, 4 vols., Grand Rapids: Baker Academic.

Murray, I. (1987) *Jonathan Edwards: A New Biography*, Carlisle: Banner of Truth Trust.

Neele, A. C. (2009) *Petrus van Mastricht (1630–1706). Reformed Orthodoxy: Method and Piety*, Leiden, Boston: Brill.

Nemansky, P. (1992) 'Jan Ross. Een achttiende-eeuwse vertaler van Engelse piëtische lectuur', *Documentatieblad Nadere Reformatie*, vol. 16, no. 1 (Spring), pp. 43–53.

Nettles, T. (1986) 'On the Road Again', in *By His Grace and For His Glory: A Historical, Theological and Practical Study of the Doctrines of Grace in Baptist Life*, Grand Rapids: Baker Books, pp. 108–30.

Noll, M. A. (1989) 'Witherspoon Comes to Princeton', in *Princeton and the Republic, 1768–1822*, Princeton, New Jersey: Princeton University Press, pp. 16–27.

Noll, M. A. (2005) 'Jonathan Edwards' *Freedom of the Will* Abroad', in Stout, H. S. *et al.* (eds) (2005) *Jonathan Edwards at 300: Essays on the Tercentenary of His Birth*, Lanham: University of Press of America, pp. 89–108.

O'Brien, S. (1986) 'A Transatlantic Community of Saints: The Great Awakening and the First Evangelical Network, 1735–1755', *The American Historical Review*, 91, no. 4 (October), pp. 811–32.

Orr, J. (1903) 'Jonathan Edwards; His Influence in Scotland', *Congregationalist and Christian World (1901–1906)*, 88 (October), pp. 467–68.

Park, E. A. (1852) 'New England Theology', *Bibliotheca Sacra*, 9 (January), pp. 170–220.

Pettit, N. (1986) 'Prelude to Mission: Brainerd's Expulsion from Yale', *New England Quarterly*, 59, pp. 28–50.

Phillips, K. (1999) *The Cousins' Wars, Religion, Politics and the Triumph of Anglo-America*, New York: Basic Books.

Robinson, J. A. (1966) 'Hume's Two Definitions of "Cause"', in Chappell, V. C. (1966) *Hume: A Collection of Critical Essays*, Modern Studies in Philosophy, New York: Doubleday, pp. 162–8.

Royce, J. (1892) *The Spirit of Modern Philosophy, An Essay in the Form of Lectures*, Boston: Houghton, Mifflin and Company.

Ryken, P. G. (1999) 'Scottish Reformed Scholasticism', in Trueman, C. R., and Clark, P. G. (eds) (1999) *Protestant Scholasticism: Essays in Reassessment*, Carlisle: Paternoster Press, pp. 196–210.

Sandeman, R. (1759) *Letters on Theron and Aspasio*, Edinburgh: Sands, Donaldson, Murray, and Cochran.

Schaff, P., and Smith, H. B. (eds) (1877) *The Creeds of the Evangelical Protestant Churches, vol. II: 'Article XIII – XVIII', The Canons of Synod of Dort*, London: Hodder and Stoughton.

Schmidt, L. E. (1989) *Holy Fairs: Scottish Communions and American Revivals in the Early Modern Period*, Princeton: Princeton University Press.

Scott, Sir W. (1815) *Guy Mannering; or, the Astrologer*, Edinburgh: Archibald Constable & Co.

Seccombe, J. (1742) *Some Occasional Thoughts on the Influence of the Spirit with Seasonable Cautions against Mistakes and Abuses*, Boston: S. Kneeland and T. Green.

Shepard, T. (1683) *De Ware Bekeering*, Utrecht: Willem Clerck.

Shepard, T. (1686) *De Gezonde Geloovige*, Amsterdam: Johannes Boekholt.

Silverman, K. (1971) *Selected Letters of Cotton Mather*, Baton Rouge: Louisiana State University Press.

Simonson, H. P. (1987) 'Jonathan Edwards and his Scottish Connections', *Journal of*

American Studies, vol. 21, no. 3, pp. 353–76.

Smith, J. E. *et al.* (eds) (1995) *A Jonathan Edwards Reader*, New Haven: Yale University Press.

Smith, T. L. (2003) *Thomas Aquinas' Trinitarian Theology: A Study in Theological Method*, Washington, D.C.: Catholic University of America Press.

Sprunger, K. L. (1966) 'Ames, Ramus, and the Method of Puritan Theology', *Harvard Theological Review*, 59 (April), pp. 148–51.

Sprunger, K. L. (1982) *Dutch Puritanism: A History of English and Scottish Churches of the Netherlands in the Sixteenth and Seventeenth Centuries*, Leiden: Brill.

Stanley, B. (ed.) (2001) *Christian Missions and the Enlightenment*, Grand Rapids: Eerdmans.

Stephenson, S. A. (1983) 'The Theological and Ministerial Influences of Jonathan Edwards', Ph.D. diss., University of Pennsylvania.

Story, R. H. (ed.) (1890?) *The Church of Scotland, Past and Present*, London: William Mackenzie.

Stout, H. (2007) 'Edwards as Revivalist', in Stein, S. J. (ed.), *The Cambridge Companion to Jonathan Edwards*, New York: Cambridge University Press, pp. 125–43.

Sweeney, D. A., and Guelzo, A. C. (eds) (2006) *The New England Theology: From Jonathan Edwards to Edwards Amasa Park*, Grand Rapids: Baker Academic.

Talbot, B. (2003) *The Search for a Common Identity: The Origins of the Baptist Union of Scotland, 1800–1870*, Studies in Baptist History and Thought, 9, Carlisle: Paternoster Press.

Taylor, W. (1887) *The Scottish Pulpit from the Reformation to the Present Day*, New York: Harper & Brothers.

Thomas, O. (2002) *The Atonement Controversy in Welsh Theological Literature and Debate, 1707–1841*, translated by John Aaron, Edinburgh: Banner of Truth Trust.

Tudur, G. (2000) *Howell Harris: From Conversion to Separation, 1735–1750*, Cardiff: University of Wales Press.

Turretin, F. (1992) *Institutes of Elenctic Theology*, ed. James T. Dennison, trans. George Musgrave Giger, Phillipsburg: P&R Publishing.

van Asselt, W. (2001) *The Federal Theology of Johannes Cocceius (1603-1669)*, Leiden: Brill.

van der Haar, J. (ed.) (1985) 'Jacobus Bortius', in *Het Blijvende Woord*, Dordrecht: Gereformeerde Bijbelstichting.

van Genderen, J. (1953) *Herman Witsius, bijdrage tot de kennis der Gereformeerde theologie*, 's-Gravenhage: Guido de Bres.

van Harten, P. H. (1986) *De Predking van Ebenezer en Ralph Erskine. Evangelieverkondiging in het spanningsveld van verkiezing en belofte*, 's-Gravenhage: Boekencentrum.

van Lieburg, F. (2008) 'Interpreting the Dutch Great Awakening (1749–1755)', *Church History*, 77, no. 2 (June), pp. 319–36.

van Mastricht, P. (1749–53) *Beschouwende en praktikale godgeleerdheit: waarin, door alle de godgeleerde hoofdstukken henen, het bybelverklarende, leerstellige, wederleggende, en praktikale deel door eenen onafgebroken schakel, onderscheidenlyk samengevoegt, voorgestelt word; hierby komt een volledig kort-begrip der kerklyke geschiedenisse, een vertoog der zedelyke, en een schets der plichtvermenende godgeleerdheit, enz.; in het Latyn beschreven; naar den laatsten druk in het Nederduitsch vertaalt, benevens de lykrede van den vermaarden hoogleeraar Henricus Pontanus, over het afsterven van den hoogwaardigen autheur; met eene voorrede van den heer Cornelius van der Kemp*, 4 vols., Rotterdam: Hendrik van Pelt; Utrecht: Jan Jacob van Poolsum.

van Mastricht, P. (1679) *Disputationum practicarum tertia de certitudine salutis, eique opposita præsumptione seu securitate carnali*, pars prima, David de Volder, Utrecht: Meinardus à Dreunen

van Mastricht, P. (1680) *Disputationum practicarum tertia, de certitudine salutis, eique opposita præsumptione seu securitate carnali*, pars secunda, Jacobus Hoog, Utrecht: Meinardus à Dreunen.

van Mastricht, P. (166?) *Methodus Concionandi*, Frankfurt an der Oder: M. Hübner.

van Mastricht, P. (1677) *Novitatum Cartesianarum Gangræna, Nobiliores plerasque Corporis Theologici Partes arrodens et exedens. Seu Theologia Cartesiana detecta*, Amsterdam: Jansson.

van Mastricht, P. (1677) *De omnisufficientia Dei, pars prior Theologiæ theoretico-practicæ disputatio sexta* Theodorus Groen, Utrecht: Meinardus à Dreunen .

van Mastricht, P. (1666) *Theologiæ didactico-elenchtico-practicæ Prodromus tribus speciminibus*, Amsterdam: Johannes van Someren.

van Mastricht, P. (1677) *Theologiæ Theoretico-Practicæ disputatio quinta, De Existentia Et Cognitione Dei*, Wilhelmus Mercamp, Duisburg: Franc. Sas.

van Mastricht, P. (1677) *Theologiæ theoretico-practicæ disputatio septima De essentia, nominibus et atrributis Dei in genere, Pars 2*, Balduinus Drywegen, Utrecht: Meinardus à Dreunen.

van Mastricht, P. (1699) *Theoretico-practica theologia: qua, per singula capita theologica, pars exegetica, dogmatica, elenchtica et practica, perpetua successione conjugantur; accedunt historia ecclesiastica, plena quidem, sed compendiosa, idea theologiæ moralis, hypotyposis theologiæ asceticæ etc proin opus quasi novum. Ed. nova, priori multo emendatior et plus quam tertia parte auctior*, Utrecht: Thomas Appels.

van Mastricht, P. (n.d. [1770?]) *A Treatise on Regeneration. Extracted from his System of Divinity, called Theologia theoretico-practica; and faithfully translated into English; With an APPENDIX containing Extracts from many celebrated Divines of the reformed Church, upon the same Subject*, New Haven: Thomas and Samuel Green.

van Valen, L. J. (1982) *Gelijk de Dauw van Hermon*, Zwijndrecht: Het Anker, tweede druk.

Vaudry, R. W. (2003) *Anglicans and the Atlantic World: High Churchmen, Evangelicals, and the Quebec Connection*, Montréal: McGill-Queen's University Press.

Voetius, G. (1736) 'Reedenvoeringe van de Nuttigheit der Akademien en Schoolen, mitsgaders der Wetenschappen en Konsten', in le Long, I. (1736) *Hondert-Jaarige Jubel-Gedachtenisse der Academie van Utrecht*, Utrecht: M. Visch.

Watson, T. (1838) *A Body of Practical Divinity, in a Series of Sermons on the Shorter Catechism*, Aberdeen: D. Chalmers and Co.

Watts, C. (1985) *A Preface to Keats*, London: Longman.

Wawrykow, J. P. (2005) *The SCM Press A–Z of Thomas Aquinas*, London: SCM Press.

Wayland, F. (1963) *The Elements of Moral Science*, ed. J. Blau, Cambridge, Massachusetts: Harvard University Press.

Webster, J. *et al.* (eds) (2007) *The Oxford Handbook of Systematic Theology*, Oxford: Oxford University Press.

Wellwood, H. M. (1818) *Account of the Life and Writings of John Erskine, D.D., Late One of the Ministers of Edinburgh*, Edinburgh: Archibald Constable and Company.

Wesley, J. (1744) *The Distinguishing Marks of a Work of the Spirit of God. Extracted from Mr Edwards. Minister of Northampton, in New England*, London: W. Strahan.

Westra, H. (1999) 'Divinity's Design: Edwards and the History of the Work of Revival', in Lee, S. H., and Guelzo, A. C. (eds) (1999) *Edwards in Our Time: Jonathan Edwards and the Shaping of American Religion*, Grand Rapids: Eerdmans, pp. 131–57.

Wheeler, R. (2003) '"Friends to Your Souls": Jonathan Edwards' Indian Pastorate and the Doctrine of Original Sin', *Church History*, 72 (December), pp. 736–65.

Wheeler, R. (2008) *To Live Upon Hope: Mohicans and Missionaries in the Eighteenth-Century Northeast*, Ithaca, New York: Cornell University Press.

White, E. M. (2008) '"I will once more shake the heavens": the 1762 Revival in Wales', in Cooper, K., and Gregory, J. (eds), *Revival and Resurgence in Christian History*, Studies in Church History, 44, Woodbridge: Ecclesiastical History Society / The Boydell Press, pp. 54–63.

Williams, C. G. (1968) 'The Unfeigned Faith and an Eighteenth Century *Pantheologia*', *Numen*, vol. 15, no. 3, pp. 208–17.

Williams, G. (1967) *Welsh Reformation Essays*, Cardiff: University of Wales Press.

Williams, G. (1970) *Reformation Views of Church History*, London: Lutterworth Press.

Williams, G. (1979) 'A Prospect of Paradise? Wales and the United States, 1776–1914', in *Religion, Language and Nationality in Wales*, Cardiff: University of Wales Press, pp. 217–36.

Witsius, H. (1677) *De œconomia fœderum Dei cum hominibus, libri quattor*, Leeuwarden, Eelcke Symons Nauta Symons for Jacob Hagenaar.

Witsius, H. (1681) *Excercitationes sacrae in symbolum quod apostolorum dicitur et in orationem dominicam*, Franeker: n.p.

Wollebius, J. (1965) *Compendium Theologiae Christianae*, in *Reformed Dogmatics: Seventeenth-Century Reformed Theology Through the Writings of Wollebius, Voetius, and Turretin*, trans. John W. Beardslee III, Grand Rapids: Baker Book House.

Yates, N. (2007) 'Wind, Rain and the Holy Spirit: Welsh Evangelicalism in a Pan-Celtic Context, 1750–1850', in *Bishop Burgess and his World: Culture, Religion and Society in Britain, Europe and North America in the Eighteenth and Nineteenth Centuries*, Cardiff: University of Wales Press, pp. 103–20.

Yeager, J. (2011) *Enlightened Evangelicalism: The Life and Thought of John Erskine*, New York: Oxford University Press.

Zakai, A. (2007) 'The Age of Enlightenment', in Stein, S. J. (ed.), *The Cambridge Companion to Jonathan Edwards*, New York: Cambridge University Press, pp. 80–99.

Index